DARE
To Be
CHRISTLIKE

Why You Must and *How* You Can

D1054051

STEPHEN P. SMITH

DARE To Be CHRISTLIKE
Why You Must and How You Can
by STEPHEN P. SMITH

Printed in the United States of America.

ISBN 978-1-4984-6830-5

www.xulonpress.com

Contents

In loving memory of Parker David Gilles,
a grandson born into the arms of Jesus
on October 21, 2012.

Dedication

"I have no greater joy than to hear that
my children are walking in the truth."'
3 John 4

To my children, Ben, Kristen, Julia, and David whom I love as much as any man could ever love his children:

From the moment I married your beautiful mother, I could hardly wait to become a father. At the young age of twenty-one, I had a prescient knowing that being a father would be the greatest experience a man could have this side of heaven. Eleven months later, Benjamin Paul Smith was born. To this day, that remains the single proudest moment of my life. But it only increased as Kristen Gabrielle, Julia Rachelle, and David Neil each entered the world!

Only once since then has my firm belief in this experience of fatherhood been challenged. Yet out of that God produced a blessing that completely erased the momentary uncertainty of such confidence. Jayli Deajean Ruth Smith, you are more like a daughter to me than a granddaughter. At the age of ten, your giving spirit is already an inspiration and blessing to others.

As John aptly wrote, there is no greater joy than to know that one's children are walking in the truth. Seeing this in all of you brings me great joy, and my heart overflows with thanksgiving to God for His grace at work in each of you and your families.

During the process of writing this book, I knew that regardless of whether I sold a single copy, I was still writing something beneficial that would be part of the legacy I would pass to you, and that you will pass to your children.

Take these words to heart. Apply them. Live them. Teach them to your children and to your children's children. Doing so will be the greatest gift you could ever give your dad.

Preface

"The greatest of these is love."
1 Corinthians 13:13

G RANDPA ENTERED THE ROOM like an actor bursting onto the stage. His sick grandson was sitting up in bed, reluctantly anticipating grandpa's arrival. The boy knew from experience he was about to be victimized by that annoying pinch of the cheek that grandparents like to give.

Grandpa did not disappoint. Cheek firmly squeezed between thumb and forefinger, he waggled his grandson's face predictably, to the boy's chagrin.

Grandpa handed his grandson a wrapped present. After opening his gift, all the grandson could muster was, "A book?" Yes, a book. But not just any book. The boy's tepid reception of the gift did not deter Grandpa in the least. "This is a special book," Grandpa replied enthusiastically. "It was the book my father used to read to me when I was sick, and I used to read it to your father. And today, I'm gonna read it to you."

Would the story be interesting? Would it contain sports, adventure, excitement? When the boy voiced his skepticism, Grandpa offered assurance that it contained all these things and more.

"Doesn't sound too bad. I'll try and stay awake." said the grandson. Grandpa then began reading aloud, *"The Princess Bride, by S. Morgenstern."*

It wasn't long before the boy had heard enough about the blossoming love between Buttercup and the Farm Boy. "Hold it, hold it. What is this? Are you trying to trick me? Where's the sports?... Is this a kissing book?"

"Wait, just wait," said Grandpa, extending his hand like a traffic cop.

"Well, when's it get good?" came the impatient response from the grandson.

"Keep your shirt on. Let me read," said Grandpa, determined to continue the story.[1]

Investment Risk

I don't know about you, but I am often like this boy when it comes to wading into a new book. Will I like this? Will it be worth my time? Will it put me to sleep? What benefit awaits me, if any?

I only know one way to find out—start reading. Or, in this case, continue reading. Only then will you know if this book is worth your time. My prayer is that you will continue, and that God will speak to you through its pages.

This is a book about love. (It's not about kissing, though.) It's a book about adventure—the adventure of a lifetime (or a lifetime adventure). It's a book about the intrinsic power of love to transform a life. This book is about my journey. This book is about your journey. It's about the lifelong pursuit of being conformed to the image and likeness of Jesus Christ.

Original Recipe?

Though I would never plagiarize another author's work, I have no problem recycling the thoughts of others if it serves my purpose in making a point. Any source is acceptable as long as what they say aligns with the timeless truth of Scripture. Pierre Bayle, a seventeenth century philosopher and writer, once said, "There is not less wit nor less invention in applying rightly a thought one finds in a book, than in being the first author of that thought."[2]

I suspect much of what you read in this book may not be new to you. I'm certainly not the first person to have a thought about the need for Christians to be more Christlike. Though I can't claim originality with respect to the subject matter, I do hope to present a fresh perspective. That said, if your point of view is such that people should only articulate original ideas and insights, then such logic would also suggest that people should only serve food they've prepared from their own recipes. But I question if anyone subscribes to such an approach when preparing meals.

In a way, I'm serving up something that's not entirely my own creation. You see, I feel as if I owe an eternal debt of gratitude to a person whose name I don't even know. On two separate occasions, separated by more than fifteen years, I found myself reading a book called *The Christlike Christian*. This now out-of-print book was written by an early twentieth century author who simply identified himself or herself as an Unknown Christian. The legacy this Christlike believer left behind has been a tool in the hands of the Holy Spirit to make me acutely aware of my shortcomings and need to pursue Christ more fully. And so it is that I thankfully and respectfully acknowledge the influence of the Unknown Christian upon my life, for much of what you will read in this book was inspired by this individual's writing.

—▸•◂—

The Christlike Christian was last published by Zondervan Publishing House in 1988. The original date of publication for this work is not known. However, it was published in 1960 as part of the Zondervan Clarion Classics series, ISBN 0-310-33461-6. This book is currently out of print and in public domain. No further information could be obtained from HarperCollins Christian Publishing (Zondervan and Thomas Nelson) concerning the original date of publication for this work.

Introduction: An Epic Enigma

"A problem well stated is a problem half solved."[1]
Charles F. Kettering, inventor and engineer (1876–1958)

INFORMATION TECHNOLOGY (IT) has been my profession for more than thirty years, and I have spent nearly half my career with an upscale women's specialty retail corporation. In the summer of 2010—after eighteen months of requirements gathering, design, development, and testing—we deployed new websites for our brands. The sites were launched prematurely, creating a maelstrom of functional and performance-related issues that resulted in numerous troubleshooting calls for our IT staff.

Our IT department then was under the direction of a man whose critical thinking and problem-solving skills were second to none. On several troubleshooting calls I witnessed his ability to gather input and observations from multiple sources regarding complex issues and articulate a summary of those artifacts so well that it truly gave a sense you were halfway to having the problem solved by the time the call ended.

I admire people who can do that. It's not one of my strengths. However, it is no great feat to articulate the problem this book addresses: *claiming to be a Christian but bearing little resemblance to the Christ we profess to follow.* I'm obviously not referring to our physical appearance, but rather how we model the character of Christ.

Jesus said, "Whoever has seen me has seen the Father" (John 14:9). Imagine how God-glorifying it would be if we could humbly and truthfully proclaim, "If you've seen me, you've seen Jesus." Is such a notion an arrogant, foolish, or presumptuous pipe dream? Not only is such a notion *possible*, it is our *responsibility* as believers in Jesus Christ to represent well the character that Christ Himself embodied during His brief incarnation upon the earth.

Paul thought it was possible. "Be imitators of me, as I am of Christ," he told the believers in Corinth (1 Corinthians 11:1). He said to the church at Philippi, "What you have learned and received and heard and seen in me—practice these things, and the God of peace will be with you" (Philippians 4:9).

Was Paul arrogant to presume his life could be imitated as a model for Christlikeness? I don't think so. This is something all believers in Jesus should aspire to. Christianity is not just some weekend activity tacked on to everything else in our lives. This *is* our life. Or is it?

Mirror, Mirror, on the Wall

It is reasonably safe to say I've lost close to three hundred pounds in my lifetime. Lose 30 pounds, gain 35. Lose 32, gain 30. Rinse, repeat. These days my weight stays consistently between 185 and 195 pounds, but it's been as high as 240.

On those occasions when my weight has ballooned, I can recall standing in front of my bathroom mirror thinking to myself, *There's a better physique in there, Steve, and you would look and feel so much better if you got yourself in the gym and stopped eating so much of the wrong kinds of food.*

Paul exhorted Timothy, his son in the faith, with these words, "Exercise yourself toward godliness. For bodily exercise profits a little, but godliness is profitable for all things" (1 Timothy 4:7–8 NKJV).

As Christians, we sometimes fail to reflect the perfect image of Christ within us. As Paul told Timothy, we must exercise ourselves toward godliness in order to remove the surrounding fatty tissue of those things in our lives that obscure the handsome physique of our Beloved, Christ Jesus.

Christlike Christian?

The expression "Christlike Christian" sounds to me like something from the Department of Redundancy Department, yet that is the premise of this book—becoming a Christlike Christian. Now, if there is such a thing as a Christlike Christian, then it's logical to conclude there exists the opposite—an un-Christlike Christian. Where I come from, we would call this an *enigma*: "a puzzling or inexplicable occurrence or situation; a person of puzzling or contradictory character."[2] It's an enigma to call myself a Christian and not be Christlike in my conversation and manner of living.

"If we could only keep all the un-Christlike Christians out of sight, the greatest hindrance to the triumph of the gospel would be gone." —Unknown Christian

Frankly, we have all been those who, at some point in our walk with Jesus Christ, have borne little resemblance to the Savior we profess to love and serve. I am painfully aware of a few specific occasions in my past when I publicly behaved in a manner that was anything but Christlike, and I hoped that no one in proximity knew I professed to be a Christian. Sadly, I resembled those of whom the Unknown Christian spoke:

> "If we could only keep all the un-Christlike Christians out of sight, the greatest hindrance to the triumph of the gospel would be gone."
>
> So said an old saint. Now that is a very arresting remark—and it is very true!
>
> Yet we read it with great trepidation. It throws us back upon ourselves. And every one of us begins to ask himself a little fearfully: "Where should I be?" Am I so unlike the Lord Jesus that it would

advance His cause if I were hidden away from my fellow man?[3]

Caveat Emptor

In some areas of my life I still fall short of Christlikeness. For those who know me well, this is not exactly breaking news. Although *caveat emptor* may sound like something my wife fixed for dinner last night, it is Latin for "Let the buyer beware."[4] So in the interest of full disclosure, *I am not yet Christlike.* I am one who is pursuing Christlikeness by the empowering grace of God, and writing as one who sees through a glass darkly, yet has confidence in the promises of a faithful and loving Father who has committed Himself to perfect that which concerns me—and every person who has taken hold of the grace of God that brings salvation (Titus 2:11).

James issues a sobering caution for those who would venture to instruct others. He writes, "Not many of you should become teachers, my brothers, for you know that we who teach will be judged with greater strictness" (James 3:1). This implies that those who teach should exemplify their teaching. This is quite an imposing thought to me—because I know me! I know how far short of Christlikeness I fall on occasion. However, I will not be less likely to have to give an account of my own pursuit of Christlikeness if I choose not to write on this subject. I am still just as accountable to be like Him whether I exhort others to be so or not. And if you call yourself a Christian, you are just as accountable to pursue Christlikeness whether you continue reading this book or not.

Christians in Crisis

If you've been on this earth long, you have no doubt experienced some crisis in your life. This book was not written to *create* a crisis in your life, but to help you *recognize* the crisis that already exists. The website Dictionary.com provides a handful of definitions for the word *crisis*, but these two are the most germane to this topic (emphasis added):

crisis[5]

- *noun.*

1. a stage in a sequence of events at which the trend of all future events, especially for better or for worse, is determined; *turning point.*
2. a condition of instability or danger, as in social, economic, political, or international affairs, *leading to a decisive change.*

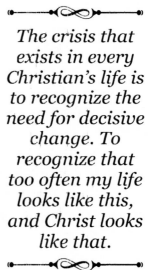

I do not think it's a stretch to include *spiritual* affairs in the list of things that may lead to decisive change. It's not God's will for Christians to meander aimlessly through life, carried along by every wind of doctrine, having no real sense of direction or purpose. He wants His children to be like Him, and yet it's altogether too easy for us to be content in the same daily routine, oblivious to how our lives affect those around us. The crisis that exists in every Christian's life is to recognize the need for decisive change. To recognize that too often my life looks like *this*, and Christ looks like *that*. One of these things is not like the other.

The crisis that exists in every Christian's life is to recognize the need for decisive change. To recognize that too often my life looks like this, and Christ looks like that.

Statement of Purpose

I believe mission statements serve to provide focus for any worthwhile endeavor, so naturally I developed one for this book:

> To challenge and convict, to encourage and inspire; to give the reader hope that becoming Christlike is not simply a noble pursuit, but possible through the grace of God at work in every believer's life.

This book is going to challenge you. It may ruffle your feathers. You may not always like—or agree with—what you read, but Ralph Waldo Emerson once said, "Our chief want in life is somebody who shall make us do what we can."[6] Oswald Chambers put it this way:

> In dealing with other people, our stance should always be to drive them toward making a decision of their will. That is how surrendering to God begins. Not often, but every once in a while, God brings us to a major turning point—a great crossroads in our life. From that point we either go toward a more and more slow, lazy, and useless Christian life, or we become more and more on fire, giving our utmost for His highest—our best for His glory.[7]

I certainly cannot *make* you be like Jesus—or even desire to be like Him—but my assumption is that you are reading this book because you *do* want to be like Him. You may already have a raging fire inside of you to become more like Jesus. Or, you may have never given it much thought. Still yet, you may find within yourself the cooling embers remnant of a bygone flame. Regardless of your situation, this book contains the inspirational insight to assist in igniting a flame—or fanning one that already exists—so that your *profession* of Christ is elevated to a *possession* of Christlikeness.

The Ultimate Pursuit

This book was written to help the reader become Christlike. That said, it admittedly falls short of addressing every aspect of how Jesus lived. Consequently, there are a number of significant omissions. If we were to attempt to cover every aspect of the life of Christ and its application to the Christian, this would quickly become a tedious and unbearable tome. Based on Paul's admonition to the church in Corinth, our primary focus is on the qualities of love listed in 1 Corinthians 13, which most aptly describe the superlative Person of Jesus Christ. For as the Nicene Creed reminds us,

Christ is "very God of very God," and God is love. Paul begins this passage on love with these arresting statements:

> If I speak in the tongues of men and of angels, but have not love, I am a noisy gong or a clanging cymbal. And if I have prophetic powers, and understand all mysteries and all knowledge, and if I have all faith, so as to remove mountains, but have not love, I am nothing. If I give away all I have, and if I deliver up my body to be burned, but have not love, I gain nothing. (1 Corinthians 13:1–3)

Do we grasp the weight of these words, or have we seen and heard them so often that they've become little more than some prosaic poetry to frame and hang on a wall as decoration? On the contrary, do they not hit us squarely between the eyes?

An untold number of books have been written for the Christian Living genre, each one designed to help us in some aspect of our walk with Christ. Pick any subject you like or any facet of Christian living; they all take a back seat to love.

The point here is that I may possess many Christlike qualities, but if I'm not walking in love, I am still falling short of the ultimate goal. Paul told Timothy the goal of his instruction was *love* from a pure heart and a good conscience and a sincere faith (1 Timothy 1:5).

When such love becomes seamlessly woven into the fabric of our lives, it not only causes people to recognize that we have been with Jesus, but our hope is that He will be so lifted up in the eyes of all who know us that they too will be drawn to Him. Therefore, my hope for you is that in the process of reading this book you will experience that psychological moment, or turning point, that inspires and urges you onward in your pursuit of Christlikeness as you discover how to extend grace and walk in love.

For Further Study

"Be imitators of me, as I am of Christ."
1 Corinthians 11:1

1. What problem does this book address?
2. What does the author state is the responsibility of believers in Jesus Christ? Share with the group* why you either agree or disagree with this statement.
3. Describe the enigma mentioned in the introduction.
4. What quote from *The Christlike Christian* suggests how the greatest hindrance to the triumph of the gospel would be remedied?
5. Share how the following question impacts you personally: "Am I so unlike the Lord Jesus that it would advance His cause if I were hidden away from my fellow man?"
6. Describe the crisis that exists in every Christian's life.
7. In your own words, summarize the distinction between professing to be Christlike and actually possessing Christlikeness.

*Possible alternatives to group study include writing your thoughts in a journal or sharing them with a close friend or family member.

Part 1

The Realization

realize[1] [**ree**-*uh*-lahyz]
—noun

1. *to grasp or understand clearly....*
3. *to bring vividly to the mind.*

1

Once Upon a Word...

*"They began to be sorrowful and to say to him
one after another, 'Is it I?'"*
Mark 14:19

"WHAT DOES THE WORD *caviling* mean?" she asked, lowering her book just enough to reveal the puzzled expression on her face.

"I don't know. Read it in context," I replied, welcoming the challenge of inferring the word's meaning from the surrounding text.

"Okay," she said.

Since I have a natural affinity for learning new words, I listened closely as she began reading the text aloud, "Such enquiries as these urgently demand our attention; and if we have been at all given to caviling, let us now turn our critical abilities to a service so much more profitable. Let us be peace-makers, and endeavor to lead others both by our precept and example."[1]

"Well," I said, "it sounds to me like the word may have something to do with being critical of others. I'll look it up on Dictionary.com."

My wife, Mindy, and I were spending a few days in her brother's cabin in Gatlinburg, Tennessee, the week before Thanksgiving, 2010. She was immersed in her daily devotional time when she came across this word while reading Charles Spurgeon's *Morning by Morning*. If I have learned nothing else in more than thirty-seven years of marriage, it is that Mindy is committed to her daily devotional time with Christ. Sometimes I think she would rather lose an arm than give up that time with Jesus. It's one of the things I admire most about her.

While waiting for the definition, I continued my attempt to derive the meaning of the word based on Spurgeon's context. Ah, finally, I was able to type it in: c-a-v-i-l-i-n-g.

cavil² [**kav**-*uh*-l]
—verb (used without object)

1. *to raise irritating and trivial objections; find fault with unnecessarily.*

A lump formed in my throat. "Okay, dear, here it is. It means to raise irritating and trivial objections; to find fault with unnecessarily."

We looked at each other and after a momentary pause, I said, "Hmm" and she said, "Hmm."

The mildly amusing but awkward silence was palpable.

As I would later come to understand, that awkward moment was a bit of an epiphany, or what I call a "Nathan moment." For that is when the Holy Spirit opened my eyes and convicted me of what had been a longstanding, recurring pattern of injurious comments and remarks to my wife about things that should be of no consequence.

As I would later come to understand, that awkward moment was a bit of an epiphany, or what I call a "Nathan moment."

For example, there had been a tug-of-war between us for years over Mindy's splashing of water around the sink—any sink, no, *every* sink... or so it seemed. She was like a bird in a bird bath. When I would point this out, she would get annoyed with me because to her it wasn't a big deal, and I would get annoyed with her for not seeing my point of view—that water is corrosive, it leaves behind stains over time, and why couldn't she just wipe it up anyway?

To be clear, I never shared any of my "observations" with a mean spirit. I was just convinced there was a better way, so I persistently tried to convince her that my way was better. Little did I realize that I was the one who needed to learn a better way.

Exam Time

It's easy to see things in others that need to change, especially when that is what you are looking for. Jesus said we should not worry about the speck in our friend's eye when we have a log in our own (Matthew 7:3–5). We would be better off if we spent more time examining ourselves instead of niggling others, not to mention the added bonus that we would not be such a bother.

Jesus did not forbid us to help our friends with speck extraction, but His point is that our primary focus should be on log extraction. Galatians tells us, "Pay careful attention to *your own work*.... For we are each responsible for *our own conduct*" (Galatians 6:4–5 NLT, emphasis added).

When speaking of people who commend themselves, Paul told the Corinthians that those who measure and compare themselves to others are unwise to do so (2 Corinthians 10:12). We should not make the mistake of comparing ourselves to others, for we can always find someone of lesser character to justify our manner of living. In doing so, we become like the self-righteous Pharisee who prayed, "I thank you, God, that I am not a sinner like everyone else. For I don't cheat, I don't sin, and I don't commit adultery. I'm certainly not like that tax collector!" (Luke 18:11 NLT). If only we had the self-awareness of the extortionist tax collector who recognized his sin and beat his breast, pleading for the mercy of God (Luke 18:13)!

It is the humble and contrite who acknowledge and accept responsibility for their sin once the Holy Spirit has opened their eyes. And only by God's Spirit do we experience grace to evoke the conviction and repentance necessary to produce lasting change.

"Is It I?"

At the Last Supper, Jesus stunned His disciples by declaring that one of them would betray Him. Each man in turn asked, "Is it I?" (Mark 14:19). Do we "betray" Christ by a life that belies His likeness? Do we have the humility to at least ask, as the disciples did, "Is it I?"

Sometimes we just don't see it. A classic illustration is the story of David and Bathsheba as chronicled in 2 Samuel 11:1–12:7. David eyes a beautiful woman bathing on a rooftop. Abusing his kingly power, he summons her to his bedchamber. When she becomes pregnant, he tries to cover his sin by bringing her husband, Uriah, home from battle to sleep with her. When Uriah refuses to lie with his wife while his comrades remain in harm's way, David sends him back to the troops with a letter instructing Joab to put him closest to the fray and "draw back from him, that he may be struck down, and die" (2 Samuel 11:15).

After Uriah is slain in battle, the prophet Nathan comes to David and tells him of a rich man with many flocks and herds who refuses to slaughter one of his own animals for a wayfaring traveler, but instead takes the only lamb of a poor man to prepare for his guest. When David hears this he is enraged:

> Then David's anger was greatly kindled against the man, and he said to Nathan, "As the Lord lives, the man who has done this deserves to die, and he shall restore the lamb fourfold, because he did this thing, and because he had no pity." Nathan said to David, "You are the man!" (2 Samuel 12:5–7a)

Yes, it is I. I am the man.
Are *you* the man—or woman?

Everyone Needs a Nathan Moment

You may not be given to caviling. You may struggle with something entirely different. You could be a longstanding member of Club Envy or the ever popular Boastmasters. Maybe you allow yourself that occasional use of profanity—because it makes you seem more like "one of the guys." Maybe you have a petulant, grumpy disposition that wears people out. Perhaps you harbor bitterness toward someone and cannot forgive them.

Need I go on? There's no need to produce a comprehensive list. The Holy Spirit knows and sees everything. He used one single word to jolt me into an awareness of un-Christlike behavior. Has He shined the penetrating light of God's Word into your soul to reveal an area of your life that is bringing dishonor to the name of Jesus Christ?

Don't shy away from your Nathan moment. Recognize it, embrace it, and let it propel you in your pursuit of Christlikeness as it did me. Like the seven churches mentioned in the opening chapters of the book of Revelation, we too need to hear what the Spirit is saying to us. What is the Spirit saying? He could be saying, "You are the man!"

For Further Study

"Why do you see the speck that is in your brother's eye, but do not notice the log that is in your own eye?"
Matthew 7:3

1. Why is it unwise to measure and compare ourselves to others?
2. Whose work are we called to examine?
3. What is a Nathan moment, and what is the significance of experiencing such a moment? Share with the group when you experienced a Nathan moment and how it affected you.
4. What is required to acknowledge and accept responsibility for sin in your life?
5. How/When does a Nathan moment occur?
6. The author suggests that everyone needs a Nathan moment. Share with the group why you either agree or disagree with this premise.

2

Aiming, Not Claiming

"We make it our aim ... to be well pleasing to Him."
2 Corinthians 5:9 (NKJV)

I AM NOT A MARKSMAN, nor do I own a firearm. I have never been a hunter of any sort, so I don't have a bow and arrow either. But I have tossed horseshoes and I own golf clubs. What do these have in common? In the hands of the user, they are all designed to accomplish the same goal: hit a target.

How strange would it be for someone to go deer hunting and shoot at anything other than deer? Who takes a firearm to a firing range and shoots at something other than a designated target? And what sense would it make for me to play golf and not focus on a target with every shot?

The answer, of course, is that it makes absolutely no sense to engage in any of these activities without aiming at the appropriate target, yet that is exactly what we do as Christians. We say we want to be like Jesus, but our lives too often testify to little more than a perfunctory pursuit of Him. We live

> *We say we want to be like Jesus, but our lives too often testify to little more than a perfunctory pursuit of Him. We live as if simply going to church and reading our Bibles is the secret to becoming a Christlike man or woman.*

as if simply going to church and reading our Bibles is the secret to becoming a Christlike man or woman.

Going to church, reading the Bible—you can even throw in supplemental devotional readings and daily prayer—all are worthy disciplines for growth in godliness, but in themselves they do not guarantee a transformation from a life governed by self to a life governed by Christ. In fact, it is dangerously possible that these very things may give us an appearance of godliness (2 Timothy 3:5) without the power of a changed life, especially if they become an end in themselves rather than a means to pursuing and possessing Christ.

So how do we ensure that our Bible reading, prayer, and church attendance, etc. result in more than just a form of godliness? We don't. We can't. We will do well to remember these words from chapter 1 of John's gospel:

> But to all who did receive him, who believed in his
> name, he gave the right to become children of God,
> who were born, not of blood nor of the will of the flesh
> nor of the will of man, but of God. (John 1:12–13)

If I can't become a child of God through blood lineage or fleshly efforts, I certainly cannot become Christlike by such means.

Willfully Aim

At this point, we must ask whether it's even possible for a man or woman to become Christlike this side of heaven. Many would claim it's not possible and may even assert it is presumptuous and prideful to suppose otherwise. They see this as unattainable as scaling a mountain twice the height of Everest.

I, however, happen to believe that a Christlike life *is* possible. Am I claiming to have attained it? Absolutely not. Am I claiming I will attain it? That is not my primary concern. What is far more important is that I am *aiming* to be like Christ, and that I have made a decision to be intentional in my pursuit of Him. To some, this may sound as if I'm trying to accomplish this through sheer power or force of will—the very approach I've stated is flawed. Not so. Allow me to illustrate.

No one gets out of bed to go to work in the morning without choosing to do so. We don't accidentally stand on our feet and commence with the activities of our day. Rather, we make a decision to get up and get going—even if we don't have much pep at first!

Does the fact that I choose to get out of bed guarantee I will be successful in getting to work on time and being productive that day? Hardly, but getting out of bed is a prerequisite to making it to work and being successful. So *choice* is important. It's not everything, but it is nonetheless an integral part of the total equation. We see this in Joshua's challenge to the Israelites, "*choose* this day whom you will serve" (Joshua 24:15, emphasis added).

Paul shared a similar mind-set, as seen in his epistle to the church at Philippi:

> Not that I have already obtained this or am already perfect, but I press on to make it my own, because Christ Jesus has made me his own. Brothers, I do not consider that I have made it my own. But one thing I do: forgetting what lies behind and straining forward to what lies ahead, I press on toward the goal for the prize of the upward call of God in Christ Jesus. (Philippians 3:12–14)

Paul was matter of fact in his admission that he had not yet *obtained*, but he was equally unapologetic in his intention to pursue and "press on toward the goal for the prize of the upward call of God in Christ Jesus." I believe he was speaking of becoming Christlike. Could there be any higher call? Oswald Chambers states, "The

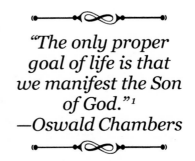

"The only proper goal of life is that we manifest the Son of God."[1]
—*Oswald Chambers*

only proper goal of life is that we manifest the Son of God."[1] He goes on to say,

> Beware of thinking of our Lord as only a teacher. If Jesus Christ is only a teacher, then all He can do is frustrate me by setting a standard before me I cannot attain. What is the point of presenting me with such a lofty ideal if I cannot possibly come close to reaching it? I would be happier if I never knew it. What good is there in telling me to be what I can never be—to be "pure in heart" (Matthew 5:8), to do more than my duty, or to be completely devoted to God? I must know Jesus Christ as my Savior before His teaching has any meaning for me other than that of a lofty ideal which only leads to despair. But when I am born again by the Spirit of God, I know that Jesus Christ did not come only to teach—*He came to make me what He teaches I should be*. The redemption means that Jesus Christ can place within anyone the same nature that ruled His own life, and all the standards God gives us are based on that nature. [2]

A Threefold Cord

Once I choose to be intentional in my pursuit of Christlikeness, the next step is to understand and embrace the healthy tension that co-exists between grace, faith, and works. I know I cannot will myself to be Christlike and I also know I can't just sit back and do nothing and expect to be transformed into His image. This creates a healthy tension. On one hand I am compelled to do something to become Christlike, but on the other hand I know it must be the work of God. So what's a person to do? What do *I* do?

Ecclesiastes 4:12 states, "a threefold cord is not quickly broken." This is because the individual strands, when woven together, form a much stronger union than when each is separate. With respect to becoming Christlike, I see a synergistic opportunity when *grace*, *faith*, and *works* combine to form a strong, threefold cord.

Much like the threefold cord, this triad of grace, faith, and works produces a total effect greater than the sum of its individual parts. Sovereign grace works in us to abandon all reliance on ourselves, implicitly trusting God to complete the work He started in us at conversion, as we also *"work out* [our] own salvation with fear and trembling" (Philippians 2:12, emphasis added).

Let's take a brief look at each of the strands that seamlessly intertwine to produce this three-stranded cord of grace, faith, and works.

1. **Grace** — "Apart from me, you can do nothing" (John 15:5).
We must not only acknowledge, but unequivocally accept, the fact that we cannot achieve Christlikeness on our own. It is completely beyond our reach. Grace, however, is the ability that God provides to do what I am otherwise unable to do in my own strength, wisdom, and understanding. Paul understood this:

> For our boast is this, the testimony of our conscience, that we behaved in the world with simplicity and godly sincerity, not by earthly wisdom but *by the grace of God.* (2 Corinthians 1:12 emphasis added)

2. **Faith** — "Without faith it is impossible to please God" (Hebrews 11:6 NIV).
If our goal is to be well pleasing to God—which we assume a Christlike life would accomplish—then we must exercise faith in the promises of God, which are said to make us "partakers of the divine nature" (2 Peter 1:4).

In his opening remarks to the Philippians, Paul writes, "And I am sure of this, that he who began a good work in you will bring it to completion at the day of Jesus Christ" (Philippians 1:6). He continues this thought in chapter 2, "For it is God who works in you, both to will and to work for His good pleasure" (v. 13). Without question, it would be pleasing to God if all of His children were living paragons of the exquisite character and virtue of Jesus Christ. With so many "great and precious promises" designed to make us like Him, how can we not be convinced that becoming Christlike is indeed possible? The challenge we face lies in our ability to answer the same probing question that Jesus asked two blind men, "Do you believe that I am able to do this?" (Matthew 9:28).

3. **Works** — "Faith apart from works is dead" (James 2:26).

It's clear from the context of James 2:14–26 that a solitary faith is a useless faith. Unless it is complemented by works, faith is as worthless as a blueprint without a builder. Verse 22 says Abraham's faith was completed by his works. Works are to faith as execution is to a plan. And although we just read "it is God who works in [us]," we are responsible for the doing. Oswald Chambers aptly describes the difference between God's work and our work in his explanation of Peter's admonition to "add to our faith virtue" (2 Peter 1:5 NKJV):

"Our work only begins where God's grace has laid the foundation."[3]
—*Oswald Chambers*

> *Add* means that we have to do something. We are in danger of forgetting that we cannot do what God does, and that God will not do what we can do. We cannot save nor sanctify ourselves—God does that. But God will not give us good habits or character, and He will not force us to walk correctly before Him. We have to do all that ourselves. We must "work *out*" our "own salvation" which God has worked *in* us (Philippians 2:12). *Add* means that we must get into the habit of doing things, and in the initial stages that is difficult. To take the initiative is to make a beginning—to instruct yourself in the way you must go.... We have to take the initiative where we *are*, not where we have not yet been.[4]

It's so true it bears repeating, "*Add* means that *we* have to do something," and "We have to take the initiative *where we are*, not where we have not yet been."[5]

Time for a Golf Lesson

In *Putting Like a Genius*, Dr. Bob Rotella, sports psychologist and author, addresses the importance of being precise in picking your target when on the putting surface. When facing long putts, many golfers will say, "I just want to get this within a three to four foot circle of the hole." It has been proven that this approach will often leave you five to six feet from the hole, whereas if you say, "I am going to try to sink this putt," you will be more likely to get within that three to four foot circle (if not closer).

Other times, like when hitting an approach shot, it is wiser— after factoring in the risk/reward—to hit into the *fat of the green* rather than take *dead aim* at the flag stick. But such logic does not apply in our pursuit of Christlikeness. The risk we take is in *not* aiming to be like Him, and the loss incurred is that the world potentially sees a misrepresentation of Jesus Christ. Conversely, the reward for *aiming* is that the world has a better chance of seeing a truer representation of the Savior who gave Himself for them so that they, too, might have life. Let us, therefore, purpose in our hearts to take dead aim at apprehending that for which we were apprehended—Christlikeness!

For Further Study

"Not that I have already obtained this
or am already perfect..."
Philippians 3:12

1. State why you agree or disagree with the premise that it is possible to be Christlike.
2. What does the author state is more important than whether or not we actually attain Christlikeness?
3. Why is choice important as it pertains to pursuing Christlikeness?
4. What three strands come together to form a strong, threefold cord?
5. Describe the healthy tension that exists between the strands in the threefold cord, and how this helps us in our pursuit of becoming like Christ.
6. What does it mean to "aim" to be like Christ, and why is that significant in the life of the Christian?

3

Day of Reckoning

"Likewise you also, reckon yourselves to be dead indeed to sin, but alive to God in Christ Jesus our Lord."
Romans 6:11 (KJV)

AIMING IS NOT ENOUGH. Being intentional is not enough. It's a good start, but there's more. This is now where the proverbial rubber meets the road: where revelation becomes reality, where truth becomes tangible, and where precept becomes practice. It's where we begin to apply the threefold cord of grace, faith, and works by aligning ourselves with God's Word and exercising ourselves toward godliness.

"I'm Back!"

I have a pair of jeans that have a particular crease in the fly, which is not visible once the pants are zipped up but is nonetheless visible to me when I put them on. Every time I take them out of the dryer I see this annoying fold, which I sometimes ignore, but at other times I am determined to eradicate. So I grab the iron and ironing board, apply lots of heat, steam, and pressure, and *voila!*—the annoying crease is gone—or not.

I can't seem to make it through an entire day before this characteristic crease is exerting its right to remain. That has also been my experience with what Paul refers to as the old man (i.e., self)—that guy that I supposedly nailed to the cross the day before but who is seemingly back from the dead.

35

Jesus said, "If anyone would come after me, let him deny himself and take up his cross daily and follow me" (Luke 9:23). There's a lot to unpack in this verse—and we'll get to that in the next chapter—but for now I wish to focus on what may well be the most significant word in His statement: *daily*. Wouldn't it be great if all I had to do was offer up a one-time prayer of dedication to deny myself and take up my cross? If only it were that simple. If only that were sufficient to put the old man to death once and for all. But it's not. Jesus said we must take up the cross *daily*. I believe He understood that while I'm asleep, the old man somehow manages to climb down from the cross and will be sitting at the foot of my bed when I awake.

"Good *Morn*-ing," he says in a singsong voice with his legs crossed and hands resting one atop the other on his knee. He then announces with a Garfieldesque grin, "I'm *ba*-ack!"

Can you relate to this? Surely, I'm not the only one to experience this phenomenon. Just like those jeans of mine with the annoying crease, I can't seem to find a way to once-and-for-all extricate myself from the influence of the old man. I'm not saying I have to *yield* to his influence; what I'm saying is that it requires a *daily diligence* on my part to "walk by the Spirit" in order to "not gratify the desires of the flesh" (Galatians 5:16).

Fore!

In Romans 7, Paul gives us a window into his own personal struggle with the old man:

> So I find it to be a law that when I want to do right, evil lies close at hand. For I delight in the law of God, in my inner being, but I see in my members another law waging war against the law of my mind and making me captive to the law of sin that dwells in my members. Wretched man that I am! Who will deliver me from this body of death? Thanks be to God through Jesus Christ our Lord! So then, I myself

serve the law of God with my mind, but with my flesh
I serve the law of sin (Romans 7:21–25).

Golf is an excellent teacher. I recall a particularly painful round
I played (during the writing of this chapter) when I carded a 95
for 18 holes. For me, this was awful. I've shot many rounds in the
70s, and for a long time rarely shot anything worse than 85. On
this day, however, I could not get the ball in play off the tee. We
were playing a difficult course; tall heather if you miss the fairway
wide left or right, and lightning fast greens. I lost more balls in this
round—ten!—than in any round I can remember.

How does this relate to the struggle against the influence of the
old man? This particular round of golf resembled everything Paul
describes here in Romans 7:

> I don't really understand myself, for I want to do
> what is right, but I don't do it. Instead, I do what
> I hate.... I want to do what is right, but I can't. I
> want to do what is good, but I don't. I don't want to
> do what is wrong, but I do it anyway. (Romans 7:15,
> 18–19 NLT)

Like Paul, I did not really understand myself that day. Wayward
shots abounded. Whatever I wanted to do, I couldn't. Whatever I
didn't want to do, I executed to perfection. I hit it in the heather
on the left. I hit it in the heather on the right. No matter how hard
I tried, I could not find the fairway.

Wouldn't it be hilarious (and telling) if every time we had a
wayward thought, launched an unkind remark, or engaged in a
selfish act, we yelled, "Fore!" in order to warn those around us they
were in harm's way? That's the standard protocol for golfers when
they hit an errant shot that's on a line to potentially hit someone.
Can you imagine all the head jerking we would see in response to
the insanity of so many people shouting, "Fore!" all day long?

All kidding aside, here's the point: We all have days when it
seems that no matter how much we reckon ourselves dead to sin

and alive to God, we seem to get it all backwards. Instead of encouraging, we berate. Instead of serving, we sit on our hands. Instead of believing God's Word, we doubt. Rather than being frustrated or overcome with condemnation, we simply need to keep in mind this truth that Paul speaks of: "But if I do what I don't want to do, I am not really the one doing wrong; it is sin living in me that does it" (Romans 7:20 NLT).

We all have days when it seems that no matter how much we reckon ourselves dead to sin and alive to God, we seem to get it all backwards. Instead of encouraging, we berate. Instead of serving, we sit on our hands. Instead of believing God's Word, we doubt.

And that should give us hope; hope that God knows and understands our struggle against sin, which is why He has shown us how to view (i.e., reckon) ourselves in the light of our crucified and risen Savior.

The Reckoning: Make It Personal and Practical

Virtually everyone who believes in Jesus Christ knows a day is coming when God will judge nations and individuals, Jew and Gentile, saved and unsaved. This is often referred to as the *day of reckoning* (see Isaiah 2:12, Romans 14:10–12, Matthew 25:31–46, Revelation 20:11–12).

Much has been written about the various judgments in Scripture, but that is not the focus here. I want to call your attention to yet another day of reckoning: *Today.*

> Take care, brothers, lest there be in any of you an evil, unbelieving heart, leading you to fall away from the living God. But exhort one another every day, as long as it is called "today," that none of you may be hardened by the deceitfulness of sin.... As it is said, "Today, if you hear his voice, do not harden your hearts as in the rebellion." (Hebrews 3:12–13, 15)

By God's perfect design, we cannot relive the past, nor can we live the future. We can only live the present. We can certainly learn from the past and plan for our future, but we can only live *today*.

May I suggest that you consider each day a *personal day of reckoning*? Every day you are afforded the opportunity to "reckon [yourself] to be dead indeed to sin, but alive to God in Christ Jesus our Lord" (Romans 6:11b NKJV).

In both English and Greek etymology the word *reckon* is an accounting term. The Merriam-Webster online dictionary[1] and the online *Blue Letter Bible* Greek Lexicon[2] use words like *count, compute, calculate, count over,* and *settle accounts,* along with expressions such as *to regard or think of as; to accept something as certain; to determine, purpose, or decide* to define what it means to reckon something as being so. The *Blue Letter Bible* definition also contains the following commentary about the word *reckon*:

> *This word deals with reality.* If I reckon (logizomai) that my bank book has $25 in it, it has $25 in it. Otherwise I am deceiving myself. *This word refers more to fact than supposition or opinion.* (emphasis added)[3]

Therefore, when Paul says we are to reckon ourselves dead to sin, he is referring to the fact that Christ has settled our account forever by paying for our sin with the blood He shed on the cross. According to the apostle John, the last words Jesus uttered on the cross were, "It is finished" (John 19:30). This makes perfect sense as we consider that Christ has made His once-for-all entry into the heavenly ledger—crediting righteousness to our account and canceling our debt of sin—thereby resulting in a balance due of zero!

It is essential that I set myself in agreement with this reality by *counting* or *accepting it as certain*. The human experience being what it is, however, suggests there will be days when this reality will be challenged, which is why I suggest a daily reckoning of this truth to serve as a continual reminder that Christ's entry written into the ledger with His own blood remains unfaded for all of time and eternity.

The Bible teaches that we are justified by faith (Romans 5:1). You may have heard this expressed as meaning *just-as-if-I'd* never sinned. It doesn't literally mean you've never sinned; it simply means that God chooses to look upon you *as though* you had never sinned. He reckons (or counts) you as righteous in His sight through the sacrificial, atoning blood of Christ.

In similar fashion, we are to count or consider ourselves as (1) *dead to sin* and (2) *alive to God*. This happens through *identification*—identification with Christ's death, but also identification with His resurrection life.

1. Dead to Sin

Oswald Chambers offers this practical explanation of what it means to be dead to sin:

> The inescapable spiritual need each of us has is...
> to sign the death certificate of our sin nature. I must
> take my emotional opinions and intellectual beliefs
> and be willing to turn them into a moral verdict
> against the nature of sin; that is, against any claim
> I have to my right to myself. Paul said, "I have been
> crucified with Christ...." He did not say, "I have
> made a determination to imitate Jesus Christ," or,
> "I will really make an effort to follow Him"—but—"I
> have been *identified* with Him in His death." Once I
> reach this moral decision and act on it, all that Christ
> accomplished *for* me on the Cross is accomplished *in*
> me. My unrestrained commitment of myself to God
> gives the Holy Spirit the opportunity to grant to me
> the holiness of Jesus Christ.[4]

Signing the death certificate of our sin nature is a fitting picture of how we can relate this spiritual concept to something practical. Although there's no literal death certificate for me to sign, I can apply my faith to this concept by having a rich understanding of what it means to identify with the death of Jesus Christ.

In Romans 7, Paul uses the analogy of a husband and wife, bound to each other as long as they both live, to illustrate that we are bound to our sin nature as long as we are *alive* to it. Upon the death of either husband or wife, the marriage contract is broken. In similar fashion, when I died with Christ my contractual obligation to the law of sin and death was broken, so sin can no longer leverage God's perfect law against me—unless I give my consent.

> For while we were living in the flesh, our sinful passions, aroused by the law, were at work in our members to bear fruit for death. But now we are released from the law, having died to that which held us captive. (Romans 7:5–6a)

Death has a sobering finality. Those of us who have lost loved ones must come to grips with the fact that they aren't coming back. They won't be "walking through that door," no matter how much we long for them to. However, we can apply that same thinking in a positive way to the daily reckoning of ourselves to be dead to sin. We can foster a mentality that puts its foot down and says, "I am crucified with Christ. My old man is dead, and sin is not walking through that door today!"

Empowered by a Watery Grave

Before we shift our focus to the importance of reckoning ourselves alive to God, I don't want to miss the opportunity to consider an underappreciated yet profound truth found in the opening verses of Romans chapter 6:

> What shall we say then? Shall we continue in sin that grace may abound? Certainly not! How shall we who died to sin live any longer in it? Or do you not know that *as many of us as were baptized* into Christ

Jesus were *baptized into His death*? Therefore we were *buried with Him through baptism* into death, that just as Christ was raised from the dead by the glory of the Father, even so we also should walk in newness of life. (Romans 6:1–4 NKJV, emphasis added)

This passage teaches us that water baptism is more than just an outward expression of our faith in Christ. Paul's question, "How shall we who died to sin live any longer in it?" appears to be rhetorical—based on how he answers it: "Or do you not know that *as many of us as were baptized* into Christ Jesus were *baptized into His death*?" Paul is teaching that baptism not only signifies our identification with Christ in His death, burial, and resurrection, it also empowers us to walk in newness of life so that we are no longer slaves to sin.

"Are you saying I have to be baptized to be saved? What about the thief on the cross?"

Baptism not only signifies our identification with Christ in His death, burial, and resurrection, it also empowers us to walk in newness of life so that we are no longer slaves to sin.

Though some teach that baptism is a *requirement* for salvation, I have never seen anything in Scripture that categorically backs up this claim. However, it is quite clear that water baptism was the common practice of the early church and was part and parcel of believing in Christ for salvation (see Acts 2:38; 8:35–38; 10:44–48; 16:31–33; 18:8, 19:1–6). In other words, all who placed their faith in Christ were exhorted to be baptized, and there's not one instance recorded in Scripture where someone refused to follow the apostles' instructions for baptism.

Now about that thief on the cross: Not only did he lack the opportunity to be baptized, there was also no *need* for this man to be baptized because he wasn't coming down from the cross (alive).

He would not be living out his days as a follower of Jesus Christ, so he didn't need to be empowered to walk in newness of life. We, on the other hand, need every advantage we can gain in putting to death the old man and living each day in the resurrection power of Christ.

If you are a believer in Jesus and have never been baptized in water, I encourage you to avail yourself of the opportunity to bury the old man and be raised in newness of life. As we see in Romans chapter 6, a significant empowerment awaits you.

Now you may be wondering how this empowerment works or if it works at all, especially if you've witnessed a less-than-Christ-like example from someone you know who has been born from above, baptized in water, and professes Christ. It is not my place to describe exactly how this works, any more than Jesus felt it necessary to explain to Nicodemus exactly how the new birth works. I can, perhaps, remove some of the mystique associated with this premise by offering a practical illustration of how water baptism can give you some firepower in reckoning yourself dead to sin and alive to God. However, as it is with any endowment—be it intelligence, wealth, spiritual gifts, or natural talents—failure to use them is to shortchange oneself of an opportunity to benefit from them.

As someone who *has* plunged beneath the waters of baptism, I can authoritatively say to the old man, "You were buried in baptism. You were laid to rest in a watery grave. You no longer have any claim to me. You have no power over me. I was raised out of the waters of baptism and empowered to walk in newness of life. I was buried in weakness and raised in power—the power of a new life!"

On the flip side, if I had never been baptized, I could not claim the old man had been buried *through baptism*—because he never was. I'm not exactly sure what biblical footing I would have at this point, but the corollary we find in Romans 6:1–4 is that those who have been baptized into Christ are in a stronger position to identify with Christ in His death and resurrection than those who have not.

This is not to imply, nor should it be inferred from this writing, that the authenticity or legitimacy of a person's salvation is being called into question if they have never been baptized. Receiving Christ by grace through faith and being baptized in water are mutually exclusive events, which more often than not were documented in Scripture as occurring at, or very near, the same time.

2. Alive to God

If all I did was to master the art of reckoning myself dead to sin, that would be quite an accomplishment. However, what good would it do to simply put the old man to death? We also need to learn to reckon ourselves *alive to God* in order to walk in newness of life—a Christlike life.

> Likewise you also, reckon yourselves to be dead indeed to sin, but *alive to God* in Christ Jesus our Lord (Romans 6:11 NKJV, emphasis added).

If I am dead indeed, then let me also be alive indeed. If I've been buried, let me also be raised. Let me be alive to God, alive to His Word, alive to holiness, alive to righteousness. Let me set my affection on things above, not on things on the earth (Colossians 3:2 KJV). Let me "put on the new man, which is renewed in knowledge after the image of him that created him" (v. 10 KJV).

We are exhorted numerous times and in various ways throughout the New Testament to adorn ourselves with Christ and His character:

> *Put on* then, as God's chosen ones, holy and beloved, compassionate hearts, kindness, humility, meekness, and patience, bearing with one another and, if one has a complaint against another, forgiving each other; as the Lord has forgiven you, so you also must forgive. And above all these *put on* love, which binds everything together in perfect harmony. (Colossians 3:12–14, emphasis added)

> For as many of you as were baptized into Christ have
> *put on* Christ. (Galatians 3:27, emphasis added)

> But *put on* the Lord Jesus Christ, and make no pro-
> vision for the flesh, to gratify its desires. (Romans
> 13:14, emphasis added)

After I have drawn the line of demarcation signaling the passing
away of the old, the focal point of my life should be this: *everything
is new*. "Therefore, if anyone is in Christ, he is a new creation. The
old has passed away; behold, the new has come" (2 Corinthians
5:17). I am no longer a slave to sin. I'm now the servant of righteousness. I now live to forgive, to show mercy, to extend grace,
and to walk in the kindness and love of God, our Savior. I live to
fulfill the plan and purpose of God for my life. I live to do His will.
I live to bring Him glory. This is what it means to be alive to God.
The NLT expresses this beautifully:

> When he died, he died once to break the power of sin.
> But now that he lives, *he lives for the glory of God*.
> (Romans 6:10 NLT, emphasis added)

Jesus lives for the glory of the Father. Should I not do the same?

It may sound trite, but there is no turning back. My gaze is forward and upward, not backward and downward. Perhaps an occasional glance in the rearview mirror helps to keep me humble, but
my focus should be on the life before me, not on what lies behind.
I choose each day *to live* for Christ. He bought me with His sinless
blood and I am completely His. I'm alive to the purpose for which I
was purchased—a purpose that begins anew each day by reckoning
myself dead to sin and alive to God through Jesus Christ, our Lord!

For Further Study

"So I find it to be a law that when I want to do right,
evil lies close at hand."
Romans 7:21

1. In Romans 7, Paul describes the struggle we all face in trying to do what's right. Where does he place the blame for failing to do what we should or doing something we shouldn't?
2. Describe what it means to you personally to reckon yourself dead to sin.
3. Christ has settled our account forever with respect to sin. With that in mind, share why you either agree or disagree with the notion that it is good to consider every day a personal day of reckoning with respect to seeing ourselves as dead to sin and alive to God.
4. Describe how Paul uses the husband and wife analogy with respect to the power of sin in our lives.
5. Is it possible to be completely free from sin? Be prepared to support your answer.
6. Though water baptism is not a requirement for salvation, the author suggests there is an empowerment available to those who have been baptized. What is this empowerment, and how does it help us? Be prepared to share why you either agree or disagree with this premise.
7. What does it mean to be alive to God? Be prepared to share at least one evidence of this in your life.

Part 2

The Foundation

foundation[1] [foun-**dey**-sh*uh* n]
—noun

1.   *the basis or groundwork of anything.*

4

A Defining Moment

"And the disciples were first called Christians in Antioch."
Acts 11:26 (NKJV)

WHAT IS A CHRISTIAN? Can you tell me what it means to be one? Even better, can you show me?

These are not the easiest questions to answer, nor are any of us perfect in our demonstration of Christ. Notwithstanding, these questions deserve and demand our attention—our *full* attention.

The world has long scorned the Church for the hypocritical and scandalous behavior of some of its high-profile leaders. Whatever the reasons, the modern day Church in large part has failed to provide a consistently clear picture of what it means to be a Christian.

> *My life proclaims a message every day. So does yours. The question we should be asking ourselves is, "What is that message?"*

In Paul's second letter to the Corinthians, he refers to them collectively as a living epistle "known and read by all... a letter from Christ... written not with ink but with the Spirit of the living God, not on tablets of stone but on tablets of human hearts" (2 Corinthians 3:2–3). Though an epistle was a handwritten letter in Paul's day, in today's ever-evolving technological world, we could describe ourselves as living texts, tweets, blog posts, or emails—known and read by all through how we live. That's both good news and bad—good news, if we are living godly, Christlike lives, and bad news, if we are living self-centered, too-much-of-me-too-little-of-Jesus lives.

My life proclaims a message every day. So does yours. The question we should be asking ourselves is, "What *is* that message?" If our words and actions belie the character of Christ, maybe we should leave our Christian T-shirts in the closet, get rid of our fish symbols and bumper stickers, and just keep quiet, rather than announce to the world we are "Christians." It would be less damaging to the reputation of Christ and His church.

We can do better. We *must* do better, if we are to reach the fallen and reconcile them to Christ.

Comic Conundrum

Riddle me this, Batman: What has a brain, walks on two legs, and identifies with a Christian religion?

According to Frank Newport, Editor in Chief of Gallup, "The large majority of Americans—77% of the adult population—identify with a Christian religion."[1] I must say I'm stumped as to exactly what that means. Does that mean 77 percent of Americans are living an exemplary Christian life? I have often accused myself of living as somewhat of a troglodyte, but even so, I come out from under my rock often enough to observe that 77 percent of Americans cannot possibly be living a Christian life as taught and modeled by Jesus Christ. Otherwise, we would be influencing our communities with the gospel far more than we are.

Think about it. If a presidential candidate won 77 percent of the popular vote, that would be a landslide margin of epic proportions. The largest ever was Warren G. Harding's 60.3 percent to James M. Cox's 34.1 percent in the 1920 presidential election.[2] It's a little easier to achieve such margins of victory in the Electoral College, but this is unheard of in the popular vote.

So with that frame of reference, if 77 percent of Americans were truly embracing and living the principles Jesus taught, I would expect us to be moving the morality needle in this country more toward Christian values than we are. Instead, in the late twentieth and early twenty-first centuries, what we have seen is the unraveling of America's moral fabric. Jesus said we would know a tree by its fruit (Matthew 7:16–20). Our actions are speaking louder than our words—and our surveys.

All Aboard!

Why do you suppose 77 percent of Americans say they identify with a Christian religion? I'll venture to say it's because they want to believe their ticket has been punched and they have a seat on the train bound for heaven when they die. Yet here's the reality: the majority of us want to have that assurance while continuing to live life on our terms rather than obeying the commandments and teachings of Christ.

We want to have our cake and eat it too. We want to do whatever we like, whenever we like, and then go to church on Sunday so we get a checkmark next to our name on the attendance roll. But how many of us truly want to be transformed into the image of Christ? How many of us want Jesus Christ to establish His kingdom in our hearts? How many of us want to please Him more than anyone or anything else? The following passage is the beginning of a parable wherein Jesus compares Himself to a nobleman whose citizens hated him:

> He said therefore, "A nobleman went into a far country to receive for himself a kingdom and then return.... But his citizens hated him and sent a delegation after him, saying, 'We do not want this man to reign over us.'" (Luke 19:12, 14)

If our eyes are open at all, we must acknowledge that the majority of Americans do not want Christ to reign over them, nor do they desire being conformed to His image. And why might that be? Because we are too vested in years of believing a gospel that conforms Him to *our* image. No wonder there are so many brands of Christianity in the world, especially in America. It has to do in large part because we want to make God look like us instead of the other way around. We deftly, albeit detrimentally, conform God to our belief systems rather than forging our beliefs in the foundry of His Word: "The words of the LORD are pure words, like silver refined in a furnace on the ground, purified seven times" (Psalm 12:6).

Show and Tell

Let's revisit those questions posed at the beginning of this chapter: What is a Christian? Can you tell me? Even better, can you show me?

It is one thing to tell people what it means to be a Christian, but if we can *show* them by our lives, then they will be more apt to accept what we *tell* them. Perhaps the simplest answer to this question is: *a follower of Christ*. A Christian is one who follows Christ.

But what does it mean to follow Christ? David said, "My soul followeth hard after thee" (Psalm 63:8 KJV). There was a time when Peter followed Him from a distance (Luke 22:54). Luke's gospel reveals that Peter was clearly conflicted after his Lord's arrest. Inwardly, he wanted to follow closely, but outwardly, he was not yet prepared to accept the consequences of being closely identified with Jesus, which led to his trey of denials.

People today follow friends and family on Facebook and Twitter. They follow celebrity tweets and online blogs because they have some level of interest in a person or a news story. Let's take a closer look at three things Jesus said concerning what it means to follow Him:

> "If anyone would come after me, let him *deny himself* and *take up his cross daily* and *follow me.* For whoever would save his life will lose it, but whoever loses his life for my sake will save it." (Luke 9:23–24, emphasis added)

1. Deny Self

To deny myself means I waive my right to self-governance. I wave goodbye to it. I waive my right to anything that is self-serving. I waive my right to pursue my interests instead of God's interests. In short, denying self means death to self.

Jesus went on to say in Luke 9:24 that those who are committed to saving (i.e., preserving) their lives end up losing them in the process, whereas those who lose their lives for His sake will find them. What did He mean by that? Quite simply that I can't live for myself and for God simultaneously. It's an either/or proposition. Either I pursue life on my terms—and miss out on a life in Christ, or I forsake worldly gain—and find true riches in Christ. Moses understood this, and his choice is chronicled for us in the book of Hebrews:

> By faith Moses, when he was grown up, refused to be called the son of Pharaoh's daughter, choosing rather to be mistreated with the people of God than to enjoy the fleeting pleasures of sin. He considered the reproach of Christ greater wealth than the treasures of Egypt, for he was looking to the reward. (Hebrews 11:24–26)

My natural tendency is to do everything in my power to preserve and protect my life—to shield myself from discomfort, pain, hardship, and tribulation. But following Jesus on His terms *guarantees* I will experience all of these things. Following Christ wherever He leads me requires a denial of self—a total rejection of the base instinct to preserve, protect, and pursue what I want or what I think is best for me. Only then will I experience the life that is found by pursuing what God has willed and purposed for me.

Oswald Chambers describes the nature of sin as "my claim to my right to myself."[3] Denying self is refusing to indulge the fleshly appetites of my selfish nature (see Galatians 5:19–21). It is saying no to my will when it opposes God's will.

To use a basketball analogy, denying self is like a defender denying the pass. When playing a man-to-man defense, coaches instruct their players to guard their man so closely, and in such a way, as to make it impossible for him to receive a pass from a team-mate. Similarly, denying self means I guard my heart and mind so tenaciously that none of Satan's devices or worldly allurements dissuades me from obeying, pleasing, and honoring Christ. Solomon's wisdom is applicable here: "Guard your heart above all else, for it determines the course of your life" (Proverbs 4:23 NLT).

In the garden of Gethsemane, Jesus demonstrated what it means to deny self. When He left the garden, everything was settled in His mind, and He was committed to enduring whatever suffering awaited Him in order to fulfill God's plan of redemption as the "Lamb of God, who takes away the sin of the world" (John 1:29). But while He was in the garden, He pleaded with His Father to explore other possibilities:

> And going a little farther, he fell to the ground and prayed that, if it were possible, the hour might pass from him. And he said, "Abba, Father, all things are possible for you. Remove this cup from me. Yet not what I will, but what you will." (Mark 14:35–36)

Jesus, the Man, did not want to suffer. And if I can borrow a thought from my friend Dr. Robert Cornwall, it wasn't just the suffering that Jesus agonized over. It was *who* He would suffer for— those who hated Him; those who were too stupid to rejoice in the healing of the sick on a Sabbath day because they would rather keep rules than extend mercy; thieves, liars, murderers, adulterers; people who are unkind, unthankful, and selfish; people like ... you and me. Is it possible Jesus asked Himself, "Why should I, having never sinned, die for such sinners?"

By reminding His Father that all things are possible for Him, and by requesting that the cup of suffering be taken away, Jesus was essentially asking the Father to consider alternative solutions.

It's just how the mind of a person works when under duress. We want to know if there is a way out. If I were to put myself in Jesus' shoes, it is easy to picture a one-sided conversation something like this:

"Father, must I drink this cup of suffering? Is there not another way we can do this? I mean, You created the universe. There's nothing too hard for You. Can't we be creative in how we solve this? Is there not some innovative thinking that would suggest another option?"

Jesus listens intently for the Father's response to His can-we-think-outside-the-box appeal, but the only sound to be heard is the drone of crickets filling the night air.

"Father... ?"

More crickets.

"Father... are You there?"

The crescendo of crickets reaches a climax, but cannot quell the deafening silence of the Father. Left with no other option, Jesus breathes a resolute sigh and says, "Father, not my will but Yours be done."

The truth of the matter is that Jesus already knew His death on the cross was the only way for God to reconcile the world to Himself (John 12:27). He had previously told a crowd in Jerusalem that He was going to be "lifted up from the earth," which He said "to show by what kind of death he was going to die" (John 12:32–33). This is most likely what He discussed with Moses and Elijah on the Mount of Transfiguration, when they spoke of His *decease*, which He should *accomplish* in Jerusalem (Luke 9:30–31 KJV). To further underscore this point, had there been another solution, Jesus would not have previously declared Himself to be the *only way* to come to the Father (John 14:6).

This was the only way and He knew it. Although He was fully Divine, He was also fully human, which is why His mind compelled Him to explore the possibility of another way. His humanity is what made it possible for Him to be "in all points tempted like as we are, yet without sin" (Hebrews 4:15 KJV).

There, in the garden, we see Jesus, the Man, wrestling with the same emotions we do whenever we are faced with the decision to deny self in order to obey God. We also see the Master's perfect example of denying Himself and choosing God's will over His own.

2. Take Up the Cross

Jesus did not tell us to take up the cross as an artifact to be carried around (literally or figuratively). However, a man by the name of Arthur Blessitt literally carried a life-size cross around the globe over a period of 44 years, visiting 321 countries, island groups and territories, and covering 40,500 miles.[4] This man's amazing feat no doubt impacted many thousands of lives all over the world with the gospel of Jesus Christ, but it's not a picture of what it means for us to take up the cross.

In no way am I questioning or disrespecting this man's work. In fact, I don't see how anyone could begin to accomplish what he did without a complete capitulation of self to the call of God. This, however, was a unique calling for one man, and certainly not applicable to all of Christ's followers.

So what *did* Jesus mean when He said to take up the cross? First, we must understand what the cross represents. Its purpose is not to accessorize our wardrobes or decorate our homes. Jesus was not encouraging us to take up the cross to wear as a piece of jewelry, or to hang it like tinsel on a Christmas tree. And it most certainly is not to be used as a good luck charm. The sole purpose of the cross is death. The cross takes no prisoners and leaves no survivors.

I'm not saying it's wrong to wear a cross on a necklace, tattoo one on your body, or hang one from the rearview mirror in your car, but you need to ask yourself what your motive is for such displays. It's a sobering thing—at least it should be—to intentionally shine a spotlight on yourself through the adornment or display of Christian symbols. You may look cool and fashionable, but you won't advance the cause of Jesus Christ if your life contradicts the Jesus you claim to represent.

For a brief period after receiving Christ, I thought everyone who had a cross hanging from their neck was a Christian. I soon discovered that was not the case. I would enthusiastically greet them and ask how long they had known Christ. Some of the strange looks I got told me the cross meant something entirely different to them than it did to me.

In his letter to the churches of Galatia, after contrasting the works of the flesh with the fruit of the Spirit, Paul concludes his exhortation by saying, "those who belong to Christ Jesus have crucified the flesh with its passions and desires" (Galatians 5:24). But how, exactly, does that happen?

Conceptually, carrying the cross has to do with an attitude or mind-set. What I *carry* is an understanding that with every inner struggle, confrontation, offense, or injustice comes an opportunity to stretch out on the cross and let such God-ordained circumstances serve as the hammer and nails that fix me to the cross so I live as one who is crucified with Christ.

Jesus carried His cross, and so should we. But there's only one reason to carry a cross, and that is to transport it to the designated place of crucifixion. For Jesus, that place was Golgotha. For us, it's whatever *place* God ordains and engineers through our circumstances. That could be a domestic dispute. It could be an inconsiderate motorist who cuts you off in traffic. It might be an undeserved reprimand from your boss,

> *Conceptually, carrying the cross has to do with an attitude or mind-set. What I carry is an understanding that with every inner struggle, confrontation, offense, or injustice comes an opportunity to stretch out on the cross and let such God-ordained circumstances serve as the hammer and nails that fix me to the cross so I live as one who is crucified with Christ.*

or perhaps an act of kindness on your part that goes completely unappreciated. It could even be the still, small voice of the Lord prompting you to do something you simply don't want to do.

A friend of mine once shared with me how he was impacted by the crucifixion scene in Mel Gibson's movie *The Passion of the Christ*. The unblemished Lamb of God, now marred, disfigured, and utterly exhausted from the merciless brutality of the Roman soldiers and uphill climb to Golgotha, collapses beneath the weight of the cross. After the soldiers strip Him of His blood-stained robe, exposing His excoriated flesh, Jesus uses His last vestige of strength to *crawl to the cross!* No coercion was necessary. He was embracing it. He was laying down His life. No one was taking it from Him.

Is this an accurate depiction of what actually happened? I don't know. I wasn't there. Regardless, I believe Gibson captured the spirit and essence of the commitment Jesus had made to give His life as a ransom for sinners.

But how was He (Jesus) able to do that? How was He able to embrace the cross? It was made possible by the decision He had already made to deny Himself in order to pursue and fulfill the will of God, which Scripture describes as "the joy that was set before him" (Hebrews 12:2).

And so it is with us. Taking up our cross daily is purely voluntary; God doesn't force it on us. It's dependent on an absolute resolution to deny ourselves the right to self-governance in order to embrace the joy that comes from obeying God and fulfilling His purpose for our lives.

Because of my IT experience, I am thoroughly acquainted with the principles of project management. One fundamental precept is to understand *dependencies*. Certain tasks simply cannot begin until other tasks are completed. Think about building a house. You can't start with the roof. You start with the foundation and build up from there.

What Jesus laid out in Luke 9:23 is a progression that goes from (1) denying self to (2) taking up the cross to (3) following Him. I will not be able to follow Christ wherever He leads me unless I am crucified in complete submission to His will, and living a crucified life is only possible when I have made the decision to deny self.

Oswald Chambers aptly stated, "The Cross represents only one thing for us: complete, entire, absolute identification with the Lord Jesus Christ."[5] I take up the cross because I choose to identify with Christ. I want to share in His sufferings. I want to bear His reproach, and I want Him to live through me.

3. Follow Me

Some meanings of the word *follow* don't need much explanation. If you are walking ahead of me on the same path, then I am following you. If I ask your opinion about something and act upon your words, then I would be following your advice. If I am inspired by what I see you doing and attempt to imitate that behavior, then I am following your example. If I agree with what you teach and try to live by it, then I would be following your teaching (and by extension, following you).

But the word *follow* also carries with it something of a copulative meaning, not in the grammatical sense, as in words that connect other words or phrases, but instead, it suggests *uniting ourselves with Christ; joining ourselves to Him.*

To be united with Christ or joined to Him is synonymous with becoming one with Him, even as He was one with the Father. Not only was Jesus one with the Father as a member of the triune Godhead, but He was fully united with and joined to the Father in will and purpose.

In his first letter to the Corinthians, Paul explains the union believers have with Christ:

> Do you not know that your bodies are members of Christ? Shall I then take the members of Christ and make them members of a prostitute? Never! Or do

you not know that he who is joined to a prostitute becomes one body with her? For, as it is written, "The two will become one flesh." *But he who is joined to the Lord becomes one spirit with him.* (1 Corinthians 6:15–17, emphasis added)

It's interesting that Paul dared to use the analogy of a consummated sexual union to describe what it means to be joined to the Lord. This is the closest two people of the opposite sex can ever be, and as Paul quoted from Genesis 2:24, is the ultimate fulfillment of what it means to become one flesh.

In my relationship with Christ, I become one with Him through the consummation of joining my spirit (my heart, my mind, and my will) with His. This happens through identification—identifying myself with *His* interests, not identifying Him with *my* interests. It's possible to have a thought or an idea about something we think would be great for the kingdom of God, so off we go with our great plans and agendas, dragging Jesus along for the ride in order to "validate" what we are doing.

It's possible to have a thought or an idea about something we think would be great for the kingdom of God, so off we go with our great plans and agendas, dragging Jesus along for the ride in order to "validate" what we are doing.

We need to do a better job of seeking, recognizing, and identifying with God's interests instead of putting His name on things we have willed. We can never forget that He is the Vine, and we are the branches (John 15:5). The branch exists because of the vine, not the other way around. Jesus also said, "You did not choose me, but I chose you" (John 15:16). He created and chose me to serve Him. He does not exist to serve me.

Joined for Service

Jesus said, "If anyone serves me, he must follow me; and where I am, there will my servant be also" (John 12:26a). The word *serve* in John 12:26 is the same Greek word from which we get *deacon*. In other places where the word *serve* is used in Scripture, the meaning has more to do with worship than actually attending someone. Not so in this case. This word means *to be an attendant*; *to wait upon.*[6] You could say it means *to be at one's beck and call.*

Let's consider for a moment Joshua, the servant of Moses. The first time he is mentioned in Scripture is in Exodus 17 where Moses instructs Joshua, saying, "'Choose for us men, and go out and fight with Amalek. . . .' So Joshua did as Moses told him, and . . . overwhelmed Amalek and his people with the sword" (Exodus 17:9–10, 13).

The next time Joshua is mentioned is in Exodus 24:

> Now the LORD said to Moses, "Come up to Me on the mountain and remain there, and I will give you the stone tablets with the law and the commandment which I have written for their instruction." So Moses arose with *Joshua his servant*, and Moses went up to the mountain of God. (Exodus 24:12–13 NASB, emphasis added)

It's not clear how Joshua became the servant of Moses, but he may have taken the initiative to join himself to Moses by simply asking, "Is there anything I can do to help you?" It's also possible that Moses asked Joshua to become his servant because of his faithful obedience in the fight against the Amalekites.

How Joshua obtained this role is not as relevant as what we're able to observe of him in this role. From the point at which Scripture identifies him as the servant of Moses, the two are seemingly joined at the hip. Wherever we see Moses, Joshua is right there with him (see Exodus 32:15–17; 33:7–11; Numbers 11:28;

27:15–21; Deuteronomy 31:14). This is noteworthy, given that Moses is a type of Christ (see Deuteronomy 18:15 and Acts 7:37).

We previously read in John 12:26 where Jesus said, "Where I am, there will my servant be also." He made this statement as part of a larger discourse concerning His approaching death:

> And Jesus answered them, "The hour has come for the Son of Man to be glorified. Truly, truly, I say to you, unless a grain of wheat falls into the earth and dies, it remains alone; but if it dies, it bears much fruit. Whoever loves his life loses it, and whoever hates his life in this world will keep it for eternal life. If anyone serves me, he must follow me; and where I am, there will my servant be also. If anyone serves me, the Father will honor him. (John 12:23-26)

"If anyone serves me, he must follow me" (v. 26). Given the context of this passage, it would seem that Jesus was telling His disciples that serving and following Him would ultimately lead to their own death. He had also just challenged them to hate their life in order to keep it. Following Christ to our death (i.e., death to self) frees us to serve His purposes rather than our own.

Following Jesus means I have joined myself to Him for the purpose to which He has called me, which is not the same as joining Jesus to a purpose or cause that I wish to pursue.

With that in mind, let's look again at the last part of verse 26, ". . . and where I am, there will my servant be also." So where, exactly, is Jesus? We know He ascended to heaven and is seated at the right hand of the Father (Mark 16:19). We also learn in Sunday school that Jesus is everywhere. How then can I, as a servant of Jesus, be where He is?

The answer lies in considering the context of His statement, which is *service:* "If anyone *serves* me. . . ." Following Jesus means I have joined myself to Him for the purpose to which He has called me, which is not the same as joining Jesus to a purpose or cause that I wish to pursue.

In an abstract sense, *where Jesus is* may be different for me than where Jesus is for you—in the context of service. It's true that wherever I go, Jesus is there because His Spirit abides in me. Plus, He promised to never leave me nor forsake me (Hebrews 13:5).

To avoid confusion, I'm speaking about what we do with our lives—and by extension what God is going to bless—rather than our physical location. Although, God's calling on my life could influence where I live, where I go, and what I do.

For example, let's say that God has called you to work with inner city youth, and me to work with college students. To fulfill our respective callings, I would expect you to spend some of your time in an urban setting, while I would spend some of my time on a college campus. By extension, I should not realistically expect that God would bless my work with inner city children to the degree His blessing would be upon my work with college students. Stated a bit differently, I would find (or experience) the Spirit of Jesus through working with college students more so than if I were to work with inner city youth. We necessarily place the answer to the question, "Where is Jesus?" in the context of service. For me the answer is, "On a college campus," while for you the answer is, "In the inner city."

Man from Macedonia

In Acts 16, we see an excellent example of this. Paul had already been forbidden by the Spirit to take the gospel to Asia, and when he attempted to go into Bithynia, God put the kibosh on that as well:

> And they went through the region of Phrygia and Galatia, having been forbidden by the Holy Spirit to speak the word in Asia. And when they had come up to Mysia, they attempted to go into Bithynia, but the

Spirit of Jesus did not allow them.... And a vision appeared to Paul in the night: a man of Macedonia was standing there, urging him and saying, "Come over to Macedonia and help us." And when Paul had seen the vision, immediately we sought to go on into Macedonia, *concluding that God had called us to preach the gospel to them.* (Acts 16:6–7, 9–10, emphasis added)

Paul could have gone into Asia or Bithynia, but it is clear from the above passage that in that situation, following Christ (i.e., being joined to and identified with His purpose) meant going into Macedonia. Had Paul followed his own heart, the Philippian jailer and his family may have never come to Christ, and your Bible may not include a book called Philippians.

Gone Fishing

John 21 gives a thought-provoking and mildly amusing account of one of the final interactions Jesus had with His disciples after His resurrection and before His ascension to the Father. John begins the anecdote as follows:

After this Jesus revealed himself again to the disciples by the Sea of Tiberias, and he revealed himself in this way. Simon Peter, Thomas (called the Twin), Nathanael of Cana in Galilee, the sons of Zebedee, and two others of his disciples were together. Simon Peter said to them, "I am going fishing." They said to him, "We will go with you." They went out and got into the boat, but that night they caught nothing. (John 21:1–3)

Peter and the other disciples don't quite know what to do with themselves. They know Jesus is alive, because He has previously appeared to them twice, but the Holy Spirit has not yet been poured out so they have not yet been "clothed with power from on high" (Luke 24:49). Their collective expectations that Jesus would immediately establish His kingdom—thus freeing them from Roman oppression—have been dashed, most likely leaving them in a state of disillusionment.

The man who insisted he was ready to go with Jesus both to prison and to death (Luke 22:33) is the same man who subsequently denied Him three times—with oaths and cursing. Luke tells us that Peter "went out and wept bitterly" (Luke 22:62) after disavowing Christ, so in addition to being devastated and disillusioned, he is likely riddled with self-disgust. At this point, he turns to fishing.

Along with James and John, the sons of Zebedee, Peter was a fisherman by trade, so when he said he was going fishing, it wasn't the same as me saying to a group of my golfing buddies, "Hey, guys, I've got a 2:24 tee time today. Anybody interested?" No, this was Peter saying, "I'm going back to work." It's possible he was doing this for the practical reason that there was no longer a money bag from which their needs were being met. If such were the case, then it makes even more sense that Peter would return to his former vocation, since that may have been the only way he knew how to make a living.

For more than three years Jesus poured Himself into these men, revealing to them the Father and preparing them to take the gospel into all the world. He told them He would be crucified and rise from the dead, but they remain obtuse in their understanding of these things. In spite of the fact that He has already appeared to them twice since His resurrection, the train is now officially going off the tracks, so Jesus appears to them a third time and uses a few fish to teach these men a poignant, life-changing lesson.

Flagged for Taunting?

Peter and the others had fished all night and caught nothing. At daybreak, Jesus stands on the shore and calls out, "Children, do you have any fish?" (John 21:5). Now this is like saying, "Boys, ya got anything yet?" (Don't you just love rhetorical questions?)

They answered him, "No."

That which they used to be successful at no longer seems to work. They don't yet recognize that the man on the shore is Jesus, and it's doubtful their crestfallen minds are conscious of the time He had spoken these words to them: "Apart from me you can do nothing" (John 15:5b).

Jesus calls out again, "Cast the net on the right side of the boat, and you will find some" (John 21:6). So they drop the net over the right side of the boat, and now they can't haul it in, because of the number of fish.

Master of the Obvious

This is where the story gets a little comical. John realizes what's happening (I can picture him digging his elbow into Peter's side) and says (I'm paraphrasing), "Dude, it's the Lord! We've seen this before! Remember when He borrowed our boat to teach the people, and then told us to launch out into the deep, and how many fish we caught?" When Peter realizes it's the Lord, he dons his outer garment and swims ashore, while the others bring in the boat, dragging along the huge catch of fish.

Once ashore, they see Jesus has already cooked breakfast for them. He tells them to bring some of the fish they've just caught, so Peter goes aboard and drags the net ashore. As they sit around the fire eating their breakfast, nobody says a word. They know it is Jesus, and they might even be a little chagrined by Him finding them fishing.

After they have finished eating breakfast, Jesus leans in and says, "Simon, son of John, do you love me more than these?" (John 21:15).

More than *these*? More than these what?

There are three possible answers as to what the pronoun *these* refers to. The first is that Jesus could have been asking if Peter loved Him more than he loved his brothers, but why would He ask this question? There is nothing written anywhere in Scripture that suggests Peter was being led astray by his brothers. If anything, Jesus could have asked the other disciples if they loved Him more than they loved Peter, given that they had followed Peter's lead to go back to fishing. Weren't they all supposed to be waiting in Jerusalem for the outpouring of the Holy Spirit (Luke 24:49)?

The second option is that Jesus was asking Peter if he loved Him more than the other disciples did. Again, why would Jesus ask such a question? The disciples, led by James and John, had previously argued as to who would be the greatest among them, so asking such a potentially divisive question would seem to reopen that Pandora's box. Moreover, what relevance would the answer have had with regard to Peter's allegiance to Christ? Peter's answer was, "Yes, Lord; you know that I love you" (John 21:16), not "Yes, Lord; you know that I love you *more than they do.*"

The third—and most plausible— explanation is that *these* refers to the *fish* and what they represented (i.e., a return to his former life). I believe Jesus was giving Peter an opportunity to remember the day when he was first called to leave his nets and follow Christ.

With that in mind, can you now picture Jesus pointing to the fish as He asks, "Simon, son of John, do you love me more than *these*?" What Jesus seems to be saying, in effect, is, "Simon, are you ready to put the past behind you and get on with the business of following Me?" Peter had denied Jesus three times, so as part of his restoration, Jesus now gives him three opportunities to change his confession and reavow his love for his Lord and Master.

Following Jesus always requires a fundamental change of direction because we are not naturally inclined to want to do anything other than what is comfortable or familiar.

Don't Miss the Message

It should not be lost on us how John introduced this seaside encounter with the risen Savior. He said that Jesus *"revealed himself* in this way" (John 21:1, emphasis added).

This is not simply a retelling of how Jesus *appeared* to them, but how He *revealed Himself* to them. He revealed *Himself* by asking some pointed questions (i.e., "Do you love Me?") and clarifying wherein *His interests* lie:

"Feed my lambs."

"Tend my sheep."

"Feed my sheep."

Fishing was still in scope for Peter, just no longer on the sea. He was now called to a land-based mission field where he would fish for men. No doubt this was outside the comfort zone of an uneducated and common fisherman (Acts 4:13), but following Jesus always requires a fundamental change of direction because we are not naturally inclined to want to do anything other than what is comfortable or familiar.

Previous Dining Experience

The last time the disciples had dined with Jesus, He spoke some hard words to Peter:

> "Simon, Simon, behold, Satan demanded to have you, that he might sift you like wheat, but I have prayed for you that your faith may not fail. And when you have turned again, strengthen your brothers." Peter said to him, "Lord, I am ready to go with you both to prison and to death." Jesus said, "I tell you, Peter, the rooster will not crow this day, until you deny three times that you know me." (Luke 22:31–34)

Here, at the sea of Tiberias, Peter is obviously not yet converted from the sifting Jesus foretold. He's not strengthening his brothers. He's distracting them. The man who boasted that he was ready to go with Jesus to prison and to death has instead decided to go fishing.

But Jesus is not there to chide them. He's not having second thoughts about the men He chose to join Him as the foundational stones upon which He would build the Church. He's there to do some course correcting. He's there to affirm them (especially Peter), and He does so by reiterating those two simple, life-altering words He spoke to them when they first heard His unwavering, clarion call: "*Follow me*" (John 21:19b).

What Say Ye?

So we conclude where we began: *What is a Christian?* I've taken my best shot at defining it, but if this were a blog and every person who read it replied with their own definition, the perspectives would share some common ground, but nevertheless be varied and unique.

Is my definition right? Whether it is or not is not so much the point as making you think about the question, because the question demands an answer—*your* answer. And perhaps *what* your answer is will determine *how* you answer—in word, deed, or both. Are you one of the 77 percent of Americans who merely identify with a Christian religion, or are you identified with Christ to the extent that your life is a convincing argument for what it truly means to be a Christian?

The world needs Jesus Christ perhaps now more than ever. If the Holy Spirit were to incline those around you to begin seeking Jesus, would you be top of mind as someone they would come to for guidance, or are you one of those "Christians" who needs to be hidden away in order to advance the gospel of Jesus Christ?

May God's transforming grace so alter our lives that people need look no further than us to find a living epistle of *Christ*.

For Further Study

"Then Agrippa said to Paul,
'You almost persuade me to become a Christian.'"
Acts 26:28 (NKJV)

1. In your own words, define what it means to be a Christian.
2. What does it mean to deny self, and why is this essential to following Christ?
3. What does it mean to take up your cross daily, and how does this differ from what many people think?
4. What does God use in our lives as the hammer and nails to fix us to the cross?
5. What does it mean to be a follower of Christ, and why is this significant in terms of serving Christ?
6. What lesson was Jesus seeking to teach His disciples at the Sea of Tiberias? How did Jesus affirm Peter in that encounter?
7. Why is it important to answer the question, "What is a Christian?"

5

Time for Some Fowl Language

"And this is eternal life, that they know you the only true God, and Jesus Christ whom you have sent."
John 17:3

I<small>T'S ONE THING TO KNOW</small> what it means to be a Christian. It's another thing to genuinely *be one*. So may I ask, *are you a Christian*? Do you know the only true God, and Jesus Christ whom He has sent? (John 17:3).

In Paul's brief letter to Titus, he issues a warning to pay no attention to those who "profess to know God, but they deny him by their works" (Titus 1:16). It is easy to say, "I believe in God," but do our lives bear witness to that claim? James tells us clearly that such faith is useless and cannot save us.

> What good is it, my brothers, if someone says he has faith but does not have works? Can that faith save him?... Do you want to be shown, you foolish person, that faith apart from works is useless? (James 2:14, 20)

Someone once said, "There are two ways to be fooled. One is to believe what isn't true; the other is to refuse to believe what is true."[1] With that in mind, some devilishly destructive notions must be debunked and disposed of before continuing this discourse on the pursuit of Christlikeness. But before we talk turkey, let's talk chicken.

Imitation or Pretense?

Paul said, "Be imitators of me, as I am of Christ" (1 Corinthians 11:1). We know, however, that this meant so much more than pretending to be like Christ. That is a fool's game. I can walk through my house with arms flapping and head bobbing forward and backward pretending to be a chicken strutting around the barnyard, but that won't transform my character into that of a chicken—though it might make for some interesting entertainment!

The word *imitate*, as defined by Dictionary.com, means "to follow or endeavor to follow as a model or example; ... to have or assume the appearance of; ... to resemble."[2]

The word *pretend* means "to cause or attempt to cause (what is not so) to seem so; to appear falsely, as to deceive; to make believe."[3]

As you can see, there is a distinct difference between these two words. Paul's imitation of Christ flowed from his relationship with Jesus, which began when he encountered the Savior on the road to Damascus. Conversely, any religious person can pretend to be pious, but the flimsy façade will eventually be exposed for what it is—a fake. The scribes and Pharisees of Jesus' day were some of the most devout people who ever lived. Their disciplined devotion to the law was unquestionable, but they knew nothing of a *personal* relationship with the God of Abraham, Isaac, and Jacob. Their religion was a tradition-bound, rules-keeping, works-based paper tiger that was completely ineffectual in transforming their stony hearts into anything resembling the heart of God. Oswald Chambers reminds us that Christ must be the Savior before He becomes the pattern:

> The New Testament example of the Christian experience is that of a personal, passionate devotion to the Person of Jesus Christ. Every other kind of so-called Christian experience is detached from the Person of Jesus. There is no regeneration—no being

born again into the kingdom in which Christ lives and reigns supreme. There is only the idea that He is our pattern. In the New Testament Jesus Christ is the Savior long before He is the pattern. Today He is being portrayed as the figurehead of a religion—a mere example. He is that, but He is infinitely more. He is salvation itself; He *is* the gospel of God![4]

Let's Talk Turkey

In Peter's second epistle, he exhorted the church to add to their faith virtue and other godly attributes (2 Peter 1:5–7). This is analogous to building a Christlike character, but before we can build or add anything to our faith we must be absolutely certain of the foundation upon which we are building. This calls for a frank, candid discussion, which means it's time to talk turkey.

Paul challenged the Corinthians with these words: "Examine yourselves, to see whether you are in the faith" (2 Corinthians 13:5a). What does it mean to be i*n the faith*? The New Living Translation expresses it beautifully:

> Examine yourselves to see if your faith is genuine. Test yourselves. Surely you know that Jesus Christ is among you; if not, you have failed the test of genuine faith. (2 Corinthians 13:5 NLT)

Genuine faith. Now there's something to ponder. Is my faith genuine? Does it pass the test? There is no point in aspiring to be a *Christlike* Christian unless or until I know that I *am* a Christian whose faith is genuine *based on what Scripture teaches*. Below is a short list of commonplace—but false—notions, which, sadly, many people are trusting in as the basis of their professed Christianity. Although this list may seem elementary to some—and possibly not worth covering—I believe it could benefit some readers.

You may think you are a Christian because:

1. . . . you go to church.
2. . . . you read the Bible and pray.
3. . . . you are a good person and do good things for others.
4. . . . you were baptized or christened as a baby.
5. . . . your parents are Christians and you grew up "in church."
6. . . . you are a member of a particular church denomination (Catholic, Baptist, Christian, Pentecostal, Holiness, Charismatic, etc.).
7. . . . you "believe in God" and defend your beliefs by saying, "This is just what I believe," as though your believing it makes it so.
8. . . . you believe that "many paths lead to God."

If you've been building on any of the above, you must allow God's wrecking ball to demolish whatever structure has been built on this sandy soil. It's then time to lay a solid foundation upon which to build a relationship with Christ as revealed in the Word of God. Let's take a closer look at these dangerous and destructive myths.

Myth #1 — I go to church

If I took a Clydesdale to Churchill Downs, fed it the same food eaten by the fastest horses in the history of horse racing, and let it run around the same track and rest in the same stall as Kentucky Derby winners past, that Clydesdale would never become a Thoroughbred. It simply is not possible.

So it is with church attendance. It doesn't matter how many church services or camp meetings you attend, or how frequently you go to Mass, that does not make you a Christian. You may presently sing in the choir, be an usher or an acolyte, or play an instrument on the worship team. You may even be the pastor of a church! But Christian service does not *make* you a Christian, nor does it validate your Christianity. You can do all of these things apart from experiencing salvation by grace through faith (Ephesians 2:8).

Myth #2 — I read the Bible and pray

Reading the Bible is essential for growth in godliness, but reading the Bible will not make me a Christian. I could spend a lifetime reading technical manuals from NASA or books and journals from the medical profession, but that would never make me an astronaut or a doctor.

What about prayer? Multitudes of people pray. In point of fact, many are praying to an "unknown god" (or they could just be talking to themselves). Most prayers offered prior to believing in the finished work of Christ are, by nature, selfish. Until we are identified with Christ in His death and resurrection and have submitted our will to His, we don't pray to see His will be done, we pray to see our will be done.

But what if I pray a lot? What if my prayers are not selfish? Jesus had this to say about prayer:

> "And when you pray, do not heap up empty phrases as the Gentiles do, for they think that they will be heard for their many words. Do not be like them." (Matthew 6:7–8)

Oswald Chambers shares this thought-provoking admonition concerning prayer:

> God does not hear us because we pray earnestly—He hears us solely on the basis of redemption. God is never impressed by our earnestness. Prayer is not simply getting things from God—that is only the most elementary kind of prayer. Prayer is coming into perfect fellowship and oneness with God. If the Son of God has been formed in us through regeneration (see Galatians 4:19), then He will continue to press on beyond our common sense and will change our attitude about the things for which we pray.[5]

Praying does not make me a Christian; neither is God impressed because I pray earnestly.

Myth #3 — I'm a good person

You're a good person, are you? No, you're not. Was that unclear? Let me say it again: You are *not* a good person. But don't take my word for it; let's see what God's Word says:

> God looks down from heaven on *the entire human race*; he looks to see if anyone is truly wise, if anyone seeks God. But no, all have turned away; all have become corrupt. *No one does good, not a single one!* (Psalm 53:2–3 NLT, emphasis added)

At a corporate dinner, I once heard a colleague say they believed everyone is inherently good. Though a convenient philosophy, it's simply not the truth. The only way to arrive at such a conclusion is to base it on something other than what the Bible teaches. Jesus Christ, the sinless Lamb of God, would not even accept being labeled *good* when a rich man once asked Him this question:

> "Good Teacher, what must I do to inherit eternal life?"
> And Jesus said to him, "Why do you call me good?
> No one is good except God alone." (Luke 18:18–19)

"Why do you call me good?" What a strange question for the perfect Son of God to ask. Jesus was masterful at asking questions—particularly rhetorical ones—to make a point. So it would seem that in asking this question, Jesus was really checking to see if the rich man understood that Jesus is, in fact, God. Jesus did not deny that He is good; He merely stated that only God is good. So I ask you, if only God is good, what on earth makes anyone wearing skin think they are good? The arrogance of such a thought should appall us!

Myth #4 — I was baptized or christened as a baby

Jesus was brought to the Temple and presented to the Lord as a baby (Luke 2:22ff), and during His years of earthly ministry He welcomed children with open arms (Luke 18:15–17). My local church invites parents to dedicate their babies to the Lord, and this passage in Luke 2 is often quoted as part of such dedications— not as a literal observance of the Old Testament sacrificial system, but more as a reference to support a modern day practice of presenting and dedicating children to the Lord.

My wife and I prayed fervently for all four of our children while they were still being formed in the womb, expressing to God our desire that they would all belong to Him and serve Him all of their days. We also publicly dedicated them to God as infants during an appointed church service. However, we never baptized any of them until they were of an age to understand and make their own profession of faith in Jesus Christ.

The twelve apostles—sans Judas—whom Jesus commissioned to go into all the world preaching the gospel, making disciples, and baptizing them in His name (Matthew 28:19) baptized individuals after they had repented and believed the gospel (see Acts 2:38; 8:35–38; 10:44–48; 16:31–33; 18:8, 19:1–6). Since it is impossible for infants to express faith in Christ, the notion of baptizing infants as a means of ensuring their eternal salvation is potentially dangerous to children as they grow older and reach that "age" of personal accountability to God. I am not categorically refuting the practice of infant baptism as part of dedicating children to the Lord. However, if they grow up believing that infant baptism saved them, they may never experience true repentance for their sins and salvation by grace through faith (Ephesians 2:8–10).

Myth #5 — I grew up in a Christian home

If you grew up in a Christian home and were blessed with a godly heritage, then that is to be celebrated! But it does not make you a Christian. John's gospel account clearly states,

> But to all who did receive him, who believed in his name, he gave the right to become children of God, who were born, not of blood nor of the will of the flesh nor of the will of man, but of God. (John 1:12–13)

No one becomes a Christian by being born to Christian parents. It is not a natural birth, but a spiritual birth that makes us children of God. No amount of parental instruction, nurture, example, and oversight—no matter how godly—can make someone a Christian. A person may be born into the most privileged circumstances imaginable—godly parents, wealth, education, opportunity, etc.—but none of that mitigates the fact that we are all born with an inherent sin nature, which cannot be rectified, reconciled, or refined simply through the influence of Christian parenting. You can put lipstick on a pig, but it will still be a pig, so the bottom line is precisely as John stated in this paraphrase, "Those who become children of God are those who believe in His name," not those who grow up in a Christian home.

Myth #6 — I'm a member of such and such Church

Church affiliation does not make you a Christian. Reread John 1:12–13. It's not by the will of the flesh or the will of man. Joining a church or being baptized into a particular denomination may add your name to a church roll, but it does not write your name into the Lamb's Book of Life (Revelation 21:27). No one becomes a Christian simply by joining a church.

Myth #7 — I believe in God

You believe in God, do you? Good for you! But you'd better have more than that to stand on. James boldly states, "You believe that there is one God. Good! Even the demons believe that—and shudder" (James 2:19 NIV).

Even demons believe in the existence of God, but only the most deceived individuals believe that demons will have a place in heaven. Many who maintain a belief in God have no biblical basis for their faith. Their faith is more ideology than theology and when challenged, they purport to say, "Well, this is just what I believe," as though that settles it; as though believing something to be so makes it so. Such thinking is beyond perilous.

Myth #8 — Many paths lead to God

Possibly the most offensive thing ever spoken by Jesus Christ was this polarizing statement recorded in John's gospel:

> Thomas said to him, "Lord, we do not know where you are going. How can we know the way?" Jesus said to him, "I am the way, and the truth, and the life. No one comes to the Father except through me." (John 14:5–6)

"No one comes to the Father except through me." Jesus was either certifiably nuts, or He was telling the truth. There's absolutely no middle ground here. When Peter stood before the Jewish council to give an account of how, by the name of Jesus, he had healed a man lame from birth, his cogent reply was without any uncertainty or apology:

> Then Peter, filled with the Holy Spirit, said to them, "Rulers of the people and elders... *there is salvation in no one else,* for there is no other name under heaven given among men by which we must be saved." (Acts 4:8, 12, emphasis added)

The world simply does not have the stomach for this, but a Christian categorically embraces and rejoices in this truth: Jesus is the only way to the Father. He is the only means for salvation and the only path to eternal life.

Have It Your Way?

As previously stated, the aforementioned list of beliefs is not comprehensive. It is nevertheless representative of the way many people think when it comes to validating their "Christianity," and it is imperative that we not resemble those whom Paul described to the church in Rome:

For they don't understand God's way of making people right with himself. Refusing to accept God's way, they cling to their own way of getting right with God.... (Romans 10:3 NLT)

Are you clinging to your own way of being made right with God? Frank Sinatra sang that I should live life *my way,* and Burger King may let you have it *your way,*[6] but in all of our dealings with God, we must do things *His way.*

I once heard Dr. Cornwall say, "The Israelites could have painted their doorways in Egypt with red paint instead of lamb's blood, but their firstborn sons would have all been dead the following morning." Why? It simply wasn't God's way.

What Is God's Way?

A certain inquisitive religious man came to Jesus under cover of darkness one night, acknowledging Him as a teacher who had come from God. I'm rather convinced he was about to ask a question similar to what the rich young ruler in Luke 18:18 asked of Jesus ("What must I do to inherit eternal life?"); only Jesus cut him off and gave him the answer before he could even ask the question. Let's read John's account of this conversation:

Now there was a man of the Pharisees named Nicodemus, a ruler of the Jews. This man came to Jesus by night and said to him, "Rabbi, we know that you are a teacher come from God, for no one can do these signs that you do unless God is with him."

Jesus answered him, "Truly, truly, I say to you, unless one is born again he cannot see the kingdom of God."

Nicodemus said to him, "How can a man be born when he is old? Can he enter a second time into his mother's womb and be born?"

Jesus answered, "Truly, truly, I say to you, unless one is born of water and the Spirit, he cannot enter the kingdom of God. That which is born of the flesh is flesh, and that which is born of the Spirit is spirit. Do not marvel that I said to you, 'You must be born again.' The wind blows where it wishes, and you hear its sound, but you do not know where it comes from or where it goes. So it is with everyone who is born of the Spirit."

Nicodemus said to him, "How can these things be?" (John 3:1–9)

"How can these things be?"

Indeed. How *can* these things be? Seems like a legitimate question to me. In fact, it's the question we would have asked, too, if we were as confused as Nicodemus. The answer to this question is the first of three characteristics that are foundational in the life of a Christian:

1. A Christian Is Born from Above

The New English Translation (NET) of John 3:1–9 translates the word *again* in verses 3 and 7 as *from above*. The NET's corresponding translator notes[7] carefully point out the dual meaning of the transliterated Greek word *anothen*, which not only means "again," but also "from above." John used this word five times in his gospel, three of which are in chapter 3—verses 3, 7, and 31. The other two references are in chapter 19—verses 11 and 23.

The translation of *anothen* in John 3:31 helps us understand what Jesus meant when He told Nicodemus, "No one can see the kingdom of God unless they are born *again (anothen)*."

> "The one who comes *from above (anothen)* is superior to all. The one who is from the earth belongs to the earth..." (John 3:31 NET)

Jesus sought to clarify His point to Nicodemus when He said, "What is born of the flesh is flesh, and what is born of the Spirit is spirit" (John 3:6 NET). In other words, *flesh cannot produce spirit.*

One of the most important things to understand about this new birth is that we don't just wake up one day and decide to be born from above, no more than a dead man can decide to get out of his grave.

> When Adam sinned, sin entered the world. Adam's sin brought death, so *death spread to everyone*, for everyone sinned. (Romans 5:12 NLT, emphasis added)

Everyone enters this world spiritually dead as a result of Adam's sin, and we remain that way unless we are born from above and made alive spiritually, thereby entering into a personal relationship with Jesus Christ through God's wonderful grace and gift of righteousness.

> For the sin of this one man, Adam, caused death to rule over many. But even greater is God's wonderful grace and his gift of righteousness, for all who receive it will live in triumph over sin and death through this one man, Jesus Christ. Yes, Adam's one sin brings condemnation for everyone, but Christ's one act of righteousness brings a right relationship with God and new life for everyone. (Romans 5:17–18 NLT)

Notice what verse 17 says about "God's wonderful grace and his gift of righteousness." It says that "*all who receive it* will live in triumph over sin and death" (emphasis added) and will be brought into "a right relationship with God" (v. 18).

"Don't *I* need to do something?" you ask. Yes, you do, but not what many presume. Our human nature compels us to think that we have to *earn* salvation through good works of some sort. The truth, however, is that you and I bring *absolutely nothing* to the table with respect to atoning for our sins and being made right with God. Here's what Jesus said *we* need to do: "The time is fulfilled, and the kingdom of God is at hand; repent and believe in the gospel" (Mark 1:15, emphasis added).

Repent and believe in the gospel. That's it! So simple that we have to complicate it. Or is it that our human nature insists on taking some of the credit for our salvation?

Think about it. How insulting is it to the Spirit of grace and the sacrifice of Jesus Christ to think for even a second that we need to add something to it? If we have to add something to His work on the cross, then by definition, His sacrifice was insufficient. Such a notion is so disrespectful to the blood of Christ that we should be repulsed by the thought. People are made right with God when they receive by faith the finished work of Christ on the cross as the only means by which they can be reconciled to God.

> *How insulting is it to the Spirit of grace and the sacrifice of Jesus Christ to think for even a second that we need to add something to it? If we have to add something to His work on the cross, then by definition, His sacrifice was insufficient.*

In chapter 2 the concept of employing the threefold cord of grace, faith, and works was introduced as a means to developing a Christlike character. When explaining the role of works, we saw where Peter exhorted believers to *add* to their faith virtue and other godly attributes. Although it is necessary for us to add to our faith godly attributes in order to develop Christlike character, we must never seek to add anything to the sacrifice of Jesus as a means for salvation. Paul's writing to the church in Ephesus makes this abundantly clear:

> For by grace you have been saved through faith. And this is not your own doing; it is the gift of God, not a result of works, so that no one may boast. (Ephesians 2:8–9)

Charles Spurgeon, in His devotional *Morning and Evening*, confronts us with the need to be brutally honest with ourselves concerning our standing in God:

> Regeneration is a subject which lies at the very basis of salvation, and we should be very diligent to take heed that we really are "born again," for there are many who fancy they are, who are not. Be assured that the name of a Christian is not the nature of a Christian; and that being born in a Christian land, and being recognized as professing the Christian religion is of no avail whatever, unless there be something more added to it—the being "born again," is a matter so mysterious, that human words cannot describe it.
>
> This great work is supernatural. It is not an operation which a man performs for himself: a new principle is infused, which works in the heart, renews the soul, and affects the entire man. It is not a change of my name, but a renewal of my nature, so that I am not the man I used to be, but a new man in Christ Jesus. To wash and dress a corpse is a far different thing from making it alive: man can do the one, God alone can do the other.[8]

May I Introduce You to Jesus Christ?

Before leaving home to attend college, I was a casual attendee of a local Protestant church. In all my years of attending that church, I never heard a single message from the pulpit that informed me of my need to repent of sin and believe in the saving gospel of Christ. From the time I was old enough to comprehend what was being preached until I was eighteen, I drew the conclusion that when I died, God would take all my good deeds and place them on one end of His scale, then take all my bad deeds and place them on the opposite end of the scale. If the good outweighed the bad, I was in!

That was *my* belief system. Yet it's not what the Bible teaches, nor could you even begin to call that *good news*.

In my senior year of high school, I had the good fortune through the providence of God—and my high school government teacher— to come into possession of a book titled *The Liberation of Planet Earth* by Hal Lindsey. It wasn't until I read this book that I understood I had been born with a sinful nature and was in need of a Savior. But the book didn't just point out my need for a Savior; it explained how Jesus provided redemption from sin and regeneration through His atonement on the cross. Here's how it went down:

I was a pitcher on my high school baseball team. In May 1976, my team had a road game in which I was to be the starting pitcher. While riding the team bus from my hometown of New Albany, Indiana, to Jasper, Indiana, I continued reading Lindsey's book in response to the tug of God's Spirit on my heart.

In order to fully appreciate the moment, you need to picture all that was happening on this bus. Up front, you've got the coaches discussing lineups and strategy, while all around me was this chaotic, juvenile foolishness, typical of a group of unregenerate high school student athletes. "Yo' Mama" jokes abounded. Strategies for *mooning* on the ride home were bandied about. And then there was me, reading this book, impervious to the nonsense around me. Get the picture?

After reading about man's debt of sin, slavery to Satan, and redemption of mankind through the cross, I was primed and ready to receive Christ. All I needed was a nudge, which these words from the final paragraph of chapter 10 on page 109 provided:

> If you've never done so before, why not right this moment thank Jesus Christ for dying for *you*, personally, and accept His gracious pardon and forgiveness. You'll be eternally glad you did![9]

My heart was convicted and I was ready to ask for God's forgiveness, so there on the bus, I quietly repented and prayed to receive Christ's forgiveness and salvation. What a glorious day!

This was *my* introduction to Christ and how I experienced the new birth, but the how and where is not what's important. Receiving Christ is not based on a formula. In fact, Jesus told Nicodemus, "The wind blows where it wishes, and you hear its sound, but do not know where it comes from or where it goes. So it is with everyone who is born of the Spirit" (John 3:8).

Don't Delay

You can receive Christ in the privacy of your home or in response to a gospel preacher's altar call. You can receive Him while driving in your car or taking a walk. You can receive Him high above the clouds on an airplane or on a bus filled with raucous teenage boys. You can receive Him as a result of reading a book like this. As long as the elements of grace, faith, and repentance are present, you can be born from above in a variety of circumstances.

As the saying goes, there's no time like the present, so if you've never received Christ's forgiveness, you can do so now. With no further delay, you can call on the name of the Lord and be born from above. Romans 10 gives us assurance that everyone who does so *will be saved*:

> If you confess with your mouth that Jesus is Lord and believe in your heart that God raised him from the dead, you will be saved. For with the heart one believes and is justified, and with the mouth one confesses and is saved. For the Scripture says, "Everyone who believes in him will not be put to shame." For there is no distinction between Jew and Greek; for the same Lord is Lord of all, bestowing his riches on all who call on him. For "everyone who calls on the name of the Lord will be saved." (Romans 10:9–13)[10]

I would love to say that some special feeling came over me on that bus when I prayed to receive Christ, but that's not the way it happened. As a matter of fact, not much change occurred in my life until I left for college that fall and made a commitment to start reading the Bible. That was when the Holy Spirit began to transform my life through the renewing of my mind by the Word of God, which brings us to the second defining characteristic of a Christian.

2. A Christian Believes the Bible Is the Inspired Word of God

The Bible is the foundation for everything a Christian believes with respect to Jesus Christ and all matters moral and spiritual. It is not my objective to convince you that the Bible is the inspired Word of God. It is, rather, to simply state that it *is*, and that a Christian does not dispute the veracity of the Bible's own claim concerning its origin:

> All scripture is breathed out by God and profitable for teaching, for reproof, for correction, and for training in righteousness, that the man of God may be complete, equipped for every good work.

> (2 Timothy 3:16–17)

In broad strokes, a Christian holds dear the belief that the Bible is God's revelation of:

. . . Himself to mankind.
. . . the sinfulness of mankind.
. . . the redemption of mankind.
. . . righteousness for mankind.
. . . Christ's triumph over death.
. . . Christ's second coming and establishment of His
    kingdom on a new earth under a new heaven.

Restated, the Bible reveals to us who God is, how sin entered the world and was passed to all men, how God provided a sacrifice for sin to reconcile us to Himself, how mankind is to live this side of heaven, and how Christ became the Firstborn to rise from the dead, preparing the way for all who believe in Him to reign with Him forever in His kingdom.

Sublime Foolishness

A Christian recognizes that without the Bible, we would not know our origin nor would we know God's will for our lives. And because a Christian believes that *all* Scripture is "breathed out by God and profitable," he or she rejects any semblance of a Jeffersonian view of the Bible.

For all of his political savvy and genius, Thomas Jefferson erred greatly in his presumptive pursuit to create what he described as "the most sublime and benevolent code of morals which has ever been offered to man."[11] It is common knowledge that Jefferson cobbled together an eighty-four-page work known as *The Jefferson Bible* (or, *The Life and Morals of Jesus of Nazareth* as it is formally titled). He accomplished this "by cutting and pasting (literally with a razor and glue) numerous sections from the New Testament as extractions of the doctrine of Jesus. Jefferson's condensed composition is especially notable for its exclusion of all miracles by Jesus and most mentions of the supernatural, including sections of the four gospels which contain the Resurrection and most other miracles, and passages indicating Jesus was divine."[12]

To say that Jefferson was a brilliant man is a monumental understatement, but the problem with some extremely intelligent people is that they lack the childlike ability to simply believe that God exists, that He created all things for His pleasure, and that He also ordained and inspired the writings of prophets and holy men of God to produce what we call the Bible. The NET expresses this in no uncertain language:

> Above all, you do well if you recognize this: No prophecy of scripture ever comes about by the prophet's own imagination, for no prophecy was ever borne of human impulse; rather, men carried along by the Holy Spirit spoke from God. (2 Peter 1:20–21 NET)

The problem with Jefferson's selective application of Scripture is that once you exclude even one verse of Holy Writ, you have created a problem that no one is able to solve. Who among us would dare declare themselves sufficient in knowledge and understanding so as to accurately discern which verses of Scripture are God's words and which are man's?

We would do well to remember how God took Job to task over his presumptive knowledge of the Holy One:

> Then the Lord answered Job from the whirlwind: "Who is this that questions my wisdom with such ignorant words? Brace yourself like a man, because I have some questions for you, and you must answer them. Where were you when I laid the foundations of the earth? Tell me, if you know so much. Who determined its dimensions and stretched out the surveying line? What supports its foundations, and who laid its cornerstone?" (Job 38:1–7 NLT)

This is but the tip of the iceberg in a series of the most pressing questions that ever a man was confronted with. It's unlikely that anyone was ever more soundly put in his place than Job. However, after two full chapters of interrogation, the Lord paused just long enough to ask Job if he wanted to effuse more of his extensive knowledge:

> Then the Lord said to Job, "Do you still want to argue with the Almighty? You are God's critic, but do you have the answers?" Then Job replied to the Lord, "I am nothing—how could I ever find the answers? I will

cover my mouth with my hand. I have said too much already. I have nothing more to say." (Job 40:1–5 NLT)

But God wasn't finished, as chronicled by two more chapters of feet-to-the-fire questioning. I encourage you to read chapters 38–42 of Job and you will see just how small Job must have felt after God put him in his place. It makes me wonder what tough questions Thomas Jefferson faced when he found himself in the presence of the Holy One who gave us His Word in the form of the Bible.

3. A Christian Points Others to Christ

The final message of Jesus Christ to His disciples, as recorded in Matthew, Mark, Luke, and the book of Acts, was to wait for the outpouring of the Holy Spirit and then go in the Spirit's power to proclaim the gospel to all nations.

Christ entrusted His followers with the greatest privilege and responsibility ever given, which was to take the greatest message of all time to all the world. We call that message the *gospel*, that is, the *good news* of salvation in Jesus Christ. Sharing this message with others is a third foundational characteristic—a fruit, actually—that should be evident in the life of every Christian.

Circa 848 B.C., Samaria came under siege by the Syrians. Ben-Hadad had mustered his army and closed off the city to all commerce, resulting in a great famine in Samaria (see 2 Kings 6:24–25). The seventh chapter of 2 Kings records how the Lord delivered Israel from the Syrian army and how four lepers were the unlikely messengers to share the news of this victory.

These leprous men discussed among themselves the logic of staying in the city and dying of starvation versus surrendering to the Syrians in hopes the Syrians would have mercy on them. By venturing out of the city, the worst that could happen is that the Syrians would kill them. Either way, their chances of dying from starvation seemed inevitable, so they decided to take a risk.

When they came to the camp of the Syrians, no one was there. The Lord had caused the Syrians to think they were being attacked by the Hittites and Egyptians, so they fled for their lives, leaving everything in their camp intact. Let's pick up the story beginning with verse 8:

> And when these lepers came to the edge of the camp, they went into a tent and ate and drank, and they carried off silver and gold and clothing and went and hid them. Then they came back and entered another tent and carried off things from it and went and hid them. Then they said to one another, "*We are not doing right. This day is a day of good news.* If we are silent and wait until the morning light, punishment will overtake us. Now therefore *come; let us go and tell the king's household.*" (2 Kings 7:8–9, emphasis added)

These four lepers made a great discovery, one that would save all of Samaria from the famine the Syrians brought upon them. God had provided a mighty deliverance from their enemy, and these men were the first to discover it. Human nature being what it is, however, their initial instinct was to hoard for themselves.

As they were pillaging the Syrian tents, there came a moment when they were convicted of keeping this good news to themselves: "We are not doing right. This day is a day of good news.... Now therefore come; let us go and tell the king's household."

All true believers in Jesus Christ should have a desire to "go and tell the King's household" about the good news of salvation they have experienced by grace through faith. Christians point others to Christ through their example, but also by actively

"It is not enough to give mental assent to the fact that God has redeemed the world, nor even to know that the Holy Spirit can make all that Jesus did a reality in my life. I must have the foundation of a personal relationship with Him."[13]
—*Oswald Chambers*

sharing the gospel through whatever means and opportunities are afforded them by the Holy Spirit.

Fowl Finish

For some readers, this chapter may have seemed unnecessary. I was concerned, however, that someone who did not yet know Christ but had an affinity for religion might read this book and attempt to apply its principles without having the proper foundation upon which to build. Therefore, I felt it necessary to take the time to talk a little chicken as well as some turkey in order to candidly dispel a number of harmful myths that hold people captive and prevent them from discovering a true relationship with Christ. It's now time, however, to discontinue the use of such fowl language and speak of things more excellent as we continue our journey toward becoming Christlike.

For Further Study

"Examine yourselves to see if your faith is genuine."
2 Corinthians 13:5 (NLT)

1. How can someone know if their faith is genuine?
2. The author lists eight myths that prevent some people from ever experiencing a genuine relationship with Christ. What are some other myths that could be added to this list?
3. Of the eight myths listed by the author, which ones either currently apply, or at one time applied, to you?
4. What three characteristics does the author list as being foundational in the life of a Christian? Do you agree with this list? How would you change or expand it?
5. What does it mean to be born from above?
6. What did Thomas Jefferson do with the Bible, and what problem does that create if we have a similar Jeffersonian view of Scripture?
7. Why is it necessary to have a solid, biblical foundation for the basis of our faith before we endeavor to be like Christ?
8. If you aren't sure whether or not your faith is genuine, allow the group to pray with you—or pray on your own—to accept and believe in the finished work of Christ once and for all as the sole basis of your forgiveness and salvation.

Part 3

The Transition

transition[1] [tran-**zish**-*uh* n]
—noun

1. *movement, passage, or change from one position, state, stage, subject, concept, etc., to another.*

6

A More Excellent Way

"And I will show you a still more excellent way."
1 Corinthians 12:31

IN THE OPENING CHAPTER of this book, I shared with you the time Mindy and I discovered the word *caviling*, and how the Holy Spirit used that Nathan moment to focus my attention on what had been a lifelong habit of carping about certain proclivities of hers that annoyed me. However, I left out a significant detail while recounting this story. Not long after this incident, I began reading (for the second time) *The Christlike Christian*, and I was hit squarely between the eyes by the following statement from the Unknown Christian: "The wife of a working-man evangelist, in a moment of confidence, said: 'My husband is more like the Lord Jesus than anyone I have ever met.'"[1]

Wow. When I read that, I knew there was no way my wife could make a statement like that about me—at least not then. I was so convicted that I asked the Lord to transform me into the kind of Christlike man about whom my wife *could* make such a statement. That may never happen, and it's really not the point. The point is that I realized my need for decisive change.

Regardless of whether it's in the home or among the masses, should it not be our aim—our resolve—to be like Jesus, and for others to view us in a light similar to how the evangelist's wife esteemed her husband?

We Are Not All Alike

Differing opinions and perspectives are a fact of life, as are differing ways of doing things. I discovered a long time ago that my wife and I are such complete opposites that if there are two ways to accomplish the same thing, she will almost always do it one way and I will do it the other. I guess you could say my thoughts are not her thoughts, neither are her ways my ways. It used to aggravate me, but it's so uncanny that I now find myself shaking my head with a wry smile whenever I recognize it.

One thing I know about people with a critical spirit is that they don't just think they are right, they know they are right—which, by definition, means *you are wrong*. And if you are "wrong," then they feel strangely beholden to let you know that you are wrong, because they believe they are actually providing a valuable service. After all, who would want to knowingly continue being wrong?

As I now remove my tongue from my cheek, hear me as I share with complete seriousness one of the many things I have learned from my pastor, Bob Hauselman:

Different is not necessarily wrong.
Sometimes, different is just ... different.

In spite of my conviction that Mindy was the one who needed to learn a better way to do certain things, God, in His goodness, revealed to me that I was actually the one who needed to learn a better way. This *better way*—or what most translations of the Bible call *a more excellent way*—now becomes our focus for the remainder of this book.

Cockles in Corinth

The church in Corinth was endowed with spiritual gifts, but they lacked understanding in how to use them to encourage and edify one another. They were also an impatient, inconsiderate, and selfish bunch, as evidenced by Paul's rebuke of their observance of the Lord's Supper (1 Corinthians 11:17–34).

In Paul's letter to the church in Ephesus, we read that Christ had offered Himself as a sacrifice "that he might present the church to himself in splendor, without spot or wrinkle or any such thing, that she might be holy and without blemish" (Ephesians 5:27). In his first letter to the Corinthians, Paul revealed the secret for ironing out the wrinkles that existed within the fabric of that church. Sandwiched between his description of the diverse gifts given by the Holy Spirit (chapter 12) and his instructions for how to use them in a corporate church gathering (chapter 14), we find what is commonly referred to as … chapter 13. Sorry, couldn't resist.

First Corinthians 13 has long been referred to as the *love* chapter, and Paul uses the following exhortation to segue from the topic of spiritual gifts to his characterization of love: "But earnestly desire the higher gifts. And I will show you a still more excellent way" (1 Corinthians 12:31). I love how the NLT expresses this:

> So you should earnestly desire the most helpful gifts. But now let me show you *a way of life that is best of all.* (1 Corinthians 12:31 NLT, emphasis added)

I cannot speak for you, but I, for one, want to experience this way of life that is best of all.

Cowed By a Chasm

Luke 16 contains a passage of Scripture commonly referred to as *The Rich Man and Lazarus.* Now Lazarus was a poor man, covered with sores, who lay at the rich man's gate longing for the scraps from the rich man's table. Both men died and Lazarus was carried to the place called Abraham's bosom, while the rich man found himself in hell. The rich man cried out to Abraham that he would send Lazarus to dip his finger in some water to cool the tip of his tongue, because he was tormented by the flames.

> But Abraham said, ". . . between us and you a great chasm has been fixed, in order that those who would pass from here to you may not be able, and none may cross from there to us." (Luke 16:25–26)

We face a similarly impossible task when we consider our prospects for becoming Christlike. It's as if we are standing at the edge of the Grand Canyon, gazing across the enormous expanse, wondering how on earth we could possibly get from here to there. We know it's not possible, so "Why make the effort?" is what we say to excuse ourselves from even trying.

I recall a time of praise and worship when our church was singing a popular song by Anthony Skinner and Chris McLarney called *Your Love Never Fails*. The second verse paints a picture of a chasm so wide as to raise significant concerns about one's ability to reach the other side. The lyric goes on to suggest that the chasm can, in fact, be crossed because of God's unfailing love. While singing this lyric, I thought of the potentially overwhelming discouragement one may face as they consider how great the gulf is between what their life looks like compared to that of Jesus Christ. As I continued singing, I began to see the unfailing love of God as the bridge that makes the seemingly impossible possible. The love of God shed abroad in our hearts is the key to bridging the gap between a life that demonstrates Christ to the world and a life that does not.

The love of God shed abroad in our hearts is the key to bridging the gap between a life that demonstrates Christ to the world and a life that does not.

Yet, how many of us truly grasp the breadth, length, height, and depth of the love of God (Ephesians 3:18)? "It is beyond my ability to comprehend that," you say. How so? It may surprise you to read again this familiar passage in the book of Ephesians and see the expectation God has for all of His saints to *know the love of Christ*:

> For this reason I bow my knees before the Father, from whom every family in heaven and on earth is named, that according to the riches of his glory he may grant you to be strengthened with power through his Spirit in your inner being, so that Christ may dwell in your hearts through faith--that *you*, being rooted and grounded in love, *may have strength to comprehend with all the saints what is the breadth and length and height and depth, and to know the love of Christ* that surpasses knowledge, that you may be filled with all the fullness of God. (Ephesians 3:14–19, emphasis added)

Would you still maintain that knowing the love of Christ is beyond our reach? After all, it says, "the love of Christ... *surpasses knowledge.*" Does that not imply that the love of God is too vast for us to comprehend?

Let's give Paul (under the unction of the Holy Spirit) the benefit of the doubt that he was not writing and praying something contradictory. He did not pray that we would be able to comprehend the impossible. God is not the author of confusion (1 Corinthians 14:33), so let's dig a little deeper to better understand two words Paul uses in the phrase, "to *know* the love of Christ that surpasses *knowledge.*"

The Greek word *know* is transliterated *ginosko* (gee-*no*-skoh), and speaks of understanding something on an intimate level. The word even applies to the sexual intercourse of a man and woman.[2] You can't get any more intimate than that.

The Greek word *knowledge* is transliterated *gnosis* (*no*-sees), and refers to general intelligence and understanding of the Christian religion; having a deeper, more perfect and enlarged knowledge of this religion, such as belongs to the more advanced. The word also conveys having an understanding of what is morally right and wrong, lawful and unlawful for the Christian.[3]

We know the Greeks were particularly fond of pursuing knowledge (see Acts 17:18–21), so Paul's prayer was teaching them (and us) that having an intimate knowledge of the love of Christ is *superior to* possessing an advanced ability to dissect the Scriptures and explain to others "the way of God more accurately" (Acts 18:26). These other writings of Paul clarify this beautifully:

> And if I ... understand all mysteries and all knowledge ... but have not love, I am nothing. (1 Corinthians 13:2)

> . . . "knowledge" puffs up, but love builds up. (1 Corinthians 8:1b)

Now that we know it's possible to comprehend the great love of God, it's likely few of us do. And I daresay that we will never experience Christlikeness until we learn to walk in the love that Paul describes in the 13th chapter of his first letter to the Corinthians:

> Love is patient and kind; love does not envy or boast; it is not arrogant or rude. It does not insist on its own way; it is not irritable or resentful; it does not rejoice at wrongdoing, but rejoices with the truth. Love bears all things, believes all things, hopes all things, endures all things. Love never ends. (1 Corinthians 13:4–8a)

What Is Christ Like?

Since our desire is to be Christlike, let's pause momentarily to consider *what* Christ is like. The Unknown Christian said, "We can scarcely be like Him if we do not know what He is like."[4] Seems obvious enough, and possibly worthy of responding with a twenty-first century, "Duh," and yet, how many of us have actually taken the time to consider "What are the distinguishing marks of the Man Christ Jesus? What makes Him 'the altogether lovely One' (Song of Solomon 5:16)?"[5]

In Paul's writing to Timothy, he describes the great mystery of godliness—that God was manifested in the flesh (1 Timothy

3:16). Christ Himself declared, "Whoever has seen me has seen the Father" (John 14:9), so we can safely conclude, as noted by the Unknown Christian, that "to be Christlike is to be Godlike. What, then, is God like?"[6]

Moses had the unique privilege of receiving firsthand the most distinct revelation ever of the nature of God. This wasn't some third party describing God, it was God Himself. Moses had the audacity on Mount Sinai to utter this request of the Almighty:

> Moses said, "Please show me your glory." And he said, "I will make all my goodness pass before you and will proclaim before you my name 'The LORD.' And I will be gracious to whom I will be gracious, and will show mercy on whom I will show mercy." (Exodus 33:18–19)

> The LORD passed before him and proclaimed, "The LORD, the LORD, a God merciful and gracious, slow to anger, and abounding in steadfast love and faithfulness, keeping steadfast love for thousands, forgiving iniquity and transgression and sin..." (Exodus 34:6–7)

Here we see God declaring Himself to be *merciful and gracious, slow to anger, and abounding in steadfast love,* and *forgiving iniquity and transgression and sin.* Nehemiah was obviously acquainted with this revelation given to Moses and even prayed it back to the Lord during a time of fasting and repentance:

> They [the children of Israel that came out of Egypt] refused to obey and were not mindful of the wonders that you performed among them, but they stiffened their neck and appointed a leader to return to their slavery in Egypt. *But you are a God ready to forgive, gracious and merciful, slow to anger and abounding in steadfast love,* and did not forsake them. (Nehemiah 9:17, emphasis added)

Is it not entirely possible for those of us who are "strengthened with power through his Spirit in [our] inner being" (Ephesians 3:16) to be just like God in demonstrating these same things? Tell me why you cannot be merciful, or why you're unable to extend grace to your fellow man? Is it so entirely impossible to be long-suffering with others, to show them goodness and forgive them of every offense? If we think such abilities are reserved for God alone, then without question such thinking

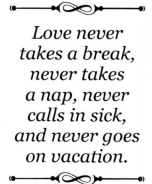

Love never takes a break, never takes a nap, never calls in sick, and never goes on vacation.

offers us a convenient excuse for maintaining our present course. But if we are to be like God, we must be transformed by the renewing of our minds (Romans 12:2) so that the very Christ who dwells in our hearts by faith can be made manifest in and through us just as transparently as light shines through glass.

No Couch Time

Like many in the IT profession, there are days when I come home from work mentally fatigued and exhausted from the grind of the day. Not surprisingly, I look forward to some couch time when I can relax, knowing that I don't have to stay *on top of my game.*

I've been blessed to be with my present employer for more than seventeen years, so I get a generous allotment of paid time off (PTO) each year, in addition to a generous number of paid holidays—and I always find a way to take *all of it.*

Imagine working a job where you had no time off—with or without pay. Imagine a grueling, seven-day work week with no breaks, no rest, and no downtime. As human beings, we require downtime; we require rest. Yet love knows nothing of the sort. Love never takes a break, never takes a nap, never calls in sick, and never goes on vacation. Love is 24/7/365 world without end. Love simply *is.* At least that's what Paul wrote to the Corinthians. Let's read the passage again, this time in the New International Version (NIV):

> Love is patient, love is kind. It does not envy, it does not boast, it is not proud. It does not dishonor others, it is not self-seeking, it is not easily angered, it keeps no record of wrongs. Love does not delight in evil but rejoices with the truth. It always protects, always trusts, always hopes, always perseveres. Love never fails. (1 Corinthians 13:4–8 NIV)

"Love is..."
and that means
whatever love is,
it always is.

"Love *is*..." and that means whatever love is, it *always* is.

These statements concerning the essence of love are categorical in nature, meaning they apply always and without exception. Love never behaves any other way. It never acts contrary to what is written here.

One of the distinguishing characteristics of love is that it is indefatigable. It never grows tired or weary of being longsuffering, of showing kindness and extending grace. It never looks for an opportunity to boast, an excuse to justify being provoked, or a reason to sing a "somebody done me wrong" song. Charles Spurgeon once noted, "The sun is not weary of shining, nor the fountain of flowing."[7] So it is with love.

Smith and Lesson

When I was much younger, I had the wonderful privilege on several occasions to hear the preaching of a dear man of God by the name of George Stormont (1909–1995). Pastor Stormont was a close friend of Smith Wigglesworth, the legendary English plumber turned healing evangelist/preacher.

Wigglesworth was known for his irascible temperament, often turning white with rage even over trivial matters. Pastor Stormont explains how God delivered him:

Setting aside ten days, he presented his body a living sacrifice (Rom. 12:1–2). He prayed, wept, soaked in the Word, and pleaded the promises. He faced up to the cross until he began to understand what Paul meant in Galatians 2:20.

This is how he described the experience to me: "God worked the old Wigglesworth-nature out and began to work the new Jesus-nature in."[8]

During his visits to our church in Sellersburg, Indiana, Pastor Stormont recounted numerous anecdotes of the life of Wigglesworth. He once told a story of the time he was shopping with Wigglesworth in a department store. Though the specifics of the incident escape me, an encounter with a store clerk provoked Wigglesworth enough for him to lament to Pastor Stormont, "I wish the Lord would give me leave of my salvation for just five minutes, so I could give this woman a piece of my mind."

The old Wigglesworth-nature would have no doubt let that woman have it, but the new Jesus-natured Wigglesworth instead held his tongue. That poor woman likely had no idea of that from which she had been spared!

Love never asks for leave from its always-on disposition. Our goal as Christians is to exhibit the love of God always and in all ways, as a natural outflow of our abiding in Christ.

In contrast to Wigglesworth's lament, love never asks for leave from its *always-on* disposition. Our goal as Christians is to exhibit the love of God always and in all ways, as a natural outflow of our abiding in Christ. Oswald Chambers describes the progression as follows:

> In the initial stages it will be a continual effort to abide, but as you continue, it will become so much a part of your life that you will abide in Him without any conscious effort.[9]

This is what we desire to attain—a life that is marked by a continual and unconscious abiding in the love of God our Savior. As we progress through the remaining chapters in this book, let us do so fueled and encouraged by this exhortation of the Lord to His servant Moses and the children of Israel:

> "For this commandment that I command you today is not too hard for you, neither is it far off. It is not in heaven, that you should say, 'Who will ascend to heaven for us and bring it to us, that we may hear it and do it?' Neither is it beyond the sea, that you should say, 'Who will go over the sea for us and bring it to us, that we may hear it and do it?' But the word is very near you. It is in your mouth and in your heart, so that you can do it." (Deuteronomy 30:11–14)

What commandment are we addressing? *Love*, of course. "This is my commandment, that you love one another as I have loved you" (John 15:12).

This commandment to love is not too hard for us. We don't have to travel far to find it. The word is very near. We need only to confess it with our mouths, believe it in our hearts, and begin to *do it*.

For Further Study

"In these last days he has spoken to us by his Son. . . .
He is the radiance of the glory of God and
the exact imprint of his nature."
Hebrews 1:2–3

1. The author openly shares his experience of coming to the realization that he needed to learn a better way, or as stated in 1 Corinthians 12:31, a more excellent way. What is this more excellent way?

2. What analogy does the author use to describe how the thought of becoming Christlike may affect some? Do you see becoming Christlike as something that is possible and worth the effort, or do you see it as a vain exercise for those who are not being realistic? Describe how you view your own prospects for becoming like Christ.

3. Explain what it means to comprehend with all the saints what is the breadth and length and height and depth, and to know the love of Christ. Share why you either agree or disagree with the author's premise that it is possible to comprehend the love of Christ.

4. Why is love superior to knowledge?

5. Hebrews 1:3 says Christ is the exact imprint of God's nature. As expressed in Exodus 34:6–7 and 1 Corinthians 13:4–8, how would you describe God's nature?

6. As human beings, we require downtime. Describe how this differs from love. What words would you use to describe love's *always on* disposition?

Part 4

The Precepts

precept[1] [**pree**-sept]
—noun

1. *a commandment or direction given as a rule of action or conduct.*

7

Take It Like a Man?

"Love is patient..."
1 Corinthians 13:4

I T WAS HAPPENING AGAIN. "Will he *ever* be able to get himself ready on time so we aren't always late? Why doesn't it bother him to be late all the time? Is it that hard to just start getting yourself ready earlier?" These and other thoughts consumed Meredith as she sat in the car waiting for Scott to make his way out the door.

Sound familiar? I know it does for some of you. You've gone through these mental gymnastics more times than you can count. And every time you've attempted to fix this problem, it has back-fired. Like Scott and Meredith, you find yourselves in a "discussion" that always seems to end with a frustrating, unresolved tension.

Keith was late for work, and he had an early morning meeting to attend as soon as he got to the office. To make matters worse, it was *his* meeting. As he pulled up to the traffic light, Keith tapped impatiently on the steering wheel. "Come on, come on already. How about a green light? Man! This is ridiculous!"

Also familiar? Of course it is.

The above examples are admittedly superficial and fall short in describing the full spectrum of opportunities life affords us to be longsuffering and patient, but they still serve as useful anecdotes to help us understand the distinction between the two. Keith doesn't need to be longsuffering with a traffic light; he needs patience while waiting for the light to change. Meredith, on the other hand, probably needs some of both. She needs patience to deal with the time element of waiting, but in the context of expressing love and forbearance, she needs longsuffering, because her frustration stems from an interaction with another human being—in this case, her spouse.

Many versions of the Bible begin 1 Corinthians 13:4 with "Love is patient..." but it doesn't matter whether your particular version says *longsuffering* or *patient*; the important thing to understand is that love puts up with *people*.

Longsuffering vs. Patience

Longsuffering and patience share some of the same characteristics, but are distinctly different in other ways—especially as we consider what it means to be Christlike. The longsuffering Paul speaks of in 1 Corinthians 13:4 has to do with the friction that is borne out of relationships and interactions with people. Waiting in a doctor's office may test my ability to sit quietly while keeping my mind and emotions in check, but that is more a function of maturity and accepting the fact that waiting is part and parcel of visits to the doctor. On the other hand, longsuffering tests my ability to repeatedly forgive a wrong, endure a character flaw, or put up with an annoying idiosyncrasy—*indefinitely* (see Matthew 18:21–22). Oswald Chambers explains our natural reaction to things that offend us:

> When a [simply] moral person is confronted with contempt, immorality, disloyalty, or dishonesty, he is so repulsed by the offense that he turns away and in despair closes his heart to the offender. But the miracle of the redemptive reality of God is that the worst and the vilest offender can never exhaust the depths of His love. Paul did not say that God separated him to show what a wonderful man He could make of him, but "... *to reveal His Son in me.*" (Galatians 1:16)[1]

God wants to reveal His Son in us, and one way we bear a great resemblance to Christ is by being longsuffering with the offenses of others. You will search in vain for a single instance in all the gospels when Jesus closed His heart to anyone because of their immorality, disloyalty, or mistreatment of Him. He loved *everyone*: His closest followers and those who rejected Him, His accusers and His betrayer, those who deserted Him and the "whitewashed tombs" who had Him crucified. We would do well to remember this exhortation in Hebrews 12: "Consider him who endured from sinners such hostility against himself, so that you may not grow weary or fainthearted" (Hebrews 12:3).

There was no end to the longsuffering of our Lord. He never retaliated or attempted to defend His sinless character. Isaiah foretold His longsuffering:

> He was oppressed, and he was afflicted, yet he opened not his mouth; like a lamb that is led to the slaughter, and like a sheep that before its shearers is silent, so he opened not his mouth. (Isaiah 53:7)

Wisdom Speaks

The world has long counseled us to "Man up" and "Take it like a man." This is all well and good if you're talking about things like learning to accept responsibility for your actions and doing the right thing—even if it means you will suffer for it. With respect to longsuffering, however, taking it like a man means I will put up with you to a point, but once you cross the line, all bets are off and it's open season—*on you.*

If we are to be like Christ, we cannot fortify ourselves to take it like a man—at least not like any man. Instead, we must allow God to transform us to the extent that we take it like *the Son of Man,* Jesus Christ.

Philippians tells us that Jesus emptied Himself, took on the form of a servant, and was born in the likeness of men (Philippians

2:7). He put on an earth suit to show us "how it's done" down here. The New King James Version (NKJV) renders 1 Corinthians 13:4 as "Love suffers long." In His humanity, Jesus demonstrated two intrinsic aspects of longsuffering, namely, that love *suffers*, and it suffers *long* (i.e., indefinitely). We must resist the temptation as mortals to take matters into our own hands when we have come to the end of ourselves. James counsels us with this superlative wisdom:

> Know this, my beloved brothers: let every person be quick to hear, slow to speak, slow to anger; for the anger of man does not produce the righteousness of God. (James 1:19–20)

The Lamb of God "opened not His mouth" (Isaiah 53:7)—and neither should we.

Rudy's Revelation

The 1993 movie classic *Rudy* is based on the true story of Daniel Eugene "Rudy" Ruettiger, a Catholic boy determined to play football for Notre Dame. There's a scene in the movie where Rudy is nearing the end of his final semester at the transfer-intent Holy Cross College in Notre Dame. After his grades fell short on his first three attempts, he is now running out of time to be accepted into the University of Notre Dame. In his desperate search for answers, Rudy goes to the church and takes a seat in one of the pews. He is soon approached by a priest who has become a friend. Pensively, Rudy asks, "Have I done everything I possibly can? Can you help me?" In what is one of the most classic movie lines ever, the priest replies, "Son, in thirty-five years of religious studies, I've come up with only two hard, incontrovertible facts: There is a God... and I'm not Him."[2]

But we sure do long to be God when it suits our purpose or justifies our passions! Scripture is rife with examples of how God was longsuffering with Israel to a point, but eventually punished them for their disobedience and hardness of heart. Shouldn't I be able to do the same with those who wear me out? Is there not a point when I have endured long enough and can finally lower the boom? Well, there is a God... and I'm not Him!

Balancing Act

I would be remiss not to point out the obvious fact that there are certain contexts in which a person does, in fact, endure a situation or circumstance to a point, and then it's time to take some action.

Consider the parent/child, employer/employee, or any other relationship involving authority or a chain of command. Sometimes a person in authority may have to "deal with a situation," which typically means dealing with a *person*.

My wife and I raised four children—two boys and two girls—and you'd better believe there were times when we put up with their nonsense to a point, and then it was time to discipline them! The following Scripture verse was often quoted in our house during our childrearing years: "Foolishness is bound in the heart of a child; but the rod of correction shall drive it far from him" (Proverbs 22:15 KJV).

Similarly, a supervisor may patiently work with a subordinate in order to improve his or her performance and productivity. Nevertheless, at times a supervisor must deal with such things as incompetence, tardiness, a bad attitude, or being unreliable—possibly culminating with termination of the individual's employment. In other words, disciplinary action is a fact of life that impacts everyone at one time or another, and such actions should not be misinterpreted as a lack of longsuffering.

To balance this thought, however, we also need to understand that whether we are in authority or under authority, it is never our place to take matters into our own hands and respond in a vengeful or retaliatory spirit. Sometimes we are simply called to suffer wrongdoing, mistreatment, and injustice, leaving the matter in the hands of the Lord to avenge us of any wrong.

Saul and David

We see a beautiful example of this in 1 Samuel 24. Insane with jealousy, Saul pursued David for several years, seeking to take his life. While David and his men were hiding in a cave in the wilderness of Engedi, Saul came in to relieve himself. Even though David had the opportunity to kill Saul, he refused to do so. Instead, he stealthily cut off a corner of Saul's robe, and when Saul left the cave, David went after him, bowed before him, and showed him the piece of cloth as proof there was no treason within him against the king.

> "May the LORD judge between me and you, may the LORD avenge me against you, but *my hand shall not be against you*." . . . And Saul lifted up his voice and wept. He said to David, "You are more righteous than I, for you have repaid me good, whereas I have repaid you evil." (1 Samuel 24:12, 16b–17, emphasis added)

It would be impossible to list everything that love is called to endure in a spirit of longsuffering, but suffice it to say that anything that stirs up a desire within you to lash out and *go off* on someone is an opportunity to be longsuffering. Peter underscores this thought in the first of his two letters to the Church:

> Do not repay evil for evil or reviling for reviling, but on the contrary, bless, for to this you were called, that you may obtain a blessing. (1 Peter 3:9)

Before continuing on—and this is reiterated in chapter thirteen—if you are in an abusive situation that is endangering your safety, I am not suggesting you should allow someone to repeatedly abuse or harm you. There may be times when you need to walk away or report the abuse to the proper authorities.

Soak It Up

Consider for a moment the absorptive nature of a sponge. Love is a lot like a sponge in that it absorbs the *messes* of others. If you've spent much time around the dinner table, there's no doubt you've either witnessed, caused, or been the victim of the proverbial spilled milk. In fact, you've likely been told at least once in your life not to cry over it.

Sometimes the messes people make around us (or on us) are a lot more difficult to deal with than a harmless glass of spilled milk. Harsh words, broken promises, lies, deceit, criticism, betrayal, unjust treatment—the list goes on of things that can be downright painful.

But in the context of longsuffering, love is like a sponge that somehow never reaches capacity as it absorbs the offenses of others, turns the other cheek, goes the second mile, and forgives seventy times seven. Love endures the foolishness and vices of others. It bears their weaknesses and shoulders their frailties. This doesn't mean that love should coddle or enable those weaknesses, or that love never confronts someone in a spirit of meekness and humility. It simply means that love consistently and persistently puts up with the personal inconveniences, frustrations, vexations, and grief experienced throughout the course of life. Love doesn't have to fix every problem or change the behavior of everyone who does things differently than we do. Sometimes love simply endures. It just keeps on soaking up the mess.

> *In the context of longsuffering, love is like a sponge that somehow never reaches capacity as it absorbs the offenses of others, turns the other cheek, goes the second mile, and forgives seventy times seven.*

But this cannot be accomplished in our own strength, or through any natural ability of our own. It is singularly accomplished by yielding to the love of God shed abroad in our hearts, as we experience the transformational progression described in Romans 5:

> We rejoice in our sufferings, knowing that suffering produces endurance, and endurance produces character, and character produces hope, and hope does not put us to shame, because God's love has been poured into our hearts through the Holy Spirit who has been given to us. (Romans 5:3–5)

Peter tells us how God is pleased when we do what is right, especially if we are treated unfairly in the process:

> For this is commendable, if because of conscience toward God one endures grief, suffering wrongfully. For what credit is it if, when you are beaten for your faults, you take it patiently? But when you do good and suffer, if you take it patiently, this is commendable before God. (1 Peter 2:19–20 NKJV)

Peter concludes this thought by telling us how our Lord Jesus responded to being treated unjustly:

> When He was reviled, did not revile in return; when He suffered, He did not threaten, but committed Himself to Him who judges righteously. (1 Peter 2:23 NKJV)

Wring It Out

For argument's sake, let's suppose our "love sponge" did have a saturation point—a point at which, after the cumulative absorption of the wrongs, offenses, injustices, irritations, annoyances, incompetence, etc. of others, it could take no more and *had* to be wrung out—what do you suppose would come out of *your* love sponge? Would it be the sweetness of the Son of God, or would it be anger, hostility, frustration, resentment, bitterness, retaliation, and the like?

You may be wondering how, after having absorbed the wrongs, injustices, irritations, and such from your interactions with others, anything but anger, frustration, resentment, etc. could come out of you when you are wrung out. If we're only talking about an ordinary sponge, then the analogy falls apart. However, we are talking about the love of God shed abroad in our hearts, which constrains us to exude the longsuffering of Jesus instead of our fleshly instincts.

Are you one of those people who gets irritated when someone asks you to repeat something you already told them? Do you get defensive when people criticize you, or challenge your authority or opinion? Are you easily exasperated by the egocentric demands of others—after all, you have your own things that need to get done, right? Do you get irked by things people say that in the grand scheme simply aren't that big of a deal? If any of these shoes fit, God is likely challenging you to exercise a greater measure of long-suffering toward those with whom you interact.

Moses, Miriam, and Meribah

Bluntly stated, being longsuffering means *putting up with the crap of others*.[3] That's about as forthright and candid as I can make it— no euphemisms, no sugar coating, just bare metal. Now before you get offended by my use of the word *crap*, please understand that one of its definitions is: "something that causes *misery, misfortune, or discomfort*."[4]

Moses experienced all of that and more during the forty years he shepherded Israel from Egypt through the wilderness, and ultimately to the threshold of the Promised Land. He experienced the *misery* of listening to their murmuring and complaining, and he experienced the *misfortune* of not being allowed to enter the Promised Land. He also experienced the *discomfort* of traipsing back up the mountain for a *second* stint of forty days and forty nights without food and water, after smashing the inaugural stone tablets inscribed by the finger of God with the Ten Commandments—all because of the idolatry he encountered when he came down from Mount Sinai the first time.

When we take a closer look at some of what Moses had to deal with, we see both *triumph* and *tragedy.*

The Triumph of Longsuffering

Like most leaders, Moses faced opposition to his authority. Sometimes people are jealous of our success. Sometimes they think they could do a better job, or they may be overly ambitious turf-grabbers. If you are a leader and honest with yourself, there have probably been times when you would have gladly let your critics have your job—at least for a day or two—just so they could see for themselves what it is like to walk in your shoes.

In Numbers chapter 12, we read of such an encounter when Miriam and Aaron approached Moses and challenged his authority:

> Miriam and Aaron spoke against Moses because of the Cushite woman whom he had married, for he had married a Cushite woman. And they said, "Has the LORD indeed spoken only through Moses? Has he not spoken through us also?" And the LORD heard it. Now the man Moses was very meek, more than all people who were on the face of the earth. (Numbers 12:1–3)

The Hebrew word translated as *meek* in verse three of this passage is translated as *humble* in other translations. The NET's parenthetical representation of verse three is one such example:

> (Now the man Moses was very *humble,* more so than any man on the face of the earth.) (Numbers 12:3 NET, emphasis added)

The translator notes in the NET provide an interesting insight into the Hebrew word translated as *meek* in some versions, but *humble* in others. A simple search through a Strong's concordance reveals that this word is translated interchangeably in the KJV as *meek* or *humble* throughout the Old Testament. In this particular passage, however, the NET translators liken the humility (or meekness) of Moses to longsuffering, which the context of this passage supports:

> The word *anav* means "humble." The word may reflect a trustful attitude (as in Pss 25:9, 37:11), but perhaps here the idea of "more tolerant" or "longsuffering."[5]

Coming back to our story... things begin to get interesting as God calls the three of them into His "office" for a quick meeting:

> And suddenly the LORD said to Moses and to Aaron and Miriam, "Come out, you three, to the tent of meeting." And the three of them came out. And the LORD came down in a pillar of cloud and stood at the entrance of the tent and called Aaron and Miriam, and they both came forward. (Numbers 12:4–5)

I don't know about you, but if I were in Miriam's or Aaron's sandals, I would've been quaking more than Dorothy and her chums standing before the Wizard of Oz. Proceeding further, we see God express His strong displeasure over their smug, presumptuous view of their own importance:

> "Why then were you not afraid to speak against my servant Moses?" And the anger of the LORD was kindled against them, and he departed.
>
> When the cloud removed from over the tent, behold, Miriam was leprous, like snow. And Aaron turned toward Miriam, and behold, she was leprous. And Aaron said to Moses, "Oh, my lord, do

not punish us because we have done foolishly and have sinned. Let her not be as one dead, whose flesh is half eaten away when he comes out of his mother's womb." And Moses cried to the LORD, "O God, please heal her—please." (Numbers 12:8b–13)

Here, we see how longsuffering moved Moses into a place of intercession on behalf of Miriam. To be fair, she was his sister, so he could also have been motivated by familial love. Nevertheless, he still could have scolded her by saying, "It serves you right for questioning my authority. You got exactly what you deserved," but instead, he extended grace and pleaded for God to mercifully heal her—leaving us a beautiful example of how longsuffering triumphs over retaliation.

The Tragedy of "Losing It"

In contrast to Moses previously showing longsuffering, we later read of a time when he finally lost his cool and *went off* on the children of Israel like a bottle rocket on the Fourth of July. This tragic outburst is summarized in a single sentence in Psalm 106:

> They angered him at the waters of Meribah, and it went ill with Moses on their account, for they made his spirit bitter, and he spoke rashly with his lips. (Psalm 106:32–33)

The full account (worth exploring) is found in Numbers 20:

> Now there was no water for the congregation. And they assembled themselves together against Moses and against Aaron. And the people quarreled with Moses and said, "Would that we had perished when our brothers perished before the LORD! Why have you brought the assembly of the LORD into this wilderness, that we should die here, both we and our cattle? And why have you made us come up out of

Egypt to bring us to this evil place? It is no place for grain or figs or vines or pomegranates, and there is no water to drink." (Numbers 20:2–5)

In other words, *"This sucks!"*

Though I'm not a fan of this expression, I believe it captures in contemporary vernacular exactly what Moses would've heard had he led a congregation of God's people through the wilderness in the early twenty-first century.

As soon as they heard this combative complaint from the people, Moses and Aaron went to the tent of meeting and prostrated themselves before the Lord:

> And the glory of the Lord appeared to them, and the Lord spoke to Moses, saying, "Take the staff, and assemble the congregation, you and Aaron your brother, and tell the rock before their eyes to yield its water. So you shall bring water out of the rock for them and give drink to the congregation and their cattle." And Moses took the staff from before the Lord, as he commanded him. (Numbers 20:6b–9)

It doesn't take much imagination based on the ensuing verses to realize that Moses was now seething over the murmuring and complaining that continued to belch forth from his fellow Israelites.

> Then Moses and Aaron gathered the assembly together before the rock, and he said to them, "Hear now, you rebels: shall we bring water for you out of this rock?" And Moses lifted up his hand and struck the rock with his staff twice, and water came out abundantly, and the congregation drank, and their livestock. And the Lord said to Moses and Aaron, "Because you did not believe in me, to uphold me as holy in the eyes of the people of Israel, therefore you shall not bring this assembly into the land that I have given them." (Numbers 20:10–12)

Although it is clear that Moses had become angry and lost his cool, I find it interesting that God chided Moses for his unbelief in striking the rock. Is one of the reasons we don't extend long-suffering to others because we don't trust God to work things out according to His plan? Is a lack of patience an indicator that unbelief is at work, causing us to take matters into our own hands? Regardless, Moses disobeyed and struck the rock instead of speaking to it, thereby tragically missing out on the Promised Land.

What a statement this makes to us about the importance of being longsuffering! It somehow seems unfair that Moses was prohibited from entering the Promised Land, but as Jesus would later say, "To whom much was given, of him much will be required" (Luke 12:48). Without question, Moses was given much. As New Testament stewards of the ministry of the Spirit, we have also been entrusted with much—perhaps even more than Moses (2 Corinthians 3:7–8).

How Does Your Garden Grow?

In Solomon's love song—an extended metaphor of the love between Christ and the Church—we see our Beloved summon the winds to blow upon His garden (His Bride, the Church) in order to unlock its fragrant spices:

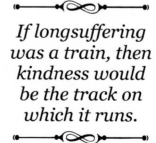

A garden locked is my sister, my bride, a spring locked, a fountain sealed.... Awake, O north wind, and come, O south wind! Blow upon my garden, let its spices flow. (Song of Solomon 4:12, 16a)

If longsuffering was a train, then kindness would be the track on which it runs.

Though not always so, north winds can be cold and harsh, and southerly winds can be hot and stifling. It's not farfetched to say these winds may represent the *stuff* that blows upon our garden through our interactions with others. What scent wafts from your garden when the irritating winds of life blow upon it? Is it the sweet fragrance of longsuffering or the pungent odor of a fleshly retaliation?

Stay On Track

If longsuffering was a train, then kindness would be the track on which it runs. "Love suffers long and is kind," we are told in 1 Corinthians 13:4a (NKJV). How could it be any other way?

It seems contradictory to think that I could be longsuffering while venting frustration in some angry tirade. It's hard to picture patiently enduring a fault or a wrong without doing so in a spirit of kindness. A train has no hope of reaching its destination without a sound track to travel on, and neither should we expect to be a compelling example of longsuffering without the supporting infrastructure upon which love travels: *kindness.*

For Further Study

"Know this, my beloved brothers: let every person be quick to hear, slow to speak, slow to anger."
James 1:19

1. Describe the difference between longsuffering and patience. Share examples of each.
2. Tell why you either agree or disagree with the premise that longsuffering primarily pertains to interactions with people. If you disagree, cite an example of longsuffering that does not involve another person.
3. How does "taking it like a man" fall short in demonstrating the longsuffering of Christ?
4. What significant difference exists between how we are to deal with people and how God deals with people? What did Rudy learn from the priest at Holy Cross College?
5. The author compares love to a sponge. Explain how this analogy works and where it falls short.
6. Describe how Moses experienced both triumph and tragedy in his dealings with Israel.
7. Complete this sentence, "If longsuffering was a train then...." Explain why you either agree or disagree with this statement.

8

Love's Secret Ingredient

"Love is ... kind."
1 Corinthians 13:4

I LIVE IN THE GREAT STATE OF INDIANA where basketball is king. Remember the movie *Hoosiers*, starring Gene Hackman? Yeah, that's about us. Corn fed and basketball bred. I was born, raised, and still reside in the southern Indiana town of New Albany, situated 105 miles south of Bloomington, Indiana, home of Indiana University. New Albany is just across the Ohio River from Louisville, Kentucky, the home of my beloved University of Louisville Cardinals, and about 75 miles west of that *other* Kentucky school known as Big Blue Nation (the University of Kentucky Wildcats). Just before this manuscript went to press, my high school alma mater—the New Albany Bulldogs—won the 2016 4A state championship title.

Basketball seems to be in our DNA around these parts, and for reasons that escape me we think that yelling at referees, coaches, opposing players, and fans is part and parcel of the game. Consequently, there seems to be this unwritten, yet universally accepted, belief that we are given temporary leave from our Christian witness in order to spew our vitriol toward referees and opponents as though it's just "part of the game."

If you're at all familiar with basketball, you've no doubt witnessed your share of truculent protests to calls made by officials, and like many—including me—you may have launched a few salvos of your own. It's never pretty. It doesn't enhance our reputation, improve our chances for getting and maintaining a good name, nor does it cause men to "see [our] good works and glorify [our] Father in heaven." In fact, it has the opposite effect.

America worships at the altar of sport as entertainment, and many Christians are caught up in that culture. That's fine to a point, but we need to be mindful of what comes out of our mouths while watching our children's Little League games, basketball games, and other sporting events. My dad was one of my greatest encouragers during my childhood years of playing baseball and basketball, but I still remember a few incidents at the ballpark when he not only embarrassed himself, but he also embarrassed me with his sideline rants. Eyes are watching and ears are hearing.

Why are we so blind to this? Can we not put ourselves in the shoes of the officials who are trying their best to get it right, and cut them a break the same as we would want if hundreds—perhaps thousands—of people were screaming at us? You may say, "Well, that's what they get paid for. If they can't stand the heat, they should get out of the kitchen."

Are you sure you want to go with that? Have you turned that same logic around on yourself with respect to what you do for a living? In your line of work, would you want people screaming at you every time you made a mistake—or what *they* thought was a mistake?

To be fair, basketball is a fast-paced sport that's difficult to watch without becoming emotionally involved. Still, that doesn't give us *carte blanche* to cast off restraint and behave contrary to Christ. According to 2 Corinthians 5:14 we are controlled (i.e., constrained) by the love of Christ.

To avoid belaboring this specific example and berating anyone who may be particularly given to this behavior, let us be reminded that this is just *one* example of many in which we spew venom instead of expressing kindness. James states it this way:

> No human being can tame the tongue. It is a restless evil, full of deadly poison. With it we bless our

Lord and Father, and with it we curse people who are made in the likeness of God. From the same mouth come blessing and cursing. My brothers, *these things ought not to be so.* (James 3:8–10, emphasis added)

What Is Kindness?

According to Dictionary.com, *kindness*[1] is the noun form of the word *kind*. To be kind is to be:

1. of a good or benevolent nature or disposition, as a person: a kind and loving person.
2. indulgent, considerate, or helpful; humane (often followed by *to*): to be kind *to* animals.
3. mild; gentle

To show kindness is to be considerate and thoughtful in both word and deed, to prefer the needs and desires of another above your own. To be kind is to share another's burden, to lessen their pain; to offer assistance or a word of encouragement.

Kindness is packaged and delivered in a variety of ways. It may even take the form of a loving rebuke: "Let a righteous man strike me—it is a kindness; let him rebuke me—it is oil for my head; let my head not refuse it" (Psalm 141:5a). Being kind to others doesn't mean we avoid confrontation or admonishment. Kindness does not have to coddle, but it should not be rude when speaking candidly about a matter. How many times have we failed in our attempts to share something helpful, simply because we spoke in a tone or spirit that caused the hearer to shut down? Solomon observed that "sweetness of speech increases persuasiveness" (Proverbs 16:21).

Kindness is to love what butter is to French cuisine— the secret ingredient.

Kindness and French Cuisine

It is widely accepted that the three secrets of French cuisine are butter, butter, and butter. It's true. Butter seemingly makes everything taste better!

Short-story writer and novelist Henry James (1843–1916) once said, "Three things in human life are important: the first is to be kind; the second is to be kind; and the third is to be kind."[2] I see here a corollary that kindness is to love what butter is to French cuisine—the *secret ingredient*.

Pierre Carlet de Chamblain de Marivaux, a seventeenth-century dramatist and novelist, said, "In this world, you must be a bit too kind to be kind enough."[3] Have you ever known anyone who was criticized for being too kind? I doubt you have, and that's because people are starved for kindness—genuine kindness—not something feigned or contrived. Leo Buscaglia, a New York Times bestselling author, is known for this quote:

> *"Three things in human life are important: the first is to be kind; the second is to be kind; and the third is to be kind." – Henry James*

> Too often we underestimate the power of a touch, a smile, a kind word, a listening ear, an honest compliment, or the smallest act of caring, all of which have the potential to turn a life around.[4]

For the Record

It's true that love keeps no record of wrongs—we'll cover that in chapter 13—but I realized one day how much easier it was for me to enumerate a list of wrongs incurred than it was to recall even a handful of acts of kindness shown to me. Talk about disturbing—and convicting! I was so ashamed of myself that I decided to set aside some time to search through the archives of my past in order to reflect upon specific acts of kindness of which I was the beneficiary. Here are a few highlights:

I married Mindy in 1979 and I can scarcely recall a time since then when she has not insisted on me having the last bite of a dessert we shared. It may hardly seem worth mentioning, but to me it is remarkably unselfish and considerate!

I remember a time early in our marriage when Mindy and I were struggling to make ends meet that I got an unexpected visit from my pastor (who is also my brother-in-law). He had been shopping for new pants, and for some reason he bought several pair for me and stopped by our house on his way home to deliver them. How thoughtful and kind!

Test yourself: how much easier is it to enumerate a list of wrongs incurred than to recall even a handful of acts of kindness?

My second job as a young IT professional was with Doe-Anderson Advertising in Louisville, Kentucky. I recall publishing my first inter-office memo for distribution. This was before the days of email, so I walked my handwritten memo to our word processing department where it was typed, printed, and then delivered via inter-office mail to department heads and senior management—including the CEO/President of the agency.

After reading his copy, CEO and President Robert S. Allison took the time to write a handwritten note on his personal stationery to let me know how impressed he was with the clarity, professionalism, and substance of my memo. I was brimming over with appreciation and confidence after receiving his note until... I received a far less glowing critique from another person within the organization. She was careful to point out some errors with grammar and punctuation, as well as the misspelling of the word *queue* (I had used *que*, which she informed me was the abbreviation of Quebec).

It didn't take me long to realize that Bob Allison[5] had likely seen those same mistakes, but he overlooked them and, instead, used the opportunity to encourage me with a personalized, handwritten note. Wow. What a powerful act of kindness!

Even though I wished the other individual had not tarnished the moment, in hindsight I'm thankful for the contrasting life lesson, which later guided me in offering encouragement instead of criticism to a young, fledgling worship leader I was mentoring. He had just experienced one of those times of leading worship when everything that could go wrong did. He berated himself and apologized profusely for doing such a poor job. Instead of needlessly confirming all the things he did "wrong" or could have done better, I directed his attention to the things he did well—things he was not even aware of doing. He deeply appreciated that I took this approach instead of highlighting all the ways he had "messed up."

I know a man who once stopped his car to remove a brand-new pair of shoes from his feet and give them to a homeless man he saw walking barefoot along the side of the road. That same man bought a hot meal for a homeless man on a cold, wintry day, and then gave him his gloves so he could keep his hands warm. Acts of kindness that can never be repaid by the recipient are some of the most precious, and are also a tremendous source of joy to the giver.

I remember a time many years ago when some folks in my church would buy groceries for needy families. The delivery method, however, was somewhat unorthodox. Under cover of darkness, these nighttime delivery agents would quietly place the groceries on the front porch, ring the doorbell, and then run away so the recipients wouldn't know whom God had used to bless them. Such acts of kindness inspire thanksgiving and praise to God rather than notoriety for individuals.

An Unexpected Surprise

One of my closest friends is a man I met in my late forties. His name is Steve Mobley (known as Mobes to his friends). Through the providence of God, we became golfing buddies a number of years before he experienced the saving grace of Christ. We met each other at a golf event, and through a series of circumstances orchestrated by God, ended up playing together for several years as a two-man team in a Friday night golf league. Some years later, I had the privilege of leading Steve in a prayer to receive Jesus Christ as Lord and Savior. Our friendship has grown and continues to this day.

About three or four years into my golfing relationship with Mobes, I received an email from him—one of those emails that circulates indefatigably throughout cyberspace. This particular email instructed me to describe him in a single word and send it back to him. After he received my word, Steve also picked a word to describe me and sent it back to me. I'm not sure what word I expected he would choose, but I was surprised by his response. The word he chose for me was *kind*. Maybe I was hoping for something a little more manly. Yet, in hindsight, of all the things I could be known and remembered for—intelligence, looks, charm, humor, success, etc.—I can think of nothing else I would rather be remembered for than being kind.

Caught in the Act of Unkindness

Unfortunately, kindness has not always been a word that would've been used to describe me. When I was twelve or thirteen years old, my best friend and I had a conversation that devastated a boy our age who lived two doors down the street from me. I lived in a typical middle income neighborhood, and our house was a Cape Cod with two upstairs bedrooms, one of which was mine and the other my brother's.

My best friend, David, lived two streets away and had come over to hang out with me, so the two of us were in my bedroom, no doubt talking about the sort of juvenile stuff that kids talk about. It was a pleasant day, and my mother informed us she was going to go visit with Doris, the mother of Dennis, the boy who lived two doors away. Since the weather was nice, my mom left the storm door unlocked and the inside front door wide open. It's just the way people lived back then.

At this point in my conversation with David, the topic shifted to Dennis. I don't recall exactly what was said, but I remember saying something about not liking Dennis because he thought he was so cool.

It wasn't long before my conspicuously upset mother returned home to inform us that Dennis heard every hateful word said about him, and that he had run back home in tears! We had no idea that when my mom went to visit with Doris, she encouraged Dennis to go to our house to hang out with Dave and me. Since the door was wide open, we never heard Dennis enter the house, and as he made his way up the stairs to my bedroom, my words pierced his heart like a dagger!

My mom promptly sent David home, and then escorted me to Dennis' house to apologize. Although I felt awful, I was too young and selfish to comprehend how damaging something like that could be, so I feigned an apology. The problem, however, was that I meant every word I had said about Dennis, even though I would have never spoken any of it to his face. And we all know that it's okay to talk behind someone's back as long as they don't hear you, right?

Dennis died at the age of forty-one, having succumbed to alcoholism. After we graduated high school, I lost touch with him, and never took the time to offer a sincere apology for my toxic words. I don't know if that juvenile conversation had anything to do with Dennis becoming an alcoholic or not, but I'm absolutely certain those unkind words of mine ripped a hole in his self-esteem that day. If only I had known these nuggets of truth from Proverbs:

> Whoever belittles his neighbor lacks sense, but a man
> of understanding remains silent. (Proverbs 11:12)

There is one whose rash words are like sword thrusts, but the tongue of the wise brings healing. (Proverbs 12:18)

My words that day cut like a sword and brought anything but healing. Yes, I was young and lacked the sense to know better, but this anecdote provides an invaluable life lesson, equally so for adults who can be just as cruel as children: unkind words begin as thoughts (Mark 7:20–23), so the place to stop them is in the mind before they reach the gate of the mouth.

Nobility Obliges

The French have an expression, *noblesse oblige*, which translated literally means *nobility obliges*. According to Dictionary.com, it refers to "the moral obligation of those of high birth, powerful social position, etc., to act with honor, kindliness, generosity, etc."[6]

"Kindness is in our power, even when fondness is not."
–Samuel Johnson

Peter described believers in Jesus as "a chosen race, a royal priesthood, a holy nation, a people for his own possession, that you may proclaim the excellencies of him who called you out of darkness into his marvelous light" (1 Peter 2:9).

Given our high birth and noble rank as citizens of God's kingdom, are we not equally obligated to extend kindness to those around us? What if I don't like a particular person? Certainly no one among us *likes* everybody, but according to lexicographer Samuel Johnson, "Kindness is in our power, even when fondness is not."[7]

The Unknown Christian said, "Kindness is the one thing we are all hungering for. And it is at the same time the easiest thing to show and the greatest thing to give. And we all ought to know that if we are unkind we cannot be Christlike."[8]

When Is Love Kind?

When is love kind? I propose answering this question with another question: When is love *not* kind? The following passage from Titus sufficiently addresses this:

> Remind the people... to be ready to do whatever is good, to slander no one, to be peaceable and considerate, and *always* to be gentle toward everyone.
>
> At one time we too were foolish, disobedient, deceived and enslaved by all kinds of passions and pleasures. We lived in malice and envy, being hated and hating one another. *But when the kindness and love of God our Savior appeared, he saved us, not because of righteous things we had done, but because of his mercy.* (Titus 3:1–5a NIV, emphasis added)

"Kindness is the one thing we are all hungering for. And it is at the same time the easiest thing to show and the greatest thing to give. And we all ought to know that if we are unkind we cannot be Christlike."
–Unknown Christian

Love is unconditionally kind. Our merciful Savior lavished His kindness upon us when we were most undeserving, so how can we not do the same? The Unknown Christian suggests that the reason we don't love unconditionally is because we either don't think or have not known to do so.[9] What excuse, then, do we yet cling to? The following words of Jesus are unqualified, without exception, and addressed to all:

If you love those who love you, what benefit is that to you? For even sinners love those who love them. And if you do good to those who do good to you, what benefit is that to you? For even sinners do the same. And if you lend to those from whom you expect to receive, what credit is that to you? Even sinners lend to sinners, to get back the same amount. But love your enemies, and do good, and lend, expecting nothing in return, and your reward will be great, and you will be sons of the Most High, for *he is kind to the ungrateful and the evil.* Be merciful, even as your Father is merciful. (Luke 6:32–36, emphasis added)

Love my enemies?
Absolutely.
Do good to them?
Without hesitation.
Lend without expecting repayment?
Certainly.

Why? The answer is simple: if we are to be like Jesus and truly act as children of our Heavenly Father, then of necessity we must also be kind to the ungrateful and evil. Anything to the contrary would be inconsistent with our profession of Christ.

"A more glorious victory cannot be gained over another man than this, that when the injury began on his part, the kindness should begin on ours."
–John Tillotson

John Tillotson, English theologian and Archbishop of Canterbury (1630–1694), once said, "A more glorious victory cannot be gained over another man than this, that when the injury began on his part, the kindness should begin on ours."[10]

The following anecdotes from *The Christlike Christian* powerfully reinforce Tillotson's premise:

"That rascal has stolen my boots!" cried a young nobleman excitedly, to Francis of Assisi. "Run after him and give him your socks," was the quiet reply.[11]

A man once knelt in prayer in a barrack-room during a time of war. The Unknown Christian describes the scene:

> A drunken and blaspheming soldier came in. Taking off his muddy boots, he flung them at the kneeler's head, and then tumbled into bed. The next morning he found his boots cleaned and polished at the foot of his bed. That loving act won the blasphemer for the Savior, when rebuke or retaliation would only have evoked further persecution.[12]

Is it not true, however, that our base instinct is to retaliate rather than to extend kindness? But that is not, nor will it ever be, the response of love. Therefore, in the end, it all comes down to this: Love is kind to the kind, and it's kind to the unkind. Love is kind to the merciful, and it's kind to the cruel. It's kind to the holy, and it's kind to the unholy. It's kind to the helpful, and it's kind to those who wouldn't lift a finger to help someone else. Love is kind to the thankful, and kind to the unthankful. Love is always kind, not just when our present disposition or circumstance accommodates it. It is kind in season and out of season, fair weather and foul, easy or difficult, convenient or inconvenient.

One of my favorite quotes is this timeless counsel from Mignon McLaughlin, a twentieth-century journalist and author (1913–1983) who said, "Don't be yourself. Be someone a little nicer."[13] That counsel remains as sound today as when it was first penned.

Love is kind, and those who would be Christlike must also be kind.

For Further Study

*"But love your enemies ... and you will be sons of the Most High,
for he is kind to the ungrateful and the evil."*
Luke 6:35

1. What is love's secret ingredient, and why is it so powerful?
2. List some ways you might demonstrate kindness to others.
3. Make a list of some of the more memorable moments in your life when you were the beneficiary of an act of kindness. How did those acts of kindness make you feel? Share at least one such experience with the group or another individual.
4. How does kindness aid our instruction and correction of others?
5. What conditions does the Bible place on extending kindness to others? When does God expect us to show kindness and when does He tell us to withhold it?
6. What impacted you most in this chapter?

9

Who Are You Sleeping With?

"Love ... does not envy."
1 Corinthians 13:4

I N CASE YOU CASUALLY SKIPPED OVER the aforementioned Scripture reference, let me restate it for you here:

Love ...
does
not
envy.

Ever.

But if there is some trace of envy within me, it simply means I'm not yet perfected in love. No big deal, right?

Of course, it's a big deal. It's huge. Let me explain.

Envy is as old as the Garden of Eden. There's hardly a literate person on the planet who is not familiar with the story, but let's look at the text anyway:

> Now Adam knew Eve his wife, and she conceived and bore Cain, saying, "I have gotten a man with the help of the LORD." And again, she bore his brother Abel. Now Abel was a keeper of sheep, and Cain a worker of the ground. In the course of time Cain brought to the LORD an offering of the fruit of the ground, and Abel also brought of the firstborn of his flock and of

their fat portions. And the LORD had regard for Abel and his offering, but for Cain and his offering he had no regard. So Cain was very angry, and his face fell. (Genesis 4:1–5)

Can you relate to this story? Have you ever become sad or angry over another person's success or recognition? Have you ever been passed over for a promotion, or watched as someone you thought had an inferior skill set to yours was presented with an award for excellence—and you got *nada*?

The Lord saw Cain's reaction and talked to him about it:

The LORD said to Cain, "Why are you angry, and why has your face fallen? If you do well, will you not be accepted? And if you do not do well, sin is crouching at the door. Its desire is for you, but you must rule over it." Cain spoke to Abel his brother. And when they were in the field, Cain rose up against his brother Abel and killed him. (Genesis 4:6–8).

Here we see the first mention of envy in Scripture. Though we don't see the word itself, we see the cause and effect. Each brother had presented an offering to the Lord, and while Abel received positive recognition for his, the Lord had *no regard* for Cain and his offering. So it is reasonable to conclude that the sin crouching at Cain's door was *envy*. God told him, "You must rule over it," but he obviously did not. Envy drove him to murder his brother. Is it now clear why this is such a big deal?

Need More Proof?

Envy, jealousy, and covetousness make terrible bedfellows. But to remove all doubt, let's go through a quick rundown of some of their more notable exploits as chronicled in Scripture:

1. Joseph being sold into Egyptian slavery by his jealous brothers (Genesis 37:3–36)

Joseph's brothers hated him because their father loved him more, so they made plans to kill him:

> They saw [Joseph] from afar, and before he came near to them they conspired against him to kill him. They said to one another, "Here comes this dreamer. Come now, let us kill him and throw him into one of the pits. Then we will say that a fierce animal has devoured him, and we will see what will become of his dreams." (Genesis 37:18–20)

We know that God had a different plan for Joseph, which superseded his brothers' plot to kill him. Were it not for that though, his brothers may have succeeded in carrying out their murderous scheme.

2. David's adulterous coveting of Uriah's wife, Bathsheba (2 Samuel 11:2–27; 12:10)

David's covetous act not only ended Uriah's life, it ended the life of other valiant men who were placed—along with Uriah—at the forefront of "the hottest battle" against Rabbah, where they became easy targets for the archers on the wall. And if that's not enough, the child born to Bathsheba also died, causing untold emotional pain to her. But that's not all that followed in the wake of this covetous adultery. This selfish act of envy brought death and destruction to David's household for generations:

> Nathan said to David, ". . . Thus says the LORD, the God of Israel, '. . . You have struck down Uriah the Hittite with the sword and have taken his wife to be your wife and have killed him with the sword of the Ammonites. Now therefore the sword shall never depart from your house, because you have despised me and have taken the wife of Uriah the Hittite to be your wife.'" (2 Samuel 12:7, 9–10)

3. Ahab's covetous acquisition of Naboth's vineyard (1 Kings 21:1–16)

Ahab was a peevish, spineless, and selfish king, whose envy precipitated Naboth's death at the hands of the wicked Jezebel, who plotted to seize Naboth's vineyard for her cowardly husband.

We read in 1 Kings 21 where Ahab approaches Naboth and offers to give him a different—in his words "better"—vineyard in exchange for Naboth's. He even comes with a contingency plan to buy the vineyard from him, in case Naboth would rather have the cash.

Ahab returns home vexed and sullen, pouting like a spoiled child after Naboth honorably refuses to give up the inheritance of his fathers. When Jezebel gets wind of this, she consoles Ahab by promising to "give [him] the vineyard of Naboth the Jezreelite." She then uses her manipulative cunning and deceit to set a trap for Naboth that ultimately leads to his demise:

> So she wrote letters in Ahab's name... "Proclaim a fast, and set Naboth at the head of the people. And set two worthless men opposite him, and let them bring a charge against him, saying, 'You have cursed God and the king.' Then take him out and stone him to death."...
>
> As soon as Jezebel heard that Naboth had been stoned and was dead, Jezebel said to Ahab, "Arise, take possession of the vineyard of Naboth the Jezreelite...." And as soon as Ahab heard that Naboth was dead, Ahab arose to go down to the vineyard of Naboth the Jezreelite, to take possession of it. (1 Kings 21:8a, 9b, 10:15–16)

4. Saul's relentless pursuit of David and his attempts to kill him (1 Samuel 18:6–26:25)

Saul hunted David and tracked his whereabouts for four years, consumed by jealousy over David's fame that spread throughout Israel after his heroic slaying of Goliath. When Saul heard that David had visited Nob, he summoned Ahimelech and all the priests in his father's household and accused them of conspiring against the king by giving aid to David and his men. Sadly, Ahimelech's attempts to convince Saul of David's loyalty to the king fell on deaf ears. Saul's unbridled envy provoked him to order the death of Ahimelech and all the priests of Nob, eighty-five in all (1 Samuel 22:6–23). And if that wasn't heinous enough, the bloodthirsty king proceeded to slaughter the entire town:

> And the king said to the guard who stood about him, "Turn and kill the priests of the LORD, because their hand also is with David, and they knew that he fled and did not disclose it to me." But the servants of the king would not put out their hand to strike the priests of the LORD. Then the king said to Doeg, "You turn and strike the priests." And Doeg the Edomite turned and struck down the priests, and he killed on that day eighty-five persons who wore the linen ephod. And Nob, the city of the priests, he put to the sword; both man and woman, child and infant, ox, donkey and sheep, he put to the sword. (1 Samuel 22:17–19)

Need I say more? Surely, by now we are convinced and understand that *envy produces hatred and hatred leads to malice.* But some may say, "I would never kill anyone out of envy or jealousy." Yet John tells us plainly that hatred for another is tantamount to murder:

> For this is the message that you have heard from the beginning, that we should love one another. We should not be like Cain, who was of the evil one and murdered his brother. And why did he murder him? Because his own deeds were evil and his brother's righteous. *Everyone who hates his brother is a murderer*, and you know that no murderer has eternal life abiding in him. (1 John 3:11–12, 15, emphasis added)

It's time to own up to the fact that if I harbor envy in my heart for another, I risk becoming like Cain, "who was of the evil one and murdered his brother." Such a vice has no place in the heart of the Christlike.

Envy Is in the Eye of the Beholder

Solomon made a number of curious observations in his pursuit to "seek and to search out by wisdom all that is done under heaven" (Ecclesiastes 1:13a). As he mused upon the vanities of man, he discerned that "all toil and all skill in work come from a man's envy of his neighbor" (Ecclesiastes 4:4a).

Much like beauty, envy is in the eye of the beholder.

Perhaps that insight is linked to another one of Solomon's observations: "the eye is not satisfied with seeing" (Ecclesiastes 1:8b). We're seldom content to just look; sometimes we want to possess what we see. If I see something you have that I don't, I may want one that's equal or better for myself.

Much like beauty, envy is in the eye of the beholder. Harold G. Coffin, professor of Paleontology and Research at the Geoscience Research Institute, Andrews University in Michigan, observed that, "Envy is the art of counting the other fellow's blessings instead of your own."[1] How true is that! If I'm focused on what you have instead of what God has blessed me with, it is

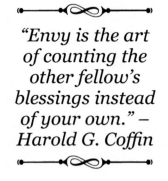

"Envy is the art of counting the other fellow's blessings instead of your own." – Harold G. Coffin

likely that I will either be puffed up because I have more than you, or I'll be envious because I don't have as much. This leads us to consider the interesting dynamic that exists between discontent and envy.

Discontent is a state of mind resulting from a restless desire or craving to have something I don't have. Envy, on the other hand, is a state of mind resulting from desiring or craving *something you have that I don't.*

Here's what I find interesting: I may be perfectly content with what I've accomplished or acquired—until I compare myself to what you've achieved or amassed. Once I make that comparison, I may either hate you for what you have that I don't, or I may despise myself for failing to attain the same (or greater) level of success. Or even worse, I despise you *and* I detest myself.

Love, however, is not concerned with what I have compared to someone else. On the contrary, love rejoices in the successes of others, realizing that God is no respecter of persons and is good to all. If I am jealous of what you have, and begin to sulk over what I don't have, is that not in some way an accusation against God— that He is not as good to me as He should be?

The Unknown Christian points out that we should not rest content with merely stifling envious thoughts. "That were a poor aim for any man!"[2] he says. Agreed. We should also be eager to encourage, and quick to congratulate people on their successes, offering kudos for even seemingly small things. Love seeks to *add* to the joy of others by rejoicing with them, but sadly, we are not naturally inclined to think and act like this.

Developing such an attitude requires a decision and commitment to allow the love of Christ to have its way in your life. It may be difficult at first. It may even seem awkward and insincere; but if you stick with it, over time it will become a beautiful evidence of the Spirit's work in your life.

> *Envy is to the soul what Drano is to the body. Consume it and it will consume you.*

The Unknown Christian went on to say, "There is nothing whatever to be gained by envy—*absolutely nothing.* All envy is self-injury! The Word of God has told us this long ago."[3]

"A tranquil heart gives life to the flesh, but envy makes the bones rot" (Proverbs 14:30). The above verse tells us envy is like a cancer. Stated a bit differently, envy is to the soul what Drano is to the body. Consume *it* and it will consume *you*.

The Key to Contentment

For as long as I can remember, I have heard well-meaning Christians misapply Philippians 4:13, using it as though it were some unconditional promise that empowers them to do anything. I've abused it on occasion myself. As often quoted, the verse reads, "I can do all things through Christ who strengthens me" (Philippians 4:13 NKJV). Yet unlike Superman, I cannot fly, leap tall buildings with a single bound, or run faster than a speeding bullet—even *after* making this positive confession.

On the surface, this verse appears to be a blank check that I can cash any time I need God's help with something. It's similar to the promise Jesus made when he said, "If you ask me anything in my name, I will do it" (John 14:14). I can ask for a million dollars or a house on the beach in Maui—*in His name*—but odds are that God's not going to give it to me, because my motives are wrong. James says, "You ask and do not receive, because you ask wrongly, to spend it on your passions" (James 4:1–3). The same is true of claiming and confessing Philippians 4:13—if my motives are misdirected. Let's look at some hypothetical examples of how this promise could be applied:

A high school basketball player stands at the free-throw line with one second left on the clock, needing to make two shots to win the game. Philippians 4:13 races through his mind over and over as he tries desperately to convince himself that he can make both of his free throws.

A ladder-climbing business executive prepares for a sales pitch that could potentially land the most lucrative account of her career. She recites the mantra for added confidence and assurance that she will nail the presentation and win the account.

A young couple waits nervously to board the plane that will begin their journey to the opposite side of the globe to serve as missionaries in Russia for five years. They know God has called them to this purpose, but do they really have what it takes? Will they fulfill this call or will they return home prematurely with their tails between their legs? The husband turns to his wife and says reassuringly, "Honey, we can do all things through Christ who strengthens us. It will be okay."

Again, *one of these things is not like the others.*

With all due respect to the Faith Movement of the 1970s and 80s, Philippians 4:13 is not a blank check. I cut my spiritual teeth on *Name it and Claim it* teaching, so I'm well experienced in misappropriating the promises of God. My point here is not to criticize; my point is for us to read this magnificent promise in its proper context.

Paul wrote from the perspective of a man who was living for only one thing:

> But I do not account my life of any value nor as precious to myself, if only I may finish my course and the ministry that I received from the Lord Jesus, to testify to the gospel of the grace of God. (Acts 20:24)

> Indeed, I count everything as loss because of the surpassing worth of knowing Christ Jesus my Lord. For his sake I have suffered the loss of all things and count them as rubbish, in order that I may gain Christ. (Philippians 3:8)

A man who had no concern for what happened to him, wanted only to proclaim the gospel of Christ, and had suffered the loss of all things in order to gain Christ is the same man who wrote, "I can do all things through him who strengthens me." That doesn't sound to me like someone who was promoting reliance on the Lord for selfish gains. Let's read the verse in its proper context:

Not that I am speaking of being in need, for I have learned in whatever situation I am *to be content*. I know how to be brought low, and I know how to abound. In any and every circumstance, *I have learned the secret* of facing plenty and hunger, abundance and need. I can do all things through him who strengthens me. (Philippians 4:11–13, emphasis added)

In his letter to the Philippians, Paul told them he had learned a secret. The man whose life was consumed with only one purpose—to take the gospel to the Gentiles—had discovered that Christ would give him the inner strength to be content in every circumstance, with however little or much he had. The lesson here is that Philippians 4:13 is as much about contentment as it is anything, and when we are content in our situation, there's less room for envy in our hearts.

Love's Great Delight

Have you ever wondered why God created mankind? Basic Christian theology teaches us that God is altogether self-sufficient and needs nothing. Psalm 50 supports this understanding:

"Hear, O my people, and I will speak; ... I am God, your God. ... If I were hungry, I would not tell you, for the world and its fullness are mine." (Psalm 50:7, 12)

If God is completely self-sufficient, then why did He create us? He certainly doesn't need us to attend Him, nor is He incomplete without our worship. I don't presume to know the answer to this age-old theological question, but I do have a theory. I believe one plausible explanation is found in 1 John 4:8, *"God is love."*

What does this have to do with envy? Much. Let me explain.

Love is incomplete without an object upon which to bestow itself. However, love in its purest form has been shared among the Godhead since time immemorial (John 17:24), so we know God did not create mankind because He needed an object to love. Yet what if God wanted to share His love outside of Himself, not because He was incomplete without this, but because it would bring Him pleasure? Revelation 4:11 (KJV) says, "Thou art worthy, O Lord, to receive glory and honour and power: for thou hast created all things, and for thy pleasure they are and were created."

Without question, one way I bring God pleasure is through a life that shows forth His glory. But I also believe God takes pleasure in loving His children (see Matthew 7:11 and James 1:17). From the moment I became a father, I have not ceased to delight in the love that I share with my children. It is one of my greatest joys in life. And if I, being evil (as Jesus says), can delight in my children, then how much more does God delight in the love He shares with all of His children, not just with Christ?

I submit to you that love's great delight is to give, which makes love diametrically opposed to envy. Envy promotes taking. Love delights in giving. Let's read the larger passage in 1 John 4 and see how John explains the love of God:

> Beloved, let us love one another, for love is from God, and whoever loves has been born of God and knows God. Anyone who does not love does not know God, because God is love. In this the love of God was made manifest among us, that God sent his only Son into the world, so that we might live through him. In this is love, not that we have loved God but that he loved us and sent his Son to be the propitiation for our sins. (1 John 4:7–10)

God demonstrated His love through the selfless act of sending His Son into the world to take our punishment and reconcile us to Himself. Love that resembles the heart of God doesn't need or covet what you have. Such love would rather give itself away, would rather enrich than be enriched, and if sued, would rather give you its shirt *and coat* rather than retaliate (Matthew 5:40).

So why did God create mankind? My subjective hypothesis is that it pleased Him to share all of His goodness and love with us—not because He needed it, but because He may have *desired* it.

Bring Back the King

A messenger comes to David, saying, "The hearts of the men of Israel have gone after Absalom" (2 Samuel 15:13). Thus begins King David's hasty exodus from Jerusalem to escape the treasonous sword of his son Absalom, who had schemed to supplant his father's rule over Israel.

On his way out of the city, David meets Ziba, the servant of Mephibosheth, son of Jonathan and grandson of Saul. Now some years prior, David had sought out a remnant of the household of Saul upon which to bestow kindness because of his close relationship with Jonathan. Mephibosheth was the lone survivor, so David had given him all that formerly belonged to Saul's household (2 Samuel 9:1–9). Ziba has brought provisions for the king's household, but Mephibosheth is not with him in support of the king.

Love that resembles the heart of God doesn't need or covet what you have. Such love would rather give itself away, would rather enrich than be enriched, and if sued, would rather give you its shirt and coat rather than retaliate.

David is curious as to why Ziba is alone, so he inquires as to Mephibosheth's whereabouts:

> And the king said, "And where is your master's son?" Ziba said to the king, "Behold, he remains in Jerusalem, for he said, 'Today the house of Israel will give me back the kingdom of my father.'" Then the king said to Ziba, "Behold, all that belonged to Mephibosheth is now yours." (2 Samuel 16:3–4)

In little more than an instant, Ziba now possesses all that David had previously given to Mephibosheth. The approval process is far less tedious when you're a committee of one whose lone member is King!

Absalom's rebellion is short-lived. Even though the king explicitly told the commanders of his army to "deal gently" with Absalom, Joab takes matters into his own hands and kills the young prince, as he dangles helplessly with his head stuck fast in the branches of a mighty oak tree.

At this point, Israel is in disarray. David has fled, Absalom is dead, and the people have no leader:

> Now Israel had fled every man to his own home. And all the people were arguing throughout all the tribes of Israel, saying, "The king delivered us from the hand of our enemies and saved us from the hand of the Philistines, and now he has fled out of the land from Absalom. But Absalom, whom we anointed over us, is dead in battle. Now therefore why do you say nothing about bringing the king back?" (2 Samuel 19:8b–10)

David does return to Jerusalem, where he is met by several individuals, some who are there simply to welcome the king, and others who are seeking mercy for various transgressions. One of those who comes to meet the king is Mephibosheth:

> When he came to Jerusalem to meet the king, the king said to him, "Why did you not go with me, Mephibosheth?" (2 Samuel 19:25)

Mephibosheth explains that Ziba had deceived him and had also slandered his name to the king. He says his intent had been to saddle his donkey and go with the king, but that he was unable to because of his crippled feet. Mephibosheth continues on about his unworthiness to receive the king's favor, but David cuts him off and says:

> "Why speak any more of your affairs? I have decided: you and Ziba shall divide the land." And Mephibosheth said to the king, "*Oh, let him take it all*, since my lord the king has come safely home." (2 Samuel 19:24–30, emphasis added)

David doesn't seem to care about determining who is telling the truth. Instead, he quickly judges between the two men and decides to divide the land equally between them. But Mephibosheth seems to have no interest in the land *now that the king has come home*. He's perfectly content for Ziba to have it all.

There's a lesson here for us. Absalom is a metaphor for just about anything that banishes Jesus from the throne of our hearts, but for the sake of this topic, let's say he represents *envy*. Do we care more about *stuff* than we do our relationship with our King, Jesus Christ? Have we supplanted His rule with the quest to acquire and accumulate possessions? As Solomon observed so long ago, is the reason we go to work every day because we are driven by envy of our neighbor? If so, then we need to welcome back our King to His rightful place as Lord of our hearts.

Content with Christ?

Paul wrote these words to Timothy: "But if we have food and clothing, with these we will be content" (1 Timothy 6:8). Ah, but in this day and age, we tend to think more like this: "If we have food and clothing [and satellite TV and Internet and a smart phone and a Tablet and a data plan and social media], with *these* we shall be content."

Am I content with only the barest of necessities as long as I have Jesus? Or do I feel as though my life is incomplete without today's technological creature comforts? Don't get me wrong. I love technology as much as the next guy; in fact, I used an iPad to write 90 percent of this book. But such questions as these give me pause to stop and consider my priorities—as well they should.

Paul exhorted the church at Colossae to "seek the things that are above" and to set their "minds on things that are above, not on things that are on earth" (Colossians 3:1–3a). This is a decision and choice that each of us can—*and must*—make, if we wish to avoid the snare of envy. As we have already seen, envy poisons our thoughts, which can lead to some downright malicious behavior. Envy eats away at our insides and affects how we think and act toward others. In Paul's letter to the church at Rome, he reminds them that love does no wrong to a neighbor:

> Owe no one anything, except to love each other, for the one who loves another has fulfilled the law. For the commandments, "You shall not commit adultery, You shall not murder, You shall not steal, *You shall not covet*," and any other commandment, are summed up in this word: "You shall love your neighbor as yourself." *Love does no wrong to a neighbor*; therefore love is the fulfilling of the law. (Romans 13:8–10, emphasis added)

Not only does love do no wrong to a neighbor, love gladly celebrates the achievements and accomplishments of others with no envy whatsoever.

A Lesson in Astronomy

Paul Bamikole, a dance instructor at Miracle Dance Centre in Abuja, Nigeria, said, "Never does the moon envy the sun, [or] the sun the moon. They both know their time and place of shining."[4] Scripture even confirms this:

> There are heavenly bodies and earthly bodies, but the glory of the heavenly is of one kind, and the glory of the earthly is of another. There is one glory of the sun, and another glory of the moon, and another

glory of the stars; for star differs from star in glory.
(1 Corinthians 15:40–41)

Not only do the stars differ from one another in their brightness and glory, the same is true of people. God, in His wisdom, has given greater "glory" to some than others. Learn to embrace your place in His order. Learn to be gracious and rejoice with others when their star shines brighter than yours.

The ancient Greek playwright, Aeschylus, said, "It is in the character of very few men to honor without envy a friend who has prospered."[5] Ah, but it *is* in the character of those who are Christlike.

For Further Study

"For we ourselves were once foolish ...
passing our days in malice and envy."
Titus 3:3

1. True or False: Being envious of others is no big deal. Cite examples to support your view.
2. Envy is the art of what?
3. Fill in the blanks: "Envy is to _____ _____ what _____ is to _____ _____. Consume it and ____ _____ _____ _____."
4. How does harboring envy in your heart potentially become an accusation against God?
5. What is an even higher aim than refusing to be jealous of the successes of others?
6. What is the primary meaning of Philippians 4:13, and how does that relate to envy?
7. What is love's great delight, and how is that a deterrent to envy?

10

Flag on the Play

"Love . . . does not . . . boast."
1 Corinthians 13:4

*"Personal foul, excessive celebration, number 27 of the offense.
Penalty to be enforced on the ensuing kickoff."*

HOW MANY TIMES during football season are we forced to endure the ostentatious displays of boasting by football players—collegiate and professional—after they score a touchdown? Or how about the defensive end who sacks the quarterback on the first play from scrimmage and thumps his chest like he's King Kong? We've all seen guys make big-time plays—I don't take that away from them—but it's ridiculous to celebrate like you've just won the Super Bowl *when only twelve seconds have expired from the game clock!* I want to say, "Pace yourself, buddy. You've got a whole game ahead of you."

We boast in many ways, but the most common is with our mouths. James aptly describes this tendency of the tongue: "So also the tongue is a small member, yet it boasts of great things. How great a forest is set ablaze by such a small fire!" (James 3:5a).

Meet Sam

Samantha (known by some as Sam) and her husband owned a highly successful and lucrative software company. She was the

CEO who ran the show, and her husband, Mack, was the technical genius behind their product.

Sam was an amazing tennis player who could work the ball all around a tennis court. Sam had an awesome backhand, and she ran her husband ragged with an impossible-to-return lob shot. In fact, she was so good she made him look stupid.

Sam had seats at MetLife Stadium in the row below John Mara, co-owner of the New York Giants. Sam also had courtside seats in Madison Square Garden to watch the Knicks play. Sam had it all.

How do I know these things about Sam? I know because she told me—and everyone else at dinner that wintry February night in midtown Manhattan, where a group of us had gathered to explore employment opportunities with her company.

I'm not sure I can adequately describe what took place in that restaurant. Sam dominated the entire conversation with one self-aggrandizing statement after another. It was the most nauseating display of boasting I've ever been subjected to in my life. One thing I knew for certain, however, is that I did not want to work for this woman. Even though my then-current work situation was extremely stressful with no immediate relief in sight, I chose to pass on the opportunity to double my income by consulting with her company.

I am certain Sam was not familiar with these words from the book of Jeremiah:

> Thus says the LORD: "Let not the wise man boast in his wisdom, let not the mighty man boast in his might, let not the rich man boast in his riches, but let him who boasts boast in this, that he understands and knows me, that I am the LORD who practices steadfast love, justice, and righteousness in the earth. For in these things I delight, declares the LORD." (Jeremiah 9:23–24)

Love does not boast—at least not in itself. It will, however, boast in the Lord. In fact, David made it his practice to do so continually:

"*In God* we have boasted continually, and we will give thanks to your name forever" (Psalm 44:8, emphasis added). On the flip side, boasting in ourselves is a practice that is discouraged in Scripture: "Let another praise you, and not your own mouth; a stranger, and not your own lips" (Proverbs 27:2).

There's something unattractive about people who brag on themselves. That is not to say you can never tell others about a recent promotion, achievement, or recognition. A lot of it has to do with the telling. Are we careful to give God the glory, or do we cut Him out of the deal and take all the credit for ourselves? Paul had it right:

> In Christ Jesus, then, I have reason to be proud of my work for God. For I will not venture to speak of anything *except what Christ has accomplished through me.* (Romans 15:17–18a, emphasis added)

I have been encouraged a number of times to toot my own horn concerning recent accomplishments within the computer systems application area for which I am responsible. This supposedly helps to *get my name out there*, but I am rather averse to it. Although I've capitulated a time or two, I always felt a bit slimy after sending such an email. Rather than boasting about our accomplishments, isn't it better to just let the work speak for itself?

> Who is wise and understanding among you? *By his good conduct let him show his works* in the meekness of wisdom. (James 3:13, emphasis added)

Love's way is to apply wisdom in the spirit of meekness and refrain from calling attention to ourselves.

Lesson in Lawn Care

It is a well-known fact that when pulling weeds, you have to dig them out root and all; otherwise, they will surely sprout again.

Pride is the root of all boasting and self-exaltation. Of the seven things that God is said to hate and that are an abomination to Him, haughty eyes (or as the KJV says, "a proud look") tops the list (Proverbs 6:16–17). Surely, we know that "God *opposes the proud, but gives grace to the humble*" (James 4:6, emphasis added). Given the choice of having God oppose us or extend grace to us, could there be any reason whatsoever not to choose the latter? You don't have to be the sharpest pencil in the drawer to make that call. A wise person would choose grace!—which also means choosing to be humble.

But how can I be humble if I have a deep-seated root of pride in my heart? Humility and pride are like light and darkness—they have no fellowship with each other (i.e., they cannot coexist). So how does a person extract the root of pride from their heart? I suggest the following approach:

1. Recognize pride for what it is: *sin.*
2. Like all sin, confess it and repent of it (i.e., turn away from it).
3. Then, ask the Lord for grace to walk in humility every day.

I realize that what I've laid out may be easier said than done, but there's no need to over-complicate this. Pride is sin. I don't want sin in my life, so I repent of it and ask God to help me overcome it. Then what follows is living it out every day, which *you and I can do* as we trust in the saving grace of Christ.

> *Humility is like a thick, healthy lawn. It's the best defense against the encroachment of the weed of prideful boasting.*

Once you have dealt with the root of pride, the best way to keep it from sprouting again is to walk in humility. A local southern Indiana sod farmer has taught me a lot about maintaining a healthy, weed-free yard. His best advice with regard to keeping a lawn free of weeds is to have a thick, healthy stand of grass. Why? Because there's no room for the weeds to come through! Humility is like a thick, healthy lawn. It's the best defense against the encroachment of the weed of prideful boasting.

The book of Proverbs counsels us to guard our heart. This is because the heart is the source from which life (or whatever it is we have in there) flows: "Guard your heart more than anything else, because the source of your life flows from it" (Proverbs 4:23 GW).

Smug Fest

Two or three years before I retired from leading worship, I was in need of a break. Pastor Bob granted me a six-month sabbatical to take some time off and recharge my batteries. We had a capable group of worship leaders who stepped in and filled the gap while I took my place in the congregation as Joe Worshipper.

I finally "came to" when it seemed as if the Holy Spirit tapped me on the shoulder, cleared His throat, and said, "What on earth are you doing?"

About three months into my sabbatical, I recall standing in the congregation on a Sunday morning noshing on some especially tasty, but disgustingly smug, thoughts with respect to my abilities as a "veteran" worship leader. As the worship team struggled a bit in my absence—which they did—I began having a conversation with myself about how much better it was when *I* led worship. After all, I'd been leading worship for more than thirty years, which clearly made me a "pro" and them ... well, you get the picture.

I finally "came to" when it seemed as if the Holy Spirit tapped me on the shoulder, cleared His throat, and said, "*What on earth are you doing?*" No one else in the room knew what was happening between the Lord and me at that moment, but I was quickly embarrassed and ashamed of my thoughts. I was boasting without so much as opening my mouth!

This internal conversation was equally as disgusting as the display of boasting I witnessed in New York City when I listened to Sam go on and on about how great she was. The only difference is that I wasn't telling others how great I was, *I was telling myself.*

As with everything else that comes out of our mouths, boasting begins in the heart (Matthew 12:33–35; Mark 7:20–23), but you don't have to verbalize it to be guilty of it. It's possible to have such an attitude without even realizing it. We look down our smug noses on the work of others as we flatter ourselves with egotistical thoughts of our superior abilities.

Monumental Mistake

"And behold, he set up a monument for himself."
(1 Samuel 15:12)

Who set up a monument for himself? King Saul—one of the most well-known Old Testament figures in the Bible. What I find intriguing is that he did this after an act of disobedience (see 1 Samuel 15:1–35), which he had convinced himself was a fulfillment of what God had commanded him to do to the Amalekites (i.e., utterly destroy them). Pride and disobedience have the potential to cloud our judgment, leading to delusional boasting.

I doubt any of us has ever erected a public monument in honor of ourselves, but our boasting bears an eerie resemblance in the sense that we're seeking recognition and honor from others whenever we tout our talent, achievements, possessions, and such. In Paul's letter to the church in Rome, he exhorted them with these words: "For by the grace given to me I say to everyone among you not to think of himself more highly than he ought to think" (Romans 12:3a).

Remembering Where We Came From

While writing the previous chapter about envy, I concluded that one reason people boast in their accomplishments is not just to garner attention but to solicit envy. I think it's mostly a subconscious thing, but it happens nonetheless. Perhaps having a better understanding of envy's destructive nature will encourage us to curtail our boasting. Or even better, we'll remember to give God the glory for what He has done in us, for us, and through us.

One reason people boast in their accomplishments is not just to garner attention but to solicit envy.

A second reason we boast is to make others think more highly of us. In other words, I want you to think I'm smarter, more athletic, more talented, or maybe I want you to like me more because of something I can do, something I possess, or something I have achieved.

A third reason for boasting is that it makes me feel better about myself. It makes me feel more important, more significant in my own eyes. The following excerpt from Paul's first letter to the church at Corinth should help to put, and keep, us in our place:

> For consider your calling, brothers: not many of you were wise according to worldly standards, not many were powerful, not many were of noble birth. But God chose what is foolish in the world to shame the wise; God chose what is weak in the world to shame the strong; God chose what is low and despised in the world, even things that are not, to bring to nothing things that are, so that no human being might boast in the presence of God. And because of him you are in Christ Jesus, who became to us wisdom from God, righteousness and sanctification and redemption, so that, as it is written, "Let the one who boasts, boast in the Lord." (1 Corinthians 1:26–31)

So there you have it—our pedigree as seen from God's point of view: *foolish, weak, low and despised.* But thank God, He says that Christ Jesus has become to us wisdom, righteousness, sanctification, and redemption. May we never forget our humble state before He chose us and made all of this possible through the blood of Christ. These words of hymn writer Isaac Watts speak to us as powerfully today as when they were first penned:

> *When I survey the wondrous cross*
> *On which the Prince of Glory died*
> *My richest gain I count but loss*
> *And pour contempt on all my pride*[1]

The cross puts every man, woman, and child in their place, and Christ Himself said that He is meek and lowly of heart (Matthew 11:29). Certainly then, none of us who are aiming to be Christlike would dare to think more highly of ourselves than our Master thought of Himself.

"I Am the Greatest!"

I'm sure most, if not all, who read this book will know of Muhammad Ali. His hometown is Louisville, Kentucky, only five miles across the river from my home town of New Albany, Indiana. Ali has been promoted, idolized, and nearly deified in this area, especially in his later years.

In his boxing heyday, the man formerly known as Cassius Clay dared to declare himself to be the greatest. *"I am the greatest!"* was his mantra. So much so that it stuck and became the moniker by which the media refers to him to this day. Only they simply refer to him as "The Greatest." In his prime, he truly was the greatest at his sport, but he somehow came to be viewed as larger than life itself—a steep precipice on which to find oneself, and where it is extremely difficult to maintain one's footing; possibly even one's sanity—as was the case with one of Ali's predecessors.

"Timber!"

History's pages are filled with the names of many great men who preceded Ali's fame as well as his claim to being the greatest. According to encyclopedia.com, one notable figure ruled the entire known world from 605 to 562 B.C. His name? Nebuchadnezzar, King of Babylon.[2]

Daniel chapter 4 tells a most intriguing account of how this man was reduced from all his kingly splendor to that of an animal living among the beasts of the field for seven *periods of time* (likely years). The story begins as follows:

> King Nebuchadnezzar to all peoples, nations, and languages, that dwell in all the earth: Peace be multiplied to you! It has seemed good to me to show the signs and wonders that the Most High God has done for me. How great are his signs, how mighty his wonders! His kingdom is an everlasting kingdom, and his dominion endures from generation to generation. (Daniel 4:1–3)

The context of these opening verses seems to coincide with the revelation given to Nebuchadnezzar after he came to his senses, so it's likely he is speaking from the perspective of a changed heart, as evidenced by the statement, "It has seemed good to me to show the signs and wonders that the Most High God has done for me." So I believe he shares this as a prologue to his recollection of how God brought him to such an understanding. He then continues, "I, Nebuchadnezzar, was at ease in my house and prospering in my palace" (Daniel 4:4).

At the outset of Nebuchadnezzar recounting his revelation, we immediately see a warning sign. Life is great. He's made it to the top and living comfortably on Easy Street. I mean, who doesn't want a life of ease and prosperity? Sign me up, right! After all, the Bible says, "The Lord be magnified, who delights in the prosperity of His servant" (Psalm 35:27b NASB). But the Bible also cautions us with these words:

> Take care lest you forget the LORD your God... lest, when you have eaten and are full and have built good houses and live in them... lest you say in your heart, "My power and the might of my hand have gotten me this wealth." You shall remember the LORD your God, for it is he who gives you power to get wealth. (Deuteronomy 8:11a–12, 17–18)

When we reach a point in life when we are at the top of our game and living comfortably, we must be wary of thinking we've somehow accomplished this on our own. As we continue reading Nebuchadnezzar's story, we see that he had previously failed to realize *God* had given him his power, wealth, and authority in the earth, instead mistaking it as his own achievement.

As the story unfolds, Nebuchadnezzar describes to Daniel a vision he had (probably within a dream) as he lay in his bed:

> "I saw, and behold, a tree in the midst of the earth, and its height was great. The tree grew and became strong, and its top reached to heaven, and it was visible to the end of the whole earth. Its leaves were beautiful and its fruit abundant, and in it was food for all. The beasts of the field found shade under it, and the birds of the heavens lived in its branches, and all flesh was fed from it.
>
> "I saw in the visions of my head as I lay in bed, and behold, a watcher, a holy one, came down from heaven. He proclaimed aloud and said thus: 'Chop down the tree and lop off its branches, strip off its leaves and scatter its fruit. Let the beasts flee from under it and the birds from its branches. But leave the stump of its roots in the earth, bound with a band of iron and bronze, amid the tender grass of the field. Let him be wet with the dew of heaven. Let his portion be with the beasts in the grass of the earth. Let

his mind be changed from a man's, and let a beast's
mind be given to him; and let seven periods of time
pass over him.'" (Daniel 4:10–16)

Daniel now has the uncomfortable and dreadful task of
explaining the king's dream:

"The tree you saw... it is you, O king, who have grown
and become strong. Your greatness has grown and
reaches to heaven, and your dominion to the ends
of the earth....

"This is the interpretation, O king: It is a decree
of the Most High, which has come upon my lord
the king, that you shall be driven from among men,
and your dwelling shall be with the beasts of the
field. You shall be made to eat grass like an ox, and
you shall be wet with the dew of heaven, and seven
periods of time shall pass over you, till you know that
the Most High rules the kingdom of men and gives
it to whom he will....

"Therefore, O king, let my counsel be acceptable
to you: break off your sins by practicing righteousness, and your iniquities by showing mercy to the
oppressed, that there may perhaps be a lengthening
of your prosperity." (Daniel 4:20, 22, 24–25, 27)

Nebuchadnezzar has been forewarned. He cannot claim ignorance of the impending judgment that's about to come upon him,
and he has been counseled to repent and practice righteousness so
that perhaps there may be a lengthening of his prosperity. Yet he
did not heed the warning or the counsel. So, as promised...

All this came upon King Nebuchadnezzar. At the
end of twelve months he was walking on the roof of
the royal palace of Babylon, and the king answered
and said, *"Is not this great Babylon, which I have
built by my mighty power as a royal residence*

and for the glory of my majesty?" (Daniel 4:28–30, emphasis added)

A lot can happen in a year's time, especially when you're the head of state, or in Nebuchadnezzar's case, monarch of the entire known world. There's little doubt he's forgotten the dream God gave him and he's twelve months removed from brushing aside Daniel's admonition to break off his sins and practice righteousness. So what happens next possibly becomes the inspiration for John the Baptist's admonition to the Pharisees and Sadducees who would later come to his baptism: "Even now the axe is laid to the root of the trees. Every tree therefore that does not bear good fruit is cut down..." (Matthew 3:10).

> While the words were still in the king's mouth, there fell a voice from heaven, "O King Nebuchadnezzar, to you it is spoken: The kingdom has departed from you, and you shall be driven from among men, and your dwelling shall be with the beasts of the field. And you shall be made to eat grass like an ox, and seven periods of time shall pass over you, until you know that the Most High rules the kingdom of men and gives it to whom he will." Immediately the word was fulfilled against Nebuchadnezzar. He was driven from among men and ate grass like an ox, and his body was wet with the dew of heaven till his hair grew as long as eagles' feathers, and his nails were like birds' claws. (Daniel 4:31–33)

It boggles the mind to picture such a transformation of a human being. This man was literally reduced to the likeness of an animal and made to dwell among the beasts of the field for seven years—because of his prideful boasting!

However, it was never God's plan to leave Nebuchadnezzar in such a state. Exactly to the day—after seven years had passed—God restored Nebuchadnezzar, re-established his kingdom, and added even more greatness to him.

> At the end of the days I, Nebuchadnezzar, lifted my
> eyes to heaven, and my reason returned to me, and
> I blessed the Most High, and praised and honored
> him who lives forever, for his dominion is an ever-
> lasting dominion, and his kingdom endures from
> generation to generation; all the inhabitants of the
> earth are accounted as nothing... and *those who*
> *walk in pride he is able to humble.* (Daniel 4:34–37
> emphasis added)

Nebuchadnezzar learned an invaluable lesson in humility, one
for which he paid a terrible price when you consider how emphati-
cally it was impressed upon him by the hand of the Lord. Wisdom
counsels us to remember that God is also able to chop us down to
size if we join the ranks of those who revel in their accomplishments as though God had nothing to do with it.

"Did we not... do many mighty works in Your Name?"

The Unknown Christian makes an astute
observation that Paul, in his first letter
to the Corinthians, seems to be writing
to Christians who were boasting of their
spiritual gifts.[3] It's hard to believe people
may even dare to boast in their Christian
service, and yet, maybe we're not that far
removed from having a similar mind-set
ourselves.

Boasting doesn't have to be verbal or demonstrative. It can reside in our heart and mind and be just as offensive to Christ as that which comes out of our mouths.

Do we boast—even if only in our
hearts—of how great our preaching or
teaching is, how many mission trips
we've been on, how many books we've
written, how many years we've led worship, how many souls we've won to Christ,
our five-fold ministry "office," or how our congregations have
grown under our leadership? At some point, do we become guilty

of taking credit for what God has built, and start to call or think of it as our own? Remember, boasting doesn't have to be verbal or demonstrative. It can reside in our heart and mind and be just as offensive to Christ as that which comes out of our mouths. More than likely, if it's in the heart, it will eventually come out—either through our speech or our actions. As previously noted, Proverbs 4:23 teaches that how I live my life flows from what's in my heart.

While writing this chapter about boasting, I had a disturbing thought concerning that day when certain people (who likely consider themselves Christians) will be shut out of the kingdom of God. When this happens, they will plead their case before the Son of God in a way that nearly smacks of boasting:

> "On that day many will say to me, 'Lord, Lord, *did we not prophesy* in your name, and *cast out demons* in your name, and *do many mighty works* in your name?' And then will I declare to them, 'I never knew you; depart from me, you workers of lawlessness.'" (Matthew 7:22–23, emphasis added)

"Look at all my Christian service, Lord. I did this, this, and this. Surely, You were impressed by all that I did in Your name, right?" Maybe not...

Love's Aim

We have not yet said much about *why* love doesn't boast, but this verse from 1 Corinthians suggests an answer: "Knowledge puffs up, but *love edifies*" (1 Corinthians 8:1b NKJV, emphasis added).

One of love's primary objectives is the building up and encouragement of others, and I am yet to understand how boasting about my gifts, talents, and accomplishments, etc. contributes in any way to the edification of the one to whom I boast. It may build *me* up—in my small, self-centered mind—but it's not going to do anything to help the other person. In seeking to bring order to the church at Corinth in their exercise of spiritual gifts, Paul exhorted them to direct their zeal toward the edification of the church (1 Corinthians 14:12). So whether it's in the exercise of spiritual gifts or the normal course of everyday living, let us do our best to walk in love and seek to excel in those things that edify others.

Jesus said it's easier for a camel to go through the eye of a needle than it is for a rich man to enter the kingdom of heaven (Matthew 19:24). It may also be easier for a donkey to speak than for a proud man to refrain from boasting. So if we must boast, let it be in the Lord; and if we seek commendation, let it come from the Lord, for God's Word reminds us:

> "Let the one who boasts, boast in the Lord." For it is not the one who commends himself who is approved, but the one whom the Lord commends. (2 Corinthians 10:17–18)

For Further Study

"Let another praise you, and not your own mouth;
a stranger, and not your own lips."
Proverbs 27:2

1. What makes fleshly boasting so unattractive, and what is the root of such boasting?
2. In what did David and Paul boast, and what was the basis of their boasting?
3. What practical measures can we take to rid ourselves from prideful boasting?
4. How is it possible to boast in ourselves without so much as uttering a single word?
5. List some reasons that people boast in themselves. Be willing to share an experience of your own such boasting.
6. What lesson(s) do we learn from King Nebuchadnezzar?
7. Why is boasting contrary to the nature of love?

11

The Secret to Becoming More Attractive

"Love is not rude, is not selfish."
1 Corinthians 13:5a (NCV)

I HEARD A MOST RIDICULOUS THING on the way to grab some lunch one day. I was listening to a sports-talk radio show when the host made this declaration about himself: "By nature, I'm not a selfish person."

I immediately burst out laughing, because what he said is absolutely not true. By nature, every human being is selfish. Granted, some are more—or less—selfish than others, but the fact remains that even the most commonplace decisions and choices we make are routinely driven by the gratification of self, and the smallest, most inconsequential of life's experiences can elicit an emotional response rooted in selfishness. Self-gratification is a core building block of the soul's DNA, as Paul alludes to in his letter to the church at Ephesus:

> *We all once lived in the passions of our flesh*, carrying out the desires of the body and the mind, and were *by nature* children of wrath, like the rest of mankind. (Ephesians 2:3, emphasis added)

Have you ever watched a couple of toddlers at play? If so, you've probably witnessed one child take something away from the other one. Where did the child learn that? It's unlikely the parents taught little Johnny or Susie to do that. The child was simply giving expression to the selfish nature that was in them from birth. They saw something they wanted, so they took it—whether it belonged to them or not. And most likely, the child from whom the toy was taken responded by lashing out, driven by their own selfish impulses.

Thankfully, as we mature, most of us learn to control such urges, but that doesn't mean we outgrow them, or that these inherent, selfish instincts mysteriously dissipate into the ether. No, selfishness exerts its influence throughout the entirety of a person's life. Why do you suppose the first thing Jesus listed as a requirement for discipleship was the denial of self (Luke 9:23)? The greatest challenge we face in obeying Jesus Christ is the love of self. His Word tells us to do *this*, but we want to do *that*.

Love, however, is not selfish because love is of God, and God is not selfish (see John 3:16). Love takes immeasurable pleasure in giving of itself. I know this to be true because on a number of occasions the grace and love of God enabled me to overcome my selfishness in order to bless someone else, and it was wonderful. It was godly. It was what Jesus Christ would do. And I don't say that to boast, because I'm ashamed of how many times I could have given of myself and didn't.

> *The greatest challenge we face in obeying Jesus Christ is the love of self.*

This will arguably be the most painful chapter for me to write, because it covers the one aspect of love at which I fail most miserably—*love is not selfish*. Much too often, I am.

Let's Get Personal

One cold November morning, I went to my local Panera Bread restaurant to buy a four-cheese soufflé for breakfast. As I approached the counter, I was second in line, and only one person was taking orders. While awaiting my turn, I spied the warming tray on which the soufflés were displayed and noticed there were three glorious four-cheese as the only soufflés available for purchase. (When they look this good, I typically buy two of them, one for today and the other for another day.)

While I was waiting for the woman ahead of me to complete her purchase, the drive-through attendant came seemingly out of nowhere to check on the soufflés for a customer outside, and I overheard her say on the radio, "All I have at the moment are four-cheese."

At this point, I started getting antsy because I wanted two of those soufflés, and I was greatly concerned that the drive-through customer was going to nab all of them. As the woman ahead of me completed her purchase, I approached the counter to place my order and saw that all three of them were still there. *This was going to be great.* However, right as I was about to open my mouth and utter the words, "I'll take two of the four-cheese soufflés," the drive-through attendant came out from the back and, to my horror, took one—and then another—as I held my breath, anxiously waiting to see if she would take all three. I breathed a sigh of relief as she walked away with only two in hand, leaving one for me.

What was happening here? I'll tell you exactly what was happening—selfishness was actively affecting my thoughts and emotions. It wasn't as if I was about to have a conniption; nevertheless, something was fomenting within me that bore no resemblance to love. I did not want someone else to have those soufflés. I wanted them for myself, thank you very much!

I recall an early morning commute to work that included a stop at my local bank to withdraw some cash from the ATM. As I turned into the parking lot, I saw a car approaching from an opposite entrance, and my knee-jerk reaction was to *punch it* so I could beat that person to the ATM. As it turned out, they went a different direction, but it didn't matter. My heart had already been revealed, and I was caught red-handed in this selfish act. Even though not another soul knew what had just occurred, my Father in heaven knew, and in His goodness He prompted the Holy Spirit to make me aware of my selfish behavior. I was absolutely ashamed of myself—and there was nobody around but me!

Does any of this resonate with you? I can't be the only person who has selfishly cut someone off in traffic, or has become grumpy or moody because my spouse wanted to watch something on television other than what I wanted to watch. Maybe you've refused to give up watching the big game when the Holy Spirit had prompted you to go minister to someone, or perhaps you've balked at an opportunity to meet someone's financial need.

I recall several times—before receiving Christ as Savior—when a cashier gave me more change than I was due and, rather than return it, I kept the excess for myself, thinking it was my lucky day. I was too selfish to realize that the associate who made the mistake might have to cover the shortfall from their own pocket. Only a selfish person would knowingly keep the extra money for themselves. I also remember the first time this happened after I became a Christian. I turned to go on my way as before, only this time the Holy Spirit prompted me to return the extra money. When I obeyed and gave it back to the cashier, I was flooded with the joy of the Lord!

Have you ever experienced that inner grinding sensation that accompanies the disappointment of wanting to do something but being denied? Here's a good example: Let's say I get a text from one of my buddies asking if I want to play golf. I check with my wife and she says she would rather I not play. *But I want to play,* so guess what... grinding sensation. For you, it may be something else, but the fact remains that there are times when we either cannot do as we please, or we find ourselves having to do something we would rather not. Either way, we experience an inner turmoil, which is nothing less than an indication of selfishness at work within us.

Meet the Leech Family

I don't know when refrigerators first started being equipped with ice makers, but when I was a boy, we had to manually fill ice-cube trays and wait several hours for them to freeze before we had ice. As simple as it was to fill an ice-cube tray, it was all too common-place in the Smith household to open the freezer for some ice only to find all the ice-cube trays empty!

Proverbs 30 records the sayings of Agur, son of Jakeh. He chronicled his observation of things that were of such fascination and amazement that they were beyond his ability to understand them. Take the following for instance:

> Three things are too wonderful for me; four I do not understand: the way of an eagle in the sky, the way of a serpent on a rock, the way of a ship on the high seas, and the way of a man with a virgin. (Proverbs 30:18–19)

I have a list of my own:

> Three things are too amazing for me; yea four I do not understand: the way of an able-bodied person too lazy to return their shopping cart to the cart return area instead of leaving it in a parking space, the way of those who make messes and leave them for others to clean up, the way of people who litter as though the earth were their personal garbage can, and the way of an able-bodied, able-minded person who refuses to work.

We see them all around us— people who always have their hand out but never is it filled with something to enrich someone else.

The types of people I am describing are members of the Leech family, and Agur aptly describes two of the children by saying, "The leech has two daughters: Give and Give" (Proverbs 30:15a).

I cannot comprehend such an approach to living, and yet we see them all around us—people who seem to know only how to consume without ever replenishing, people who are content to take and never give, people who always have their hand out but never is it filled with something to enrich someone else. Such an attitude could never be found among the Christlike.

True Beauty

Thankfully, not everyone caters to their selfish instincts. We realize now that selfishness is the underlying reason why people aren't longsuffering, why they aren't kind, why they envy, why they get provoked, and so on. On the other hand, an unselfish person is more likely to be longsuffering, more likely to be kind, more likely to be generous, and less likely to be provoked or keep a record of wrongs. And herein lies the true beauty of love—*unselfishness*.

Few things in life are more attractive than an unselfish person. Unselfish people are more likable, endearing, inspiring, and worthy of emulation than those who clutch and grab and hoard for themselves. And I'm not simply talking about possessions. One of the things I struggle most with is giving of my time. I would often rather give money to a cause than devote my time to it, unless I have a particular affinity for—or vested interest in—the cause. It's one thing to purchase the plow; it's another thing to put your hand to it.

Paul said of Timothy, "For I have no one like him, who will be genuinely concerned for your welfare. For they all seek

> *Few things in life are more attractive than an unselfish person. Unselfish people are more likable, endearing, inspiring, and worthy of emulation than those who clutch and grab and hoard for themselves.*

their own interests, not those of Jesus Christ" (Philippians 2:20–21). I know some people who embody this same Timothy spirit—people who genuinely put the welfare of others above their own.

For nearly forty years, I have been privileged to know Bob Hauselman as my pastor and brother-in-law. He and his wife, Sara, are two of the most unselfish and generous people I personally know. They aren't perfect, but they have lived exemplary lives when it comes to being hospitable, visiting the sick, giving to the poor, and giving up personal time to counsel folks in need. On more than one occasion, they abruptly cut short their vacation and returned home to comfort the bereaved or minister to someone in a crisis. Cutting short a vacation usually means a loss of money in addition to giving up the personal enjoyment, rest, and recreation you were so looking forward to. I see the beauty of Christ in them—the beauty of unselfishness.

I have also had the privilege of knowing Tony and Sherry Stopher for nearly thirty-five years. Tony and Sherry have served the Lord selflessly in numerous ways. Sherry has served on our worship team as a gifted pianist, which comes with the added "bonus" of being asked to play in people's weddings, at funerals, for school plays, and so on. In all my years of leading our worship team, I never knew Sherry to say no. I'm sure there were times when she did, but they were so few and far between that they went unnoticed.

Tony is the head of maintenance at a nursing home. He is gifted to do most anything related to plumbing, electrical, and HVAC work, and much the same as it is with musicians—when people know you have trade skills, they will call you for help. Such phone calls typically come when it's inconvenient. Tony has taken on many a frigid crawl space to repair broken pipes, often accepting nothing more than a "Thank you."

I could go on, but I suspect you can produce your own list of unselfish people who, like Bob and Sara and Tony and Sherry, have impacted your life and the lives of others by demonstrating a Christlike example of Paul's statement to the Corinthians, "I will most gladly spend and be spent for your souls" (2 Corinthians 12:15a).

The Rich Man's Legacy

Jesus was a marvelous communicator, and He effectively used stories to impart His message. In chapter 6 we made a passing reference to the story of *The Rich Man and Lazarus*. The full account is found in Luke 16:19–31, a portion of which follows:

> There was a rich man who was dressed in purple and fine linen and lived in luxury every day. At his gate was laid a beggar named Lazarus, covered with sores and longing to eat what fell from the rich man's table. Even the dogs came and licked his sores.
>
> The time came when the beggar died and the angels carried him to Abraham's side. The rich man also died and was buried. In Hades, where he was in torment, he looked up and saw Abraham far away, with Lazarus by his side. So he called to him, "Father Abraham, have pity on me and send Lazarus to dip the tip of his finger in water and cool my tongue, because I am in agony in this fire."
>
> But Abraham replied, "Son, remember that in your lifetime you received your good things, while Lazarus received bad things, but now he is comforted here and you are in agony. And besides all this, between us and you a great chasm has been set in place, so that those who want to go from here to you cannot, nor can anyone cross over from there to us." (Luke 16:19–26 NIV)

Need rarely has a pretty face, and it typically shows up on our doorstep at an inopportune time.

The above story illustrates a painful truth for those who have the wherewithal to help others but not the heart to do so. It reveals an attitude of, "I've got mine, and I really don't want to be inconvenienced by you or your situation." The man who lay at the rich man's gate was described as "a beggar... covered with sores." He was (1) needy and (2) repugnant in appearance. Many times the two go hand in hand. Need rarely has a pretty face, and it typically shows up on our doorstep at an inopportune time.

The Holy Spirit has used this parable of Jesus to impress upon me how easy it is to turn away from the less fortunate because of their encroachment upon my time, my energy, and my finances, which can ultimately interfere with *my plans.*

The rich man had the means to help the beggar but did not. We're not told exactly why he didn't, but it's obvious from the context that he knew Lazarus by name, yet still chose not to give him so much as the scraps from his table. We also learn from this story that God expects the haves to share with the have-nots. So much so, that God reversed the two men's circumstances in the afterlife. Lazarus now had the comforts and the rich man was destitute.

This is a stern warning. We could easily—and conveniently—assume the rich man would have been an unbeliever, but Jesus offers no color commentary to support such an assumption. I consider myself a Christian, and yet I know how many times I have not wanted to be bothered by that person who randomly "shows up on my doorstep" with a need. I mean, just leave me alone so I can watch the football game, or eat my dinner, or continue with whatever it is that I want to do. I don't want to be bothered by you, okay? Can you come back when it's convenient? Or better yet, can you just go bother someone else? This mind-set is not only held by those with mountains of money, but the caution also applies to anyone who is in a position to help someone else, no matter how large or small the need may be.

This story gives me great pause when I consider how callous I can be at times with respect to the needs of others. The rich man's legacy was that of regret. May we all learn from his legacy and take to heart the message of Jesus, which is to be unselfish and compassionate toward the destitute.

In his parting address to the elders in Ephesus, Paul exhorted them with a similar message:

> In all things I have shown you that by working hard in this way we must help the weak and remember the words of the Lord Jesus, how he himself said, "It is more blessed to give than to receive." (Acts 20:35)

Aim Higher

Love does not seek its own—its own advantage, its own honor, its own success, etc., especially if it comes at the expense of another. It is one thing to put in the time and effort to be successful in one's career, but if I'm using people in the process, or taking credit for work they've done, this certainly cannot be Christlike.

One of the finest bosses I have ever worked for used to go out of his way to sing the praises of his direct reports—never taking credit for the work done by his team—although he could have conveniently attributed our accomplishments to the strength of his leadership.

Let's take this a step further. If you were credited with an accomplishment that was largely due to the input and effort of another, would you remain quiet and accept the recognition for yourself, or would you set the record straight and make sure the other person received the credit?

And do we now dare test the limits of our sensibilities by asking ourselves if we would be willing to let someone else receive praise for work we had done? That would unquestionably be a bitter pill to swallow, though nowhere near the gall our Lord tasted when He was falsely accused as a transgressor and nailed to a cross for our sins.

As admirable as recognizing the work of others may be, such selflessness could be rooted in nothing more than a humanistic, altruistic motive that is completely detached from any desire to glorify God. So it is one thing to seek the good of others, but entirely another to aim higher and seek the glory of the Father and His Christ. In quoting a portion of Psalm 40:7–8 (KJV), the Unknown Christian said, "'Lo, I come to do thy will. I delight to do thy will, O my God.' Our Lord sought only the Father's glory.... This is the Christlike life.... [And] if Christ [lives] in me, I shall be Christlike, and my great aim will be to glorify the Father and speak only the Father's Word, and do only the Father's will. And all this is possible only by the inspiration of the Holy Spirit."[1]

What about in the home? Do we serve unselfishly; do we delight in glorifying the Father there? The below excerpt from *The Christlike Christian* describes how godliness in the home is often neglected, taking its toll on the members of the family. Like an unmaintained fence that over time becomes rough to the touch, the splinters not always visible to the naked eye have the potential to inflict pain on the unsuspecting:

> Even notably successful Christian workers often feel at liberty to be cross, and ugly, and selfish, and un-Christlike in the privacy of their homes.
>
> After an address to a crowded congregation on the Christlike life two fashionably-dressed ladies stopped a servant-maid at the church door, and said, "Are you not a maid in the house where the preacher is staying?" "Yes," was the reply; "I am." "Well—tell us—what is he like in the house?"
>
> Yes—that is the crucial test. But it is not enough to know about the speaker's behavior when he is the privileged guest of godly people. Tell me—what is he like in his own home?—then I shall be in a position to gauge the depth of his spirituality.
>
> "He is seen at his best in his own home and parish," said a lady of a clerical friend of the writer's.
>
> That is praise indeed....
>
> Yet the happiness of so many homes is wrecked and ruined by the selfishness of one member of the family. For the sake of peace and quietness, perhaps,

nothing is said—it is just taken for granted that the "self" in that one member of the family must be gratified; whilst that member just—

Lives for himself and thinks of himself,
For himself, and none beside,
Just as if Jesus had never lived,
And as if He had never died.[2]

Did You Really Ask Me That?

Mindy is a paraprofessional at a charter school (i.e., she is a teacher's aide). In October 2014, she was enjoying some time off during the school's fall break, and we had previously discussed the possibility of me also taking a day or two off so we could spend some time together during her two-week hiatus. This was not particularly good timing for me because of the current demands of my work. I was two months away from the implementation of an eighteen-month project, and had been unable to take hardly any of my PTO. We were heading into the final push before go-live, and I was focused on the goal before me—a successful implementation.

While eating dinner on a Tuesday evening, Mindy asked, "Are you going to be able to take some time off this week?"

I said, "I don't think so." Within two minutes—I kid you not—I received an email from a friend asking if I could play golf at Valhalla that Thursday. For the uninitiated, Valhalla is owned by the PGA of America and has been host to several PGA Championships as well as the 2008 Ryder Cup matches. Ergo, it is exclusive and private, and an opportunity like this does not often present itself to a peasant like me. It had been approximately seventeen years since I last played there, so naturally—as anyone would understand—I immediately replied to the email and said, "I think I can make that happen."

Since I was using my phone to communicate while we were eating dinner—I know, rude behavior—Mindy asked who I was emailing, so I explained to her that an opportunity to play golf at Valhalla had just come up, and that I was going to take off work Thursday in order to play.

She said nothing—at that moment.

The following day, Mindy came to my workplace so we could eat lunch together. During our meal, she said she needed to get something off of her chest. She then described what had happened the night before and, to my amazement, I didn't even remember her asking me the question, "Are you going to be able to take some time off this week?" She found it interesting how quickly I just cleared everything off my schedule in order to play golf. I found it interesting too—and a bit disturbing. As a man aspiring to be Christlike, it would seem I have some room for growth when it comes to being unselfish.

What If?

If all people embraced this one commandment universally known as *The Golden Rule*, it would solve nearly every one of the world's problems in singular, categorical fashion: "So whatever you wish that others would do to you, do also to them, for this is the Law and the Prophets" (Matthew 7:12).

If people would only ask themselves how they would like to be treated—and answer the question honestly—immeasurable good would come of it. If I were hungry, I would hope that someone would feed me. If I were naked, I would want someone to clothe me, and if I were sick or in prison, I would want someone to visit me. If I were dying, I would hope that someone would pray for me. Aren't these all practical examples of what it means to love my neighbor as myself? Jesus summarized both of these commandments as the essence of the Law and the Prophets. Re-read Matthew 7:12, and then read the following passage from Matthew 22:

> And one of them, a lawyer, asked him a question to test him. "Teacher, which is the great commandment

in the Law?" And he said to him, "You shall love the Lord your God with all your heart and with all your soul and with all your mind. This is the great and first commandment. And a second is like it: You shall love your neighbor as yourself. On these two commandments depend all the Law and the Prophets." (Matthew 22:35–40)

I have heard it said that people cannot love their neighbor unless they first love themselves. The implication is that some people do not love themselves, and therefore, need some type of inner healing before they will be able to love others. To me, this sounds more analogous to people not *liking* themselves—which is completely believable and understandable—but I have to question if this is what Jesus meant.

In the context of normal psychology—which Dictionary.com defines as "approximately average in any psychological trait, as intelligence, personality, or emotional adjustment; free from any mental disorder; sane"[3]—every living, breathing human being loves him/herself.

What Jesus is talking about here is not whether a person is happy with what they've become or what their life is presently like, but rather the innate motivation to satisfy our most basic needs. Give me food, give me shelter, give me clothing, give me comfort, and give me pleasure. Even in the context of abnormal psychology, unless we are talking about an extreme—possibly demonic—abnormality, people will love themselves with respect to having their essential needs met. These verses in Ephesians 5 make this perfectly clear:

In the same way husbands should love their wives as their own bodies. He who loves his wife loves himself. *For no one ever hated his own flesh, but nourishes and cherishes it,* just as Christ does the church. (Ephesians 5:28–29, emphasis added)

Walk in Love

Paul exhorted the church at Ephesus to "be imitators of God, as beloved children. And walk in love, as Christ loved us and gave himself up for us, a fragrant offering and sacrifice to God" (Ephesians 5:1–2). Oswald Chambers says, "The word *walk* is used in the Bible to express the character of a person."[4] If Chambers is right—and I believe he is—then walking in love enables me to express the true character and nature of Jesus Christ, which is selfless love.

Christ set the gold standard by sacrificially giving Himself—and we should follow His example. May we not be like the self-seeking Diotrophes, whom Paul said "likes to put himself first" (3 John 1:9). Rather, "Let each of us please his neighbor for his good, to build him up. For Christ did not please himself" (Romans 15:2–3a)—and neither should those who would be like Him.

For Further Study

"Do nothing from selfish ambition or conceit, but in humility count others more significant than yourselves."
Philippians 2:3

1. The author asserts that every human being is selfish by nature. State why you either agree or disagree with this statement.
2. What is the greatest challenge we face in obeying Jesus Christ, and how do we overcome that challenge?
3. In Proverbs 30, Agur, son of Jakeh lists four things that are difficult for him to comprehend. Make your own list of three or four selfish behaviors you have witnessed (or practiced).
4. How does unselfishness make us more attractive?
5. What was the rich man's legacy? Write down a time when you failed to recognize the Lazarus lying at your gate.
6. Where is the one place we sometimes neglect to serve? Who suffers the most as a result?
7. Jesus said to love your neighbor as yourself. What, exactly, does it mean to love yourself in this context?

12

No Pets Allowed

"Love ... is not provoked."
1 Corinthians 13:4–5 (NASB)

S OME OF MY FONDEST CHILDHOOD MEMORIES are from the summer
vacations spent at my great-aunt Jessie's home in Pensacola,
Florida. Each year, as soon as my brother and I finished playing
Little League baseball, my family piled in the station wagon and
drove eleven hours down I-65 from New Albany, Indiana, to spend
two weeks at Aunt Jessie's.

One of the things I did to pass the time in the car was to read
signs—road signs, outdoor boards, signs on buildings, bumper
stickers, and the like. One thing that sticks out in my memory is
the hotel marquees from the 1960s that would let travelers know
whether or not they had vacancies and whether or not they allowed
pets. We never took our dog with us on vacation, but if we had, the
NO PETS ALLOWED signs would have signaled us to stop elsewhere.
Hotel owners know that pets—no matter how well trained—are
potential liabilities, so most hotels prohibit them. All who seek to
be Christlike should take a page from their playbook and implement their own NO PETS ALLOWED policy.

If you haven't already figured out this analogy, I am alluding
to *pet peeves*—those pesky annoyances that precipitate becoming
provoked, and yet we perversely treat them as sacred.

For most of my life I had a number of such pets under my care.
I fed them well, I nurtured them, and I gave them ample attention.
I routinely boasted of them to my friends, family, and colleagues.

But when God brought to my attention how easily I got provoked, I became acutely aware of how often I used some form of the expression, "One of my pet peeves is...." One day, the Lord whispered to me that I should not have any pet peeves—none, zero, *nada*. That was eye-opening, because such household pets are commonplace among the skin-wearing, yet they can hardly be considered man's best friend. Many of my former pet peeves gave me a foretaste of what weeping and gnashing of teeth could be like. Certainly anyone at all familiar with the teachings

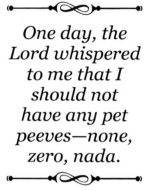

One day, the Lord whispered to me that I should not have any pet peeves—none, zero, nada.

of Jesus knows that weeping and gnashing of teeth is not something we want to experience when this life is over—so why engage in it now?

Speaking of gnashing of teeth, allowing oneself to be provoked can lead to Temporomandibular Joint Dysfunction (TMJ), high blood pressure, and other physical maladies. Worst of all, it mars our Christian witness and testimony, making it more difficult to influence others—including our enemies—with the saving power of the gospel.

Each day life presents me with opportunities to be provoked: the way other motorists drive, the way people treat me or the way they disappoint me; the way a slow Internet connection affects my productivity, the way a cancelled airline flight delays my travel, the way the fast-food guy messes up my order, and the way the toilet paper roll is on *backwards*.

Not all, but many of these provocations originate with co-workers, spouses, family members, and friends—people with whom we frequently rub elbows—which is why it is imperative that we take these pets for a long ride into the countryside and dump them in some remote place where they can't find their way back home!

Standing Guard

All kidding aside, the love that Paul speaks of in 1 Corinthians 13:4–8 is the same love that controls us (2 Corinthians 5:14) and is unmoved by life's irritations and vexations of spirit. This is possible because of what we covered in the previous chapter—that such love is not selfish and does not seek its own way. I am not saying that to be Christlike is to be immune to ever being provoked. However, when the screws of life are tightened, the Christlike man or woman is constrained by the love of Christ to exhibit a composure that can only be explained as the result of a life that is wholly yielded to Christ, and which keeps them from taking out their frustrations on others.

When I was in the ninth grade, my class went on a trip to Washington, D.C., to tour our nation's capital. One of the sites we visited was the Tomb of the Unknown Soldier in Arlington National Cemetery. I still remember the precision, focus, and imperturbable composure of the tomb guards as they executed their charge to perfection in honoring their unknown fallen comrades. The day we visited the monument a few knuckleheads disrespectfully and intentionally tried to break the concentration of the guards. Despite their antics, there wasn't so much as a flinch or change of expression on the guards' faces. This is undeniably an extreme example, but nonetheless useful in providing a vivid picture of the kind of composure we should demonstrate when things begin to get under our skin, rather than being provoked and saying or doing something we will later regret.

We should have no buttons to push, no peeves for pets, and nothing that gets our proverbial goat.

Where the tomb guard analogy falls short is that it tends to resemble stoicism more than Christlikeness. I am not suggesting that a Christlike man or woman should never experience emotion when faced with an opportunity to be provoked. What I am saying, however, is that we should have no buttons to push, no peeves for pets, and nothing that gets our proverbial goat. So if something happens that triggers a sudden spike in blood pressure, we must quickly remind ourselves that love does not get provoked, and subsequently exhibit that fruit of the Spirit called self-control.

One final interesting thing of note about the tomb guards is that they choose this life of rigor in order to honor those who died serving their country. How much more should we seek to honor Jesus Christ, who gave Himself for the sins of all mankind?

Cause and Effect

As I have considered this topic, I find two primary reasons that explain why people get provoked:

1. *Offense* (somebody does, or says, something that riles me)
2. *Disappointment* (somebody fails to do, or say, something I expect them to)

The first is active, the second is passive, and I would be willing to bet your paycheck that you have experienced both at one time or another—as have I. The stories that follow serve to illustrate either active or passive forms of provocation.

Wipe That Girn off Your Face

No, that is not a typo in the subheading for this section. Girning is something I did often as part of a Sunday morning ritual in preparation for leading worship. Romans 12:1 exhorts us to "present your bodies as a living sacrifice . . . which is your spiritual worship," but this ritual of mine could hardly pass as anything spiritual.

Anyone who knows me well knows that I have a natural proclivity to be a bit fastidious. Some would consider this a monumental understatement. I can just imagine the eye rolling, sighing, laughing, and remarks like, "Ya think?" or the sarcastic, "I had no idea." What can I say? I like things to be tidy, organized, and kept in a certain place, largely for the sake of efficiency, not because I'm a neat freak—though some may even debate that!

Consider for a moment what it would be like if you didn't have a designated silverware drawer in your kitchen. If you needed a knife or fork, you would never know which drawer to open. Trial and error, lost time, frustration—all words that describe the result of never knowing with certainty which drawer to open when it was time to set the table.

For a little more than thirty-five years, I had the privilege of leading praise and worship at Restoration Christian Church (RCC) in Sellersburg, Indiana. Each Sunday, the worship team would arrive between 8:00 and 8:30 AM to *set the worship table* for our congregation. There were times when I could not find a knife or a fork—um, I mean a microphone or a music stand—because someone had been in the kitchen and did not put things back where they found them!

For thirty-two years, RCC was host to a Christian school. In addition to sharing real estate with the church, some of the church's assets were also used by the school—most notably the sanctuary where school plays and musicals were performed. Sharing the platform, the music stands, the sound system, and the peripheral sound reinforcement equipment became a significant source of irritation for me. Whenever the school was working on a play, or if they were offering after-school music lessons in the sanctuary, it invariably resulted in a rearrangement of the platform "furniture."

Many Sunday mornings the microphone cables were so tangled that it took me a full ten to fifteen minutes to sort out the mess, and much of the time while doing so, I was whining to anyone who would listen about how I could not understand how people could use the platform and not put things back the way they found them.

I finally wised up and bought some wireless microphones, which solved the cabling issue, but with respect to me not being provoked... well, it only addressed the symptom, not the disease.

There were plenty of other things for me to girn about. As defined by Dictionary.com, *girn¹* means:

1. to snarl
2. to grimace; pull grotesque faces
3. *to complain fretfully or peevishly*

Bingo! How pleasant it must have been for the rest of the worship team to listen to me complain about my pet peeve of expecting things to be returned to their place. Should those who used the platform have made the effort to put things back as they found them? Yes. Was it wrong of me to expect this of them? Absolutely not. Was it a foolish and unrealistic expectation? Apparently so.

Some of you will be 100 percent in my corner and will quickly think back to similar experiences of your own. And though it may seem perfectly justifiable to let off steam in such situations, it is not. *Love is not provoked.* Those of you who are not naturally wired to put something back where you found it simply expect others to build a bridge and get over it, and although that attitude is conveniently self-serving to excuse such behavior, it is nevertheless apropos of what people should do in such situations. Rather than being provoked, we do, indeed, have to get over it; we have to let it go. If we don't, we sentence ourselves to a lifetime of frustration, and we soil our Christian testimony before those who suffer through our peevish complaints.

When our children were small, Mindy would not tolerate murmuring and complaining from any of them. To reinforce this biblical truth (see Philippians 2:14), she made up a little song and used it as a correctional device whenever she heard them complain. It goes like this:

No Murmuring

By Mindy Smith

No Thank You

Let's consider for a moment how disappointment affects our emotions and entices us to be provoked. Not only must we guard against being annoyed by something someone says or does, we must also stand at the ready to resist the temptation to become irritated by what people don't say or do. Have you ever done something nice for someone and they showed no appreciation whatsoever? In such situations you may be tempted to think or say, "Well, after all I did for them and they never even said, 'Thank you.' Of all the nerve!"

You might expect to receive kudos for a job well done, and it never comes. I certainly have. Let's read a passage in Luke 17 where Jesus teaches us not to expect recognition or even a "thank you" for doing what is asked or required of us:

> "When a servant comes in from plowing or taking care of sheep, does his master say, 'Come in and eat with me'? No, he says, 'Prepare my meal, put on your apron, and serve me while I eat. Then you can

eat later.' And does the master thank the servant for doing what he was told to do? Of course not. In the same way, when you obey me you should say, 'We are unworthy servants who have simply done our duty.'" (Luke 17:7–10 NLT)

This may be true in other cultures as well, but in Western culture, we are taught at an early age to say "Please" and "Thank you." That ingrains within us the expectation that we should also be thanked when we do something we are asked (or told) to do—especially if we do something nice for someone without being asked. But Jesus doesn't even pause for effect before answering His own question: "Does the master thank the servant for doing what he was told to do? Of course not."

Of course not?

Wow. That's a punch to the gut. Jesus is so matter-of-fact as to imply that no one would ever expect to be thanked for doing what they are commanded (or expected) to do. And yet, that's exactly the opposite of how we think in Western culture.

My employer compensates me financially for fulfilling the responsibilities of my job description. My paycheck is my "Thank you." Do I like it if my boss verbally thanks me and encourages me for a job well done? You better believe it! A pat on the back sometimes provides more positive motivation than the paycheck. So what do I do if I don't receive the praise and recognition I think I deserve? Do I sulk? Do I get upset? Do I feel underappreciated? To help me approach my work with an attitude of humility, I can remind myself that I've "simply done my duty." Love is not provoked by a lack of praise or recognition.

Town Hall

In October 2010 I flew to New York City for an IT town hall meeting. In such gatherings, we hear about the progress of current projects and long range plans, we celebrate our fellow associates' milestone anniversaries, and we typically conclude by recognizing individuals for outstanding contributions on projects or in support of systems.

On this particular occasion, I was five months into a challenging and stressful period of hypercare support for a project that launched in early June of that same year. In January of 2009, I began working with a team of people on this project to migrate our corporate websites to a new system hosted by another company. The initial timeline was slated as a six-month project. However, the project's complexity was so greatly underestimated that we did not implement the new sites until eighteen months later—*and they were still not ready for primetime.*

Our senior management made the decision to implement the new sites prematurely, resulting in the inability to settle any credit-card transactions for nearly three weeks. Translation? We had sold millions of dollars of merchandise and could not collect payment from our customers! Not so good for cash flow.

To exacerbate the situation, our company had just completed its fourth round of head-count reductions as part of an outsourcing of IT support to a third-party organization. As an outlying casualty of this initiative, some associates left voluntarily for greener pastures, which meant much of our knowledge base was gone, and that left some of us having to support applications we knew nothing about.

I distinctly recall working with my boss for more than forty hours on Father's Day weekend in an effort to settle the outstanding credit-card transactions. Neither of us knew the credit-card settlement system, but it nevertheless fell on our shoulders to work with our business clients in Finance, our new third-party support organization, and a software vendor to solve this problem.

As if this were not difficult enough, we had the additional challenge of learning to communicate with our new India-based support staff. I have since come to have a great appreciation for this relationship, but in the early going it was quite nerve-racking, for even though my Indian friends speak English well enough, my ears were not yet accustomed to the nuance of their dialect—especially over a sketchy cell phone connection. It made for a situation that was beyond frustrating, especially being under the gun to resolve such a business-critical situation involving these outstanding credit card transactions.

Her name was Suja. She was the new third-party support resource I had to track down in order to have her verify some transactions. When our Operations staff finally reached her and she called me back, I began explaining what I needed from her. She said nothing. I repeated myself, and she remained silent. At this point, I began to raise my voice, "Suja, are you listening? Are you there?" (*Why, God, am I stuck in this situation? What sins have I committed to bring such calamity upon me? Please forgive me and get me out of this!*) But... there was no escape.

To cut the story short, by the end of that fateful Father's Day, we had resolved the matter and were able to settle the outstanding credit-card transactions. It seemed nothing short of a heroic effort on the part of my boss and me, and yet it was somehow lost on others.

As the October town hall meeting began to wind down, our IT leadership started doling out the customary recognition to associates who had performed admirably since the last town hall. One by one, people made their way up front to receive their certificates of recognition and have their photos taken with senior leadership.

As the awards presentation drew to a close, the speaker began describing one final award that was being given to recognize an individual for their support of the new E-Commerce websites. Could he be describing me? Could this be my moment of recognition? (I knew it wasn't my boss, since he had left the organization about a month prior.)

My heart began to beat faster as I listened to the description of the individual's contributions, and I found myself nervously anticipating the announcement of my name. In preparation of walking up front to receive my certificate, I began tugging on my pant legs and shirt to remove any grotesque wrinkles, only to hear the speaker announce, "So it is my pleasure to recognize Suja for her outstanding support of our E-Commerce platform."

Suja? Are you kidding me? I nearly fell out of my chair. What could they have possibly seen to make them think she had done a good job supporting this new system? And how could they have been so blind to *my* contributions since the new system went live? *Stunned* barely begins to describe how I felt in that moment. I don't believe I would have been upset simply for not being recognized—disappointed, yes, but upset, no. But giving an award to Suja—when I knew first-hand how painful it had been to work with her that Father's Day weekend—now that was a bitter pill to swallow.

In all fairness to Suja, my knowledge of her support of the new E-Commerce system was largely limited to this one isolated incident. I'm sure she deserved the recognition she received. It just didn't seem like it at the time, at least not from my vantage point.

Finally Recognized

The following spring, my moment arrived, only this time I participated in the town hall remotely via Conference Bridge from my office in Louisville, Kentucky. I was now reporting to my third boss in less than a year, and since I had started transitioning back to more of what I would call my normal job responsibilities, the E-Commerce project was officially behind me. Nevertheless, as the awards for outstanding contributions were announced, I was pleasantly surprised to hear my name called for what I had contributed to the E-Commerce project. Though it felt anticlimactic, I still appreciated the acknowledgement... until a couple of days later when I received my certificate of recognition via inter-office mail.

As I removed the certificate from its envelope, I didn't know whether to laugh out loud or be mad. In the past, these certificates had always been printed on official Certificate of Recognition paper stock and signed by the Chief Information Officer (CIO), but mine was printed on plain white 8 ½ x 11 paper and signed by ... no one!

Our CIO and his Administrative Assistant had recently left the organization, and our Chief Financial Officer was now the acting head of IT, so it was actually not surprising that something like this could happen. *But to not even sign the thing?* As Miracle Max lamented in *The Princess Bride*, "While you're at it, why don't you give me a nice paper cut and pour lemon juice on it?"[1]

I've shared these stories in hopes of making you laugh, but also to illustrate how God uses such things to refine us and to see how we will respond in such situations. There is no way this was a coincidence; God was engineering my circumstances. I also know that in the end, all that matters is that I am performing my job in a way that is pleasing to Him. I have since been recognized—with appropriate paper stock—for other project contributions, but these two stories are priceless with respect to the lessons I learned.

Tempest in Target

It seems as though we have barely scratched the surface on what could be said concerning this Christlike quality of not being provoked. Said the Unknown Christian:

> It is curious to see how many different renderings modern versions give us for this word *provoked*. We are told that "love is never irritated and resentful"; "does not blaze out in passionate anger"; "is not irritable, touchy and unwilling to hear criticism or suggestion"; "does not get peevish"; "is never angry without a cause."
>
> May we sum them all up in a well-understood word? Love is not bad tempered. We are not dealing with isolated—even if repeated—acts; but with a dread and terrible disease which is both fatally injurious and amazingly infectious.[2]

In chapter 1, we made a passing reference to those who carry within themselves a petulant disposition—the tendency to be "moved to or show sudden, impatient irritation, especially over some trifling annoyance."[3] Petulance is that terrible disease noted by the Unknown Christian that injures and infects those with whom it comes in contact, and the man consumed by it has little chance of portraying a Christlike image to those around him. Those who wear their feelings on their sleeves or fly off the handle at the slightest matter are a detriment to the cause of Christ. No matter how godly we may be in other areas, if we routinely over-react to certain situations—especially trivial ones—we significantly lessen our chances of being a positive influence for Christ to others. Solomon observed the folly of anger and wrote this admonition for us: "Be not quick in your spirit to become angry, for anger lodges in the heart of fools" (Ecclesiastes 7:9).

"But it's healthier to let off steam than to keep things bottled up on the inside." For whom? The Unknown Christian tells of a lady who, upon excusing her ill temper, said to evangelist Billy Sunday, "It's all over in a minute."

"So is a Gatling gun," he replied, "but it blows everything to pieces in that minute!"[4]

I recall making quite a scene about fifteen years ago while attempting to return some merchandise at a local Target store. I had purchased a suit for my youngest son for Christmas, but it did not fit him well. Instead of returning it promptly, we let it hang in his closet for several months until one day it dawned on me that $110 was hanging there. So with receipt in hand I decided to take the suit back to the store.

The associate at the customer service desk informed me that, even though I still had the receipt, the store's returns policy prohibited her from refunding cash for merchandise that had been purchased more than ninety days prior.

"Why?" I asked. "I have the receipt. There's nothing wrong with the suit. It just didn't fit my son."

"I'm sorry, sir, but I cannot give you cash. All I can do is give you an in-store credit for the amount."

But I didn't want an in-store credit, I wanted my money back, so I asked to speak to a manager. She gladly obliged, given that I was becoming noticeably belligerent.

When the manager arrived, I rehashed everything for him, but to my dislike, he reiterated the store's returns policy and said he could only give me an in-store credit. At this point, I lost it . . . and said, "I don't give a (rhymes with spit) what your returns policy is, I want a refund!" I suddenly became aware of the scene I was making and could not believe what had just come out of my mouth. But it was too late. As they say, you cannot un-ring a bell, and the bell had tolled—in stentorian fashion.

I finally relented and agreed to take the in-store credit. As I turned to walk away, I was stricken with a horrific sense of what had just transpired, and I hoped against hope that no one within earshot knew anything about me, my God, or my church. I thought to myself, "Dear God, what if someone who just witnessed this knows that I claim to be a Christian or that I lead praise and worship at Restoration Christian Church!" It felt as if all eyes were on me as I shamefully slinked away from the customer service desk.

Although I was still angry over what I thought was an illogical returns policy, I knew I had blown it, and I now wanted to do whatever I could to make things right. I went to the back of the store and picked up a few items to purchase with my in-store credit. As I made my way through the checkout line, I saw the manager who had absorbed the brunt of my rant. As soon as I

As I turned to walk away, I was stricken with a horrific sense of what had just transpired, and I hoped against hope that no one within earshot knew anything about me, my God, or my church.

finished my transaction, I walked over to him and apologized for my outburst. I told him that he did not deserve to be spoken to like that, and I understood he was just doing his job. He thanked me for apologizing, and I went home feeling ashamed and wondering how on earth that had happened. I repented for my sinful rant and I thank God that I have never repeated—and rely on His grace that I never shall repeat—such un-Christlike behavior.

Are You Smarter Than a Canine?

I think it beneficial to reiterate the gracious words of the Unknown Christian who said, "We are not dealing with isolated—even if repeated—acts;"[5] but rather a person's general disposition or *modus operandi* (M.O.). I have known individuals who toss their head, sigh, and look at you with disgust simply because you called their name to ask them a question. Or how about the sorry individual who gets annoyed if someone asks them to repeat themselves? I have drawn the look of ire from others when asking them to reiterate something they previously said. I've also worked for people who expected others to understand every instruction the first time it was given, and asking for clarification was to invite retribution for assumed incompetency to listen. Such people are the reason for the expression "walking on eggshells."

As stated by the Unknown Christian, we are not so much concerned with isolated incidents as we are a resident surly disposition. If we discover that we are given to such mercurial behavior, let us "draw near to the throne of grace, that we may receive mercy and find grace to help in time of need" (Hebrews 4:16), lest we repeat our foolishness like the proverbial dog that returns to its own vomit (Proverbs 26:11).

Road Rage

Do we dare venture into an examination of how we behave behind the wheel of our automobiles? Even Christian people can be downright mean behind the wheel of a car, supposing that anonymity gives them immunity from being Christlike on the road. Would Christ intentionally drive up on someone's bumper in order to bully them to get over?

Are you the kind of person who lays on your horn if someone cuts you off in traffic or does something you think is unsafe or just plain stupid? Have we not been guilty of the same things at least once or twice? Paul said in Romans 2:1 that when we judge others we actually condemn ourselves because we, in fact, do the same things. So if your favorite term of endearment for fellow motorists is *Idiot*, it could be an indication that you need to work on this.

Appetite for Grace

I enjoy eating a good meal at a nice restaurant, but the dining-out experience does not always meet expectations. Whenever that happens to you, do you leave a penny to indicate your service was subpar? Why not go ahead and bless your server anyway? Maybe they're new on the job, or so slammed with customers that it's difficult for them to provide the kind of service they otherwise would. Do you ever have an "off day" in your line of work? "But I paid good money for this meal, so I have a right to good food and good service!" I used to think this same way until I came to realize that such an attitude would never be tolerated by the Christlike man or woman. It is far superior to extend grace rather than to let such a pet peeve rule your life.

The World's Longest and Shortest Showers

Once again, I am grateful to Mindy for allowing me to share some of our life's experiences, especially when they aren't quite as funny to her as they are to me.

We both prefer showering in the morning before going to work, and on most days she takes hers while I am at the gym working out. On one particular morning, I returned home from the gym right as

Mindy was getting in the shower. I waited (mostly) patiently as she took a thirty-minute-plus shower, nearly draining our fifty-gallon hot water tank. Though I lacked understanding at the time, I have since learned that this is the SOP (standard operating procedure) whenever she has to wash her hair and shave her legs.

When it was finally my time to shower, there was hardly any hot water left in the tank—and I also needed to shave. Now I've always been a blade man myself, which means hot water is a must if you want to keep your face from feeling like you just shaved with a piece of broken glass.

My first instinct was to fuss at Mindy for using up all the hot water, but since I had been spending time meditating on these wonderful verses in 1 Corinthians 13, I chose to remind myself that love is not provoked. Instead of berating her for taking such a long shower, I simply washed as quickly as I could with what little hot water was left and decided not to shave. I figured if anyone didn't like my appearance, they could just look at something else.

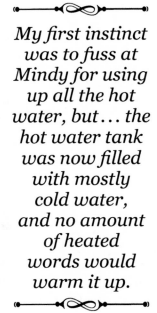

My first instinct was to fuss at Mindy for using up all the hot water, but ... the hot water tank was now filled with mostly cold water, and no amount of heated words would warm it up.

Before we left for work, Mindy apologized for using up the hot water, but I told her it wasn't a problem and that I had what I needed. Here's the practical takeaway from this: Fussing at her would have had *no positive outcome.* It would have only gratified a selfish desire to complain; she would have felt bad, and I would have ended up feeling just as bad if not worse. The hot water tank was now filled with mostly cold water, and no amount of heated words would warm it up.

Turn Your Pets into Pearls

Jesus said in Luke 17:1 (KJV), "It is impossible but that offences will come." In other words, try as we may to avoid it, life is rife with stumbling blocks and temptations to sin, which means we will experience ample opportunities to be provoked. However, if instead of becoming peeved we yield to the Spirit of God, He will take life's irritations and use them like sand in the oyster to produce a beautiful pearl from our lives.

Are you easily irritated by petty things? Don't be. Do you over-react to things of little consequence? If so, what good has it ever done you, or those around you? The Unknown Christian referenced a Hindu sadhu by the name of Sundar Singh who once exclaimed, "The true Christian is like sandalwood, which imparts its fragrance to the axe which cuts it, without doing any harm in return."[6] Such is the beauty of the love of Christ at work in a believer, and "is so miraculous in the eyes of un-Christian men [that it], more than anything else, draws them to Christ."[7]

The Unknown Christian goes on to tell of a Japanese workman who, "in a fit of anger, seized a tool and made a gash in a Christian man's head. When he had cooled down, he was overwhelmed with shame and cried out, 'If only he had not forgiven me I should not have minded so much! Why did he not strike back?' Such Christian forbearance completely won that man for the Lord Jesus Christ."[8]

"Nobody Gets to Me Like You Do"

It is equally important to not give offense as it is to not take offense. I've already established the fact that I seem to have been born with a gift for finding fault with others when instead I should be looking for the good in them. The following anecdotes provide further evidence of that.

In the game of golf, a number of scoring terms are used to describe a player's score in relation to par on any given hole. In addition to par, bogey, double bogey (or worse), bird references are used to describe subpar scoring on a hole. For instance, we have the birdie (one under par), eagle (two under par), and double eagle (three under par). The double eagle is also known as an albatross (for its rarity), but unknown to many, there is an even rarer bird—the *grouse*—which is used for scoring the overall enjoyment level of a round of golf.

A golfer's round is deemed to be a grouse whenever another golfer in his group effectively ruins his round by complaining incessantly throughout the game. I am grieved when I recall how many times I spoiled a friend's round of golf by grousing for eighteen holes about whatever peeve *du jour* was currently eating at me.

One day, while driving to one of our favorite restaurants in Madison, Indiana, Mindy startled me by saying, "Nobody gets to me like you do." On the surface, this might sound like a compliment—or a catchy title for a hit pop song—but I assure you it was neither. I don't recall what I had said or done, but the message to me was loud and clear: I was still saying things that she perceived as criticism. And I thought I was doing so much better! This incident reminds me of one of my favorite verses in Proverbs: "The one who states his case first seems right, until the other comes and examines him" (Proverbs 18:17).

It stung when she told me that, but after prayerfully considering her statement, I came to see this from a different perspective. True, I still needed to watch my words, but on the flip side of the coin was this matter of learning not to be provoked. I realize this may seem like I'm throwing my wife "under the bus," but the fact is that no one—not I or anyone else—should "get to her," and the same holds true for us—because love is not provoked.

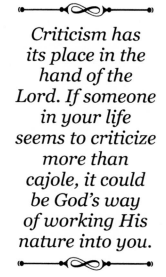

Criticism has its place in the hand of the Lord. If someone in your life seems to criticize more than cajole, it could be God's way of working His nature into you.

Mindy is tender-hearted, empathetic, and she has a low tolerance for hearing criticism about anyone or anything. Whenever she hears what sounds like criticism, she will invariably find something positive to say in response. For instance, I could say something like, "Look at the rust on that lamp post," and she would say, "But look how straight it is!" She's been that way ever since I've known her and although this is a beautiful quality, it has frustrated me numerous times when I was making what I considered to be a worthwhile, objective observation—and she would have none of it. God has greatly used her to teach me to keep my mouth shut when I don't have something positive to say.

But criticism has its place in the hand of the Lord. If someone in your life seems to criticize more than cajole, it could be God's way of working His nature into you. That certainly doesn't excuse them, but neither does it give you license to unequivocally dismiss or censure their critique.

"But Lord, that person has a reputation for being critical of everyone. Use anybody but them, Lord, to point out my flaws. I would certainly welcome it from anyone else." Does the wood on the lathe object to the tool the craftsman uses to shape it? When criticized, we should be less quick to defend and justify our position, and more willing to examine ourselves to see if the critique is legitimate. We can always do as Paul said and "test everything; hold fast what is good" (1 Thessalonians 5:21), and if, after examination, we find there is no merit, we can overlook it in a spirit of longsuffering and grace.

The Purview of God

Questions come to mind when I think about being Christlike and not being provoked. For instance, if God is love and love is not provoked, then how do we explain God becoming provoked with the children of Israel, or Jesus Christ driving the money-grubbing money changers from the temple with a whip? And why is God "angry with the wicked every day" (Psalm 7:11 KJV) if He loved the world so much "that he gave his only Son, that whoever believes in him should not perish but have eternal life" (John 3:16)?

The following passage from Psalm 78 is just one of several in Scripture that documents how God was moved to provocation by the rebellious acts of His people:

> Their heart was not steadfast toward him; they were not faithful to his covenant. Yet he, being compassionate, atoned for their iniquity and did not destroy them; he restrained his anger often and did not stir up all his wrath. He remembered that they were but flesh, a wind that passes and comes not again. How often they rebelled against him in the wilderness and grieved him in the desert! They tested God again and again and *provoked the Holy One of Israel.* They did not remember his power or the day when he redeemed them from the foe, when he performed his signs in Egypt and his marvels in the fields of Zoan. (Psalm 78:37–43, emphasis added)

While seeking the Lord for greater understanding concerning this seemingly contradictory conundrum, I shared some preliminary thoughts with Mindy as to what I thought was a plausible explanation. I told her that I had discovered through some cursory research that the Hebrew word translated as *provoked* in the Old Testament is translated in many other places as *rebelled*, and that you see both words used interchangeably throughout the Old Testament. The same Hebrew word is also translated as *grieved* in many places, so my early speculation was that in places where it said God was *provoked*, He may have

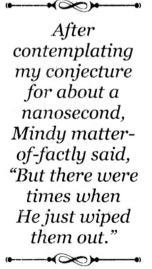

After contemplating my conjecture for about a nanosecond, Mindy matter-of-factly said, "But there were times when He just wiped them out."

simply been *grieved*, which could imply something altogether different.

I proceeded to explain to her that when God was provoked, He acted in such a way as to discipline His people in order to bring about their restoration, and that it was not His intent to destroy them. After contemplating my conjecture for about a nanosecond, Mindy matter-of-factly said, "But there were times when He just wiped them out." Well, she was right, so how *was* I going to explain this?

First, let's be clear on this point: God doesn't need me to defend His actions. He sovereignly does as He pleases, yet in no way is He unjust. He alone is the standard for all that is holy, righteous, and perfect, and as such is the only One qualified to define sin and determine its consequences.

Romans 6:23 tells us the wages of sin is death. This is a governing truth that God established for His universe, and He watches over His Word to perform it (Jeremiah 1:12). So the resulting consequence of the rebelliousness of certain individuals documented in Scripture is simply the fulfillment of God's decree that the wages of sin is death. These individuals labored in sin, and they earned the paycheck for their work.

Scripture says that God cannot deny Himself (2 Timothy 2:13), so He is obligated to enforce the principles He has decreed for righteousness, truth, and judgment. It now seems like we are venturing into similar territory that we covered in chapter 7 in our perusal of longsuffering. There are certain things that God can— and must—do that we are unqualified to do. We must remember the priest's advice to Rudy, "There is a God... and I'm not Him,"[9] or to put it another way, this is in God's purview, not mine.

The reason we must leave judgment and retribution to God is because only He sees into the depths of a person's heart and knows what's in there. My information is limited and based solely on surface evidence, but God's Word is "living and active, sharper than any two-edged sword, piercing to the division of soul and of spirit, of joints and of marrow, and [discerns] the thoughts and intentions of the heart" (Hebrews 4:12). This makes Him the only One with sufficient information to pronounce a final verdict and impose a just punishment.

Be Angry and Sin Not

The Unknown Christian acknowledged in his writing that the Bible exhorts us, "Be angry without sinning" (Ephesians 4:26 GW). He astutely said that "we do well to be angry against sin, but never with the sinner. That anger which is against sin is without sin if coupled with love for the sinner."[10] This explains how it was not sin for Jesus to make a whip and use it to drive out the den of thieves from His Father's house. It also explains how it is no contradiction for God to be angry with sinners every day even though He loves them so much that He sent His only Son to die in their place.

When our children were small, they had to be taught not to run out into the street without first looking in both directions to check for oncoming cars. I'm also fairly certain that all four of them had to have this lesson reinforced at least once via a good ol' fashioned paddling. When they ran out into the street without looking, the tremendous love I had for them made me angry enough to want to *kill them*—once I knew they were safe. Even though I was angry with them, it did not alter the fact that I loved them. In fact, it was because of my love for them that I became angry with them.

Pièce de résistance

How does all this fit together, and what does it have to do with love not being provoked? As with all of the other qualities of love, it comes down to the nature of love. Love is always more concerned with the welfare of others than itself, which is why when the opportunity arises to become provoked, love considers the impact upon those around it. Christ is our example, and His love seeks reconciliation, redemption, and restoration, not retaliation and retribution. If I allow myself to be peeved and provoked by every trifling offense, then I limit God's ability to effectively use me as His minister of reconciliation to others, and the opportunity for Christ to be showcased in me is lost.

The common practice of the carnal man is to retaliate when provoked. When someone slaps us on the cheek, we want to slap them back, and yet Jesus said not to resist an evil person (Matthew 5:39). However, if we *resist* the temptation to respond in kind and instead demonstrate the longsuffering nature of Jesus, then what is revealed becomes the *Pièce de résistance*—a best, most outstanding manifestation of the love of Christ.

Camping Lesson

When I was a senior in high school, I had a front row seat to witness what it is like—literally—to be slapped on the cheek and not retaliate. My six closest buddies and I went camping one Saturday night, rolling out our sleeping bags within the safety of an alcove in Floyds Knobs, Indiana, several hundred feet above the Ohio River bank. That night, we were just seven ordinary coming-of-age boys out to have a good time drinking a few beers away from the watchful eyes of our parents.

I do not remember the exact details of how this incident unfolded, but after a few too many beers, my friends Brian and Greg got into an argument. I also don't remember what they were arguing about—it's not important. What is important, however, is that when things reached a boiling point, Greg slapped Brian across the face... *hard*. Absolute silence ensued as those of us looking on waited anxiously to see what would happen next.

> *When things reached a boiling point, Greg slapped Brian across the face... hard. Absolute silence ensued as those of us looking on waited anxiously to see what would happen next.*

To my astonishment, Brian just stood there. He said nothing. He did nothing.

Greg didn't know what to say, or do—nor did the five of us with ringside seats. I'm pretty certain, though, that like me the other guys were greatly relieved that Brian didn't strike back—because we were all really close friends and none of us wanted to see two of our buddies fighting. Within a matter of minutes, Greg apologized, and the two made up. Then the seven of us, tucked away in the security of that alcove, sat back and watched in fascination and awe as a thunderstorm rolled in and created an amazing lightshow for us before we slipped into our sleeping bags and fell asleep.

To this day, I don't know how Brian managed to restrain himself from striking back—I never asked him. But the image of him just standing there saying nothing was etched into my memory forever as a picture of what it looks like for love not to retaliate. Proverbs 15:1a says, "A soft answer turns away wrath." In this case, the answer was so soft it never even made a sound.

Last Word Concerning Pets

We began this chapter using a figure of speech to bring to light how easy it is to adopt a number of pet peeves over time, and that we should mercilessly kick these pets out of the house. It would be futile to try to address all of them, but you most likely already know which ones have made themselves at home in your heart.

I was with a group of friends a number of years ago, and we somehow found ourselves discussing our preferences for how toilet paper should be dispensed from the roll. Should it hang over the front of the roll or should it hang from the back? This is no doubt a burning question that will be debated by all future generations. One young man's perspective, however, silenced all the rhetoric that evening when he astutely said, "I'm just happy to find some paper on the roll."

For Further Study

"Be not quick in your spirit to become angry, for anger lodges in the heart of fools."
Ecclesiastes 7:9

1. What are the two primary reasons that people get provoked? Which is active and which is passive?
2. Make a list of your pet peeves. What do you need to do in order to stop feeding and caring for these pets?
3. What does it mean to girn, and have you ever been guilty of this?
4. Why is it difficult to do certain things without receiving recognition, even if it's only a simple "Thank you."?
5. Which is better, keeping your emotions bottled up on the inside or letting off steam so you don't internalize everything? What is better than either of these options?
6. How does God work through the criticism of others?
7. What explanation would you give as to why love is not provoked when the Bible clearly tells us God was provoked by the children of Israel?

13

Scoreboards, Journals, and Do-overs

"Love... keeps no record of wrongs."
1 Corinthians 13:4–5 (NIV)

I DON'T KNOW WHOSE IDEA THIS WAS or when it actually began, but since my childhood there has been a shift in youth sports to de-emphasize the scoreboard. It's not important who wins or loses, it's about having fun and learning the fundamentals of the game. That's what we seek to instill in our children, but anyone with even a shred of competitive spirit in them finds this maddening. Of course, you have to keep score; otherwise, you won't know who wins!

Here's a news flash for you: *Love does not keep score.* Or, as the New Century Bible (NCV) states in 1 Corinthians 13:5b, "Love does not count up wrongs that have been done."

I won't waste time making arguments for or against keeping score in youth sports. I'll leave that to young parents to sort out. However, this chapter is devoted to recognizing that quality of love that refuses to keep a stat sheet of the wrongs inflicted upon us by others. Imagine how ludicrous it would be if we kept statistics on the people we spend the most time with—family members, co-workers, and our brothers and sisters in Christ—breaking down the numbers of selfish and hurtful actions per day/week/month/year:

- Unkind remarks made
- Failed expectations
- Broken promises
- Times they were late
- Stupid decisions they made
- Times they gave you the silent treatment
- Other infractions

Keeping such a box score would be the pinnacle of foolishness as it relates to this topic, yet to some degree it's exactly what we do. Though we tend to do this subconsciously, an honest self-evaluation may reveal a conscious, deliberate harboring of a grudge or two. Christ was despised, rejected, misunderstood, wrongly accused, and unjustly put to death, yet on the cross He asked the Father to forgive His persecutors. He chose not

One of the more significant ways we build and maintain a Christlike character is by developing our forgiveness muscle.

to keep score. One of the more significant ways we build and maintain a Christlike character is by developing our forgiveness muscle, because walking in forgiveness guards our heart against keeping a record of wrongs. Paul exhorted the church at Ephesus with these words:

> Let all bitterness and wrath and anger and clamor and slander be put away from you, along with all malice. Be kind to one another, tenderhearted, forgiving one another, as God in Christ forgave you. (Ephesians 4:31–32)

Therein is the standard that must govern our hearts with respect to how we forgive others… *as God in Christ forgave us.* We are also to base how we love others on how we have been loved by Jesus: "This is my commandment, that you love one another *as*

I have loved you" (John 15:12, emphasis added). It is possible that no other characteristic more aptly depicts the nature of Jesus Christ than His forgiveness of sinners, and this potentially becomes the greatest challenge we face in our pursuit of becoming Christlike. In all of our interactions with skin folk we must consider how Christ has forgiven us, and extend the same grace and mercy to others that we have freely received from Him. Otherwise, we put ourselves in a precarious position. As noted by Confucius, "Those who cannot forgive others break the bridge over which they themselves must pass."[1]

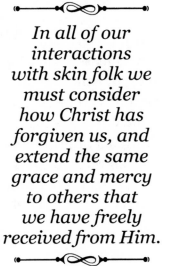

In all of our interactions with skin folk we must consider how Christ has forgiven us, and extend the same grace and mercy to others that we have freely received from Him.

New Math

In Matthew 18, Peter asks Jesus how many times he should forgive his brother for sinning against him. Peter seems to think that forgiving someone up to seven times would be beyond what even Jesus would expect, but Jesus responds with this hyperbole in answer to Peter's question: "I do not say to you, up to seven times, but up to seventy times seven" (Matthew 18:22 NKJV). By using such an exaggerated figure of speech, Jesus was teaching us a couple of things:

1. There is never a time when we stop forgiving someone—no matter how many times they have wronged us.
2. Anyone who is determined to keep count of such a ridiculous number of offenses has obviously never forgiven in the first place.

Jesus continues his lesson on forgiveness by telling a story about a servant who owed his master a huge sum of money. Upon the servant's pleading for mercy and additional time to repay a debt he could never pay, his master "was moved with compassion, released him, and forgave him the debt" (Matthew 18:27 NKJV). But the servant immediately went out and found a fellow servant who owed him just a few dollars and demanded repayment. When his fellow servant pleaded for mercy and requested additional time to repay his debt, the servant whose debt had been forgiven refused to show mercy and threw him into prison to satisfy the debt. When the master discovered what he had done, he issued this stern rebuke:

> "You wicked servant! I forgave you all that debt because you begged me. Should you not also have had compassion on your fellow servant, just as I had pity on you?" (Matthew 18:32–33 NKJV)

But the story doesn't end there. Jesus goes on to say that the servant's master became angry "and delivered him to the torturers until he should pay all that was due to him" (Matthew 18:34 NKJV). Jesus then punctuates the lesson with this bone-chilling statement, "So My heavenly Father also will do to you if each of you, from his heart, does not forgive his brother his trespasses" (v. 35 NKJV).

When we throw others into a debtor's prison created by our unforgiveness, we effectively end up shackling ourselves.

This lesson teaches us that when we throw others into a debtor's prison created by our unforgiveness, we effectively end up shackling ourselves. Although the meaning of this passage is perfectly clear in my mind, some interpret it euphemistically in order to soften its blow. Regardless of your interpretation, suffice it to say that refusing to forgive someone who has sinned against us makes our own standing with the Father tenuous at best, and at worst raises the possibility that God may rescind His forgiveness of us. And I will leave it to the reader to conclude the eternal ramifications of that.

No Exception Clause

How much pain we carry and how long we carry it is influenced by whether or not we choose to forgive in order to release the transgressor from an imprisonment of bitterness and resentment in our hearts. I realize I'm stating the obvious when I say that some transgressions are easier to forgive than others, but here's what we must come to grips with: no matter how heinous an offense may be—and some actions are so heartbreaking and egregiously vile as to test the uttermost limits of our faith—the love of God shed abroad in our hearts is greater than all bitterness, anger, hatred, and resentment, and it urges and obliges us to forgive the offender.

I have been unable to find anywhere in Scripture where we are excused from forgiving someone, even if the offense is notably nefarious. Yet some would assert that Jesus taught His disciples to forgive only when the person who has sinned repents (Luke 17:3–4). They purport that to forgive unconditionally (i.e., if the transgressor has not repented) is to cheapen the value of forgiveness and misrepresents God's forgiveness of us—because (they are quick to point out) God doesn't forgive anyone unless they first repent.

Hebrews 12:1 says we are surrounded by a great cloud of witnesses. My research of this topic suggests we are also surrounded by a great cloud of confusion. Famed photographer Ansel Adams said, "There is nothing worse than a sharp image of a fuzzy concept,"[2] which is why I think it is worth the time and effort to clear up some of the misconceptions that potentially blur the truth about forgiveness.

In no way is it my intent to marginalize the importance of repentance for sin—and I am absolutely not teaching nor am I endorsing universal reconciliation. However, categorically requiring someone to repent before *we* forgive them is a position that is untenable and, as I intend to show, logistically becomes unmanageable and contradictory to Paul's teaching that love keeps no record of wrongs. This is no doubt a difficult topic to exegete, but the following six points serve to provide a holistic view of Scripture to aid us in acquiring a proper understanding:

1. "Father, Forgive Them"

Luke's gospel account tells us that Jesus uttered these words on the cross, "Father, forgive them, for they know not what they do" (Luke 23:34). No one as of yet had repented for crucifying the Son of God, yet Jesus asked the Father to forgive them. Jesus did not literally say, "Father, *I* forgive them," but isn't it a bit ridiculous to think that Jesus would ask the Father to extend forgiveness while withholding it Himself? "Father, I sure hope *You* can forgive them, because I'm unable to since they haven't repented yet." The same can be said of Stephen's dying words when he was stoned, "Lord, do not hold this sin against them" (Acts 7:60). Does it make any sense to think Stephen was not also forgiving them, even as he breathed his last?

2. To Forgive, or Not To Forgive, That Is the Question

Luke 17 begins as follows:

> And he said to his disciples, "Temptations to sin are sure to come, but woe to the one through whom they come! It would be better for him if a millstone were hung around his neck and he were cast into the sea than that he should cause one of these little ones to sin. Pay attention to yourselves! If your brother sins, rebuke him, and if he repents, forgive him, and if he sins against you seven times in the day, and turns to you seven times, saying, 'I repent,' you must forgive him." (Luke 17:1–4)

In verses 3 and 4 Jesus describes a situation where the offender has come in repentance to seek forgiveness. In such cases, we are clearly obliged to forgive them. However, it is a mistake to infer from this passage that if the offender does not repent we are equally obliged to withhold forgiveness. In these verses—even if we doubt the sincerity of their repentance—Jesus is clearly instructing us to forgive; He's not laying out a prescription for withholding forgiveness.

Many scenarios could be enumerated where the sinner/offender is simply never going to repent and seek forgiveness, and this makes withholding forgiveness problematic.

Mark's gospel suggests that repentance is not a constant in the forgiveness equation, especially in the *horizontal relationship* of people forgiving people. In Mark 11, Jesus uses a withered fig tree as an object lesson to teach the disciples about faith and forgiveness:

> As they passed by in the morning, they saw the fig tree withered away to its roots. And Peter remembered and said to him, "Rabbi, look! The fig tree that you cursed has withered." And Jesus answered them, "Have faith in God. Truly, I say to you, whoever says to this mountain, 'Be taken up and thrown into the sea,' and does not doubt in his heart, but believes that what he says will come to pass, it will be done for him. Therefore I tell you, whatever you ask in prayer, believe that you have received it, and it will be yours. And whenever you stand praying, forgive, if you have anything against anyone, so that your Father also who is in heaven may forgive you your trespasses." (Mark 11:20–25)

There's nothing in Mark's writing that suggests we should only forgive someone after they have repented. Jesus simply says we are to forgive if we have *anything against anyone.*

Luke and Mark are in perfect agreement with each other because they both teach that we should forgive, not that we should ever withhold forgiveness. Luke simply points out what is altogether obvious: If someone sins—and repents—*tell them* that you forgive them. I have no problem conceding that if someone does not repent, it is okay not to *tell them* you forgive them, but between you and the Lord, you must forgive them if you expect your Father in heaven to forgive you.

Craig Groeschel, in his book *The Christian Atheist*, tells a poignant real-life story that lends credence and plausibility to the argument for extending forgiveness in the absence of repentance.

Craig's baby sister, Lisa, by God's design was born on Craig's third birthday. They developed a special bond, and as they grew Craig assumed the role of protector, always looking out for his little sis.

Blindsided by the news, Craig was devastated when he learned that his little sister had been molested for years by a man named Max, who had been her sixth-grade teacher, and was also a close friend of their family. Craig wanted nothing more than for Max to die and suffer an eternal torment. In his personal account of the story, Craig confessed, "Although the words *rage, hate,* and *revenge* come to mind when I think about Max, the English language simply doesn't have a word for what I felt."[3]

Craig understood the concept of forgiveness, but there was no way he could begin to consider forgiving Max for something so despicable. Although Craig acknowledged the bitter hatred that began to grow in his heart, he felt completely justified to hate Max the way he did. Craig described himself at this point in the story as a Christian Atheist—someone who believes in God but lives as if He doesn't exist. In this specific instance, living as if God doesn't exist meant refusing to forgive.

Craig described how he fed the root of bitterness in his heart, "Love keeps no record of wrongs, but bitterness keeps detailed accounts. And that's what I did. Over and over I played the story in my mind. Each time I pictured Max, my hatred grew."[4] Sound familiar? I suspect it will resonate deeply with some who read this.

Sometime later, Max developed muscular dystrophy, and Craig naturally concluded this was God's punishment for what Max had done. But as he found himself celebrating Max's crippling disease, he knew it was time for a heart check.

Craig tells of how one Sunday morning his "pastor preached a convicting message on forgiveness, explaining how we should release those who've wronged us."[5] Everything within Craig resisted forgiving and releasing Max. It just wasn't right. It couldn't be right. God nevertheless slowly began to chip away at his hard heart. Over a period of weeks and months, Craig finally managed to pray this "grudging but obedient three-second prayer: 'God, I pray you work in his life.'"[6]

As Craig continued praying that prayer, he eventually began to mean it, and he describes the change that began to occur within him, "Praying for Max over time changed me. It made me a different person, so different that I began to contemplate the impossible: asking God to help me forgive Max."[7] But he continued to be torn between wanting to obey God and wanting to continue hating Max.

Craig's heart was stone cold, and he knew only God could soften it to the point where he could actually forgive his sister's molester. He continues, "Miraculously, that's what God did. To this day, I don't know exactly how or when it happened. But it did. By God's grace, I had forgiven Max for his sin and abuse. With God's help I'd done the humanly impossible, and I felt as though a spiritual weight had been lifted."[8]

Craig then took the next step of writing a letter to Max expressing his forgiveness. He explained how much God had forgiven him (Craig), and shared the story of Jesus and His love for us. He told Max that he had forgiven him and that God could also forgive him. He also included a short prayer that Max could pray to repent for his sins and receive forgiveness.

Craig had no idea that Max's sickness had progressed to the point at which he was now under the care of a hospice nurse. Months after Max's passing, his nurse sent Craig's family a letter asking if she could talk to them. They agreed to meet with her, and they listened intently as she told them about the last days of Max's life. Craig punctuates the ending of this story as follows:

> The caregiver explained that Max's eyesight had deteriorated and that he had asked her to read him my note. Although she wasn't aware of what he had done (and I never told her), it was obvious to her that he had done something grievously wrong. According to the nurse, he listened with tears streaming down his face. He asked her to pray the prayer with him. She recalled that his whole countenance changed as he asked Christ to forgive him and make him new. He died a few days later.[9]

I fail to see in this story how forgiveness was devalued in any way by Craig's willingness to extend forgiveness before hearing a confession of repentance from Max. One could almost make an argument that the exact opposite occurred: forgiveness was viewed as a most undeserved, yet precious gift, which was ultimately received amid tears of repentance.

3. Timing Is Everything

Though not universally agreed upon by all Bible scholars, the New King James and other versions of the Bible translate Revelation 13:8 in such a way as to suggest that God counted Jesus Christ, the Lamb of God, as having been *slain* (implying the provision of *atonement, reconciliation,* and *forgiveness*) before the creation of the world:

> And all who dwell on the earth will worship him [the beast], whose names have not been written in the Book of Life of *the Lamb slain from the foundation of the world.* (Revelation 13:8 NKJV, emphasis added).

In Peter's first epistle, he appears to support this notion when he says in chapter 1, verses 18–20 that we were redeemed by the precious blood of Christ, as of a lamb without blemish or spot who was indeed *"foreordained before the foundation of the world,* but was manifest in these last times for you" (1 Peter 1:20 NKJV). Peter makes it clear that although the physical offering of the Lamb of God as a sacrifice for sin occurred at a specific point in time (i.e., *these last times),* in the mind of God our redemption was provided for and completed before He ever uttered the words, "Let there be...." It's almost as if God said, "Let there be a provision of redemption and reconciliation before I create the earth or anything else."

So from God's perspective, *when* was I pardoned? *When* was I reconciled? *When* was my debt of sin paid for in full? *When* was I forgiven? Do we still not know the answer? Let us then consider Paul's writing to the church in Rome:

> For if while we were enemies we were reconciled to God by the death of his Son, much more, now that we are reconciled, shall we be saved by his life. (Romans 5:10)

Here, we find the answer—in unmistakable language: *while we were enemies we were reconciled to God by the death of His Son.* Paul tells us in 2 Corinthians 5:18–19 that God was in Christ reconciling the world to Himself. God transacted with Himself on the cross to reconcile us before we ever uttered one word of repentance. This, of course, is not meant to imply that repentance is unnecessary to experience the *reality* of being reconciled to God. The ministry and message of reconciliation referred to by Paul in 2 Corinthians 5:18–19 most certainly includes repentance, but we find something even more poignant in this passage:

> All this is from God, who through Christ reconciled us to himself and gave us the ministry of reconciliation; that is, in Christ God was reconciling the world

to himself, not counting their trespasses against them, and entrusting to us the message of reconciliation. (2 Corinthians 5:18–19)

When he says that "*in Christ* God was reconciling the world to himself, not counting their trespasses against them," does this not remove all doubt as to *when* this occurred in the mind of God? And, equally important, if God is no longer counting their trespasses against them, then why are we? Love does not keep score.

4. Receiving the Gift

Let us now take a look at the difference between being unconditionally forgiven and receiving that forgiveness.

Before I can be born from above, I must recognize I am a sinner and that Christ is the only One who can save me. At that point, repentance from sin, belief in Christ's atoning sacrifice, and His resurrection from the dead become the doorway by which I enter into a relationship with Jesus Christ. The book of Hebrews offers emphatic testimony that Christ's once-for-all sacrifice has atoned for all my sins—past, present, and future (see Hebrews 7:27; 9:12, 25–28; and 10:10–18).

This does not imply, however, that I can live a careless, sin-indulgent life, based on the knowledge that my future sins have already been atoned for (Romans 6:1). Nor does it suggest that I don't need to immediately repent and ask for forgiveness if I knowingly sin after my conversion to faith in Christ. But neither

The problem with making categorical statements such as, "God only forgives us when we repent," is that it suggests for the believer a relationship with God akin to walking through a minefield for the rest of a person's life— one misstep, one failure to repent of a specific sin, and outer darkness awaits.

must I live in fear that I will be lost for eternity if I sin unknowingly and fail to repent for a specific sin.

The problem with making categorical statements such as, "God only forgives us when we repent," is that it suggests *for the believer* a relationship with God akin to walking through a minefield for the rest of a person's life—one misstep, one failure to repent of a specific sin, and outer darkness awaits where there is weeping and gnashing of teeth. Such a view contradicts the very spirit of what we read in Romans 5:10, "Much more, now that we are reconciled, shall we be saved by his life."

Again, if this sounds like I'm discounting or disregarding the importance or necessity of repentance, I assure you that is not the case. I am simply making the point that repenting of a sinful nature and a life of sin prior to the new birth, and repenting for sins committed after I have entered into a saving relationship with Jesus Christ serve two different purposes. The first enables me to experience the reality of being reconciled to God thereby entering into a right relationship with the Father and His Son, whereas the second serves to restore fellowship with God if I sin. Without the first, I will never become a member of God's family; but once saved, although a specific occurrence of sin may disrupt my fellowship with God, it does not change the relationship. I remain His son and He remains my Father, even as the prodigal remained a son while his father watched with longing for his return from the hog lot (Luke 15:11–24).

5. Forgiveness versus Reconciliation

I'm convinced that some of the confusion surrounding this topic stems from conflating our understanding of forgiveness and reconciliation and treating them as synonymous when, in fact, they are not. According to Dictionary.com, to *forgive*[10] means: "1) to grant pardon for or remission of (an offense, debt, etc.); absolve, 2) to give up all claim on account of... 4) to cease to feel resentment against," whereas to *reconcile*[11] with someone means: "1) to win over to friendliness; cause to become amicable; 2) to bring into agreement or harmony; make compatible or consistent; 3) to restore."

I can choose to pardon, to give up all claims against others, and to cease feeling resentment toward them without becoming friends with them, coming into agreement or harmony with them, or being restored to fellowship with them. Many times, however, forgiveness is the first step toward reconciliation. And if repentance precedes the act of forgiveness, so much the better! There is no doubt in my mind that repentance is a necessary key to reconciliation and restoration of fellowship in relationships that have become strained due to sin.

6. The Letter Kills, but the Spirit Gives Life

Luke's gospel account (9:52b–56) tells of how Jesus and the disciples entered a village of the Samaritans, but were not received by the people because His face was set toward Jerusalem. This evidently offended James and John, so they said, "Lord, do you want us to command fire to come down from heaven and consume them, just as Elijah did?" Not impressed, Jesus turned and rebuked them, "You do not know what manner of spirit you are of. For the Son of Man did not come to destroy men's lives but to save them" (Luke 9:54–56 NKJV).

To anyone who insists upon withholding forgiveness apart from repentance or an apology, I would ask you to consider if that is in keeping with the spirit of Jesus, who came not to destroy men's lives but to save them. Would you rather imprison the unrepentant in your heart or forgive them, and let God sort out the rest? Harboring unforgiveness can only contribute to tearing down men's lives, not saving them.

Alexander the Not-So-Great

Paul wrote to Timothy about Alexander the coppersmith who, Paul said, "did me great harm; the Lord will repay him according to his deeds. Beware of him yourself, for he strongly opposed our message" (2 Timothy 4:14–15).

For those who may be wondering about Paul's remembrance of Alexander the coppersmith and the great harm done by him, it is worth noting that Paul said, "The Lord will repay him." Paul was clearly not vindictive but was leaving this in God's hands to deal with. Moreover, it appears from verse 15 that rather than keeping a record of wrongs, Paul is simply warning Timothy of this man's potential to be disruptive and hinder the proclamation of the gospel. I see this as similar to a person being wronged by another person and simply warning others to be cautious around that same individual. Just because I'm warning others doesn't mean I am keeping a record of the offense and holding it over someone's head. I'm simply being circumspect and offering prudent advice.

The Little Black Book

The mind is a beautiful—and mysterious—thing. The ability to remember events is something to treasure, although memories are a collection of things pleasant and painful. Choosing to forgive someone does not erase the memory bank, and that can easily lead to confusion as to whether or not I have sincerely forgiven them.

While discussing this topic of forgiveness with my daughter Kristen, she shared an insight with me that she had heard concerning what it means to forgive: *to forgive means that I accept the consequences of another's actions and choose to move forward with my life without harboring hatred or resentment toward the individual who wronged me.*

> *To forgive means that I accept the consequences of another's actions and choose to move forward with my life without harboring hatred or resentment toward the individual who wronged me.*

This implicitly means I choose not to keep a record of past hurts, even if the memory of those hurts triggers a recurrence of the emotional pain associated with them.

Let us now consider in practical terms the notion of keeping a record of wrongs—what it means and how to avoid it. Keeping a record of wrongs is similar to keeping a diary or journal. Keeping a diary involves intentionally documenting personal experiences, events, and observations *for the express purpose of remembering them at a later date and time.*

Remembering events—logging them, if you will—is something our mind does subconsciously. It's completely involuntary, and the more emotional the experience is, the more likely it gets stamped into our memory. Keeping a record of wrongs is the equivalent of writing them in a "little black book," only this book is without pen and paper. It occurred to me one day how frequently I got out my little black book to thumb through its pages and rehash select experiences. Without realizing it, I was feeding something I should have been starving.

Not long after picturing this mental image of the little black book, I concluded it was time to surrender mine to the Lord. When memories of offenses would surface in my mind, I would literally pray something to the effect of, "Lord, I refuse to keep a record of this wrong. Here's the book. I surrender it to you. Please take it and destroy it. I will not continue to rehearse this or hold anything against this person."

When a situation triggers a reminder of wrongs against us, love chooses to hand over the book instead of ruminating on the tasty delicacies of the past. Paul wrote these liberating

It occurred to me one day how frequently I got out my little black book to thumb through its pages and rehash select experiences. Without realizing it, I was feeding something I should have been starving.

words to the church at Colossae concerning the record of charges against us:

> And you, who were dead in your trespasses and the uncircumcision of your flesh, God made alive together with him, having forgiven us all our trespasses, by *canceling the record of debt that stood against us* with its legal demands. This he set aside, nailing it to the cross. (Colossians 2:13–14, emphasis added)

When we put these same words into practice and cancel the record of wrongs we hold against others, we are now truly becoming Christlike. However, this presents another conundrum to solve. If God is love and love keeps no record of wrongs, then we can logically conclude that God keeps no record of wrongs. *Au contraire.* As logical as that may seem (If A=B and B=C, then A=C), Scripture as a whole does not support that rationale.

Once again, I am going to invoke what I will now simply refer to as the "Rudy clause": *There is a God… and I'm not Him.* Or as David said, "I don't concern myself with matters too great or too awesome for me to grasp" (Psalm 131:1 NLT).

There are certain things that God can—and must—do, but are simply off-limits for me. Keeping a record of wrongs is one of them. As noted by Solomon, "The eyes of the Lord are in every place, keeping watch on the evil and the good" (Proverbs 15:3). God knows everything we've done and everything we are yet to do, and He *does* keep detailed accounts in order to determine just judgment (Matthew 25:31–46) and distribute righteous rewards (2 Corinthians 5:10). However, even though God knows the wrongs we've done, He doesn't hold them against us. For those who believe in the finished work of the cross and have had their sins washed away by the blood of Christ, there is no condemnation (Romans 8:1); there is no longer a remembrance of sins (Hebrews 10:3).

The Do-over

The concept of the do-over was an implicit rule in all my childhood backyard games. It was most often invoked whenever competing sides could not agree on the outcome of a call. Was the ball fair or foul? Did the guy travel with the basketball or not? Did he drop the football or was it a catch? In the absence of a consensus, the ruling was simple: *it's a do-over*. The do-over settled all disputes. You simply acted like the previous play never happened. In golf, this is called a *mulligan*. It is grace to replay the previous shot without penalty.

Love approaches a situation that has some history as though that history did not exist.

The NKJV renders 1 Corinthians 13:5b as love "thinks no evil." Until now, we've only examined this verse from the perspective of not keeping a record of wrongs (i.e., not keeping score). However, these two thoughts represent something of a corollary. The reason love thinks no evil toward another person is that it has no record of wrongs previously inflicted by that person. In other words, love approaches a situation that has some history as though that history did not exist.

Stated another way, if similar circumstances arise wherein I was previously offended, irritated, frustrated, or wronged, I must be willing to approach the situation as though there were a blank slate and essentially give the other person a do-over. A do-over in this context is an extension of grace that gives the individual the opportunity to do one of two things:

1. Get it right this time.
2. Offend me again.

Expressions like, "You always..." and "You never..." are key indicators that we are keeping detailed accounts of the wrongs we have suffered. But love doesn't assume or expect—because of past history—that the person will say the same things or repeat the same behavior. Love gives the other person the benefit of the doubt and says, "Instead of pre-judging the outcome of this conversation, situation, or circumstance, I'm going to give them the opportunity to get it right this time. And if they don't, then I trust God for the grace to be longsuffering and forbearing."

Now before we go any further with this line of thought, we must pause long enough to clarify what is—and what is not—being said here. Jesus said we are to "be wise as serpents and innocent as doves" (Matthew 10:16), and Paul echoed this thought when he said, "Look carefully then how you walk, not as unwise but as wise" (Ephesians 5:15). If you are in an abusive situation that is endangering your safety, I am not suggesting you should give others an opportunity to repeatedly abuse or harm you

> *Expressions like, "You always..." and "You never..." are key indicators that we are keeping detailed accounts of the wrongs we have suffered.*

as though they had never done so in the past. Rather, you should be wise, listen to God, and *do what He tells you to do*, which could mean that you distance yourself from them and seek safety with others. You may even need to contact the proper authorities to report the abuse.

Time for the Old Dog to Learn a New Trick

It is one thing to cultivate the habit of keeping no record of wrongs, but how many of us are eager to look for the best in others? Jesus said, "And if anyone forces you to go one mile, go with him two miles" (Matthew 5:41). As cited in *The Christlike Christian*, Samuel Chadwick once said, "I hate to think the worst of others when I might think the best."[12] There always seems to be more to the story than we know—two sides to the same proverbial coin—yet we often zero in on the negative and assume the worst about a person. The Unknown Christian penned these convicting words for us to ponder:

> It is so easy for self to creep into the soul and lead to a miserable readiness to censure, criticize, and depreciate others. Even those who have received great blessing from God may be defiled before they are aware of it. It is only hateful vanity and conceit of our own superiority that leads us to think ill or speak ill of others. Or is it that we feel ourselves better when we prove others to be worse? It is, of course, only a delusion, for we steadily go down in the opinion of those who listen to our unkind remarks.[13]

The Unknown Christian continues his exhortation by saying, "Love [doesn't] just coldly [ignore] an injury. If we love we shall not merely not strike back, but we shall love back, as one puts it.... To influence people for good we must not only love them, but believe in them—must expect great things of them. And how delightful it is to feel that we are not searchers after evil, but seekers after good in others!"[14]

The Conclusion?

Keeping a record of wrongs fosters within me a bitter spirit, which is contrary to Christ, and when I hold the record of the past over people's heads, it causes me to pre-judge how they will act. That bias makes it nearly impossible to extend grace to them for a clean slate do-over. Since Christ has canceled the record of my wrongs, how can I justify keeping a record of the wrongs of others?

It will undoubtedly take much grace and the work of the Holy Spirit to come to the place where we can treat each person and situation as though there were no prior history—especially if a person has a longstanding proclivity toward a certain ill behavior. Regardless, no matter how many times we have been hurt, wronged, or offended by the same person, the love of Christ within us—if we yield to it—will enable us to forgive the individual and extend grace to them. You never know when they might surprise you and actually get it right. Likewise, if we were to flip this around on ourselves... we might discover that we also are in need of some do-over grace in some particular area(s) of our lives. It's time we stop keeping score, hand over our ledger to the Lord, and ask Him to help us go that extra mile to begin thinking the best of others instead of the worst. Doing so will keep our hearts free from bitterness and foster within us a greater understanding of those things in which love delights.

For Further Study

"Lord, do not hold this sin against them."
Acts 7:60

1. What lesson was Jesus teaching Peter in Matthew 18:21-22?
2. Discuss the possible ramifications of withholding forgiveness from others. What does God think of that, and how might that affect our standing with Him?
3. In what circumstance or scenario does the Bible encourage us to withhold forgiveness?
4. True or False: We are only supposed to forgive after the offender has repented. Be prepared to support your position.
5. Why does love keep no record of wrongs?
6. What is the difference between forgiveness and reconciliation?
7. Explain the following concepts as they pertain to keeping track of offenses:
   • The "little black book"
   • The do-over

14

Joseph and Mrs. P.

"Love does not delight in evil but rejoices with the truth."
1 Corinthians 13:6 (NIV)

THERE ARE SO MANY THINGS in which to delight, and no shortage of reasons to rejoice. You may delight in chocolate, or walking along a beach with the warm ocean breeze blowing in your face. You may rejoice at the birth of a child, or in receiving a long-awaited promotion or an unexpected raise in pay. Paul, however, makes a curious statement as to what love delights in and what it rejoices with. He tells us love does *not* delight in evil, but it does rejoice with the truth.

Since love does not delight in evil, we can presumably say that love delights in what is good. We are also told that love rejoices with the truth, so we can safely conclude that love would never celebrate falsehood or dishonest dealings. It is also reasonable to say that love would never compromise truth for the sake of expediency or selfish advantage. After much prayer and waiting on the Lord, I came to understand better what this sixth verse in 1 Corinthians 13 represents in the life of a Christian. Though this verse speaks to us on

> *Integrity is of such consequence in the life of a Christian that to violate it is to forfeit a good name and effectively perpetuate the list of excuses that many give for not following Christ.*

several levels, its primary message can be summed up in a single word: *integrity.*

Someone once said, "Honesty is the best policy."

"Not so fast," said another. "Honesty is the *only* policy."

Love does not bend the rules or skim off the top to lower its tax bill or pad its wallet. Love knows only one scale—a just scale. These Proverbs of Solomon describe how seriously God takes this matter of honesty and integrity:

> A just balance and scales are the LORD's; all the weights in the bag are his work. (Proverbs 16:11)

> Unequal weights are an abomination to the LORD, and false scales are not good. (Proverbs 20:23)

> A false balance is an abomination to the LORD, but a just weight is his delight. (Proverbs 11:1)

This scale Solomon speaks of is a metaphor that applies to more than simply business dealings. The above verses tell us that God is concerned with "all the weights in the bag," not just a few. Every aspect of my conduct is important to Him. He is concerned with how I do my job, how I prepare my tax return, and how I honor my marriage vows. He watches to see whether I will record all the strokes for my team, or write down a lower number in order to win a golf scramble. He detests double standards, and a false balance (scale) is an abomination to Him. These are strong words, and should not be taken lightly. Yet juxtaposed with His disdain for dishonesty is His delight in those who deal

Some—even professing Christians—use the Bible to support their ungodly choices rather than searching for the light of truth to illuminate the path of righteousness before them.

236

justly, and in order to deal justly one must be truthful, which also requires that one must not delight in evil.

Integrity Personified

Joseph has always been my favorite biblical character. We can learn so much from this young man's life, from how he handled adversity to how he responded to temptation, and how he was possibly the greatest project manager, overseer, and governor who ever lived. No matter who or where he served, he quickly earned the reputation for being implicitly trustworthy and faithful in his management and oversight of everything he was entrusted with. From Potiphar to the prison warden to the Pharaoh himself, none feared that Joseph would ever deviate from his integrity or abuse his office, no matter how punitive or privileged his circumstances. His unwavering integrity and faithfulness to God amid some of the most troubling and discouraging circumstances make him one of the most inspirational and exemplary figures in all of Scripture.

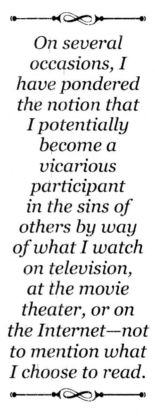

On several occasions, I have pondered the notion that I potentially become a vicarious participant in the sins of others by way of what I watch on television, at the movie theater, or on the Internet—not to mention what I choose to read.

When faced with the temptation to lie with Potiphar's wife, Joseph refused to "do such a wicked thing and sin against God" (Genesis 39:9b NIV). When Mrs. P. falsely accused him of trying to force himself upon her, he immediately found himself in a no-win situation. He could not accuse her to his master concerning her unrelenting sexual advances. For a slave to make such an accusation would have resulted in certain punishment; and to capitulate to her wishes would have likely meant death—given the fact that he was immediately imprisoned based solely on the false accusation of an *attempt* to lie with Mrs. P. Whether considering such consequences or not, Joseph refused to violate the moral compass God had placed within him. He did not know it at the time, but his path to becoming the governor over all of Egypt and a savior to the nation of Israel was about to take a turn for the worse because of his resolute integrity.

Lesser men would have tried to find a way to justify having an affair with Mrs. P. Andrew Lang, a Scottish poet, novelist, and literary critic (1844–1912) is generally credited for saying, "[Some people] use statistics like a drunken man uses lamp-posts... for support rather than for illumination."[1] Sad as it is, some—even professing Christians—use the Bible in a similar manner. They search for verses to support their ungodly choices rather than searching for the light of truth to illuminate the path of righteousness before them. I know this to be true, because there was a time many years ago when I was that lesser man who searched the Scriptures to find a way to justify leaving my wife for another woman. Yet the goodness of God shown to me through loving counsel, confrontation, and much prayerful intercession pulled me back from the precipice of destruction. God did for our marriage what all the king's horses and all the king's men could not do for Humpty Dumpty— He put us back together again! As of this writing, Mindy and I recently celebrated thirty-seven years together, but it would be a glaring omission not to point out that this is also largely due to the fact that Mindy is such a great forgiver. Robert Quillen, journalist and cartoonist (1887–1948), once said, "A happy marriage is the union of two good forgivers."[2] After all, what is love, and what is it to be Christlike if not to forgive?

"I Could Be Persuaded to Partake..."

Paul wrote many things to Timothy, his son in the faith, concerning his conduct and oversight of the church. One such charge reads:

"Do not be hasty in the laying on of hands, nor take part in the sins of others; keep yourself pure" (1 Timothy 5:22).

One of the ways we keep ourselves pure is by not partaking in the sins of others. This is another facet of love's refusal to delight in evil, setting apart the Christlike Christian from the un-Christlike.

At the end of Acts chapter 7, Luke chronicles the stoning of Stephen, the first Christian martyr. He tells us that those who dragged Stephen out of the city and stoned him "laid down their garments at the feet of a young man named Saul" (Acts 7:58). Luke goes on to say, "Saul approved of his execution" (Acts 8:1)—though his account suggests that Saul did not throw a single stone. The King James Version says it like this: "And Saul was consenting unto his death."

By condoning this act, Saul was just as guilty of Stephen's death as those who threw the stones—his own writings attesting to this fact (Acts 22:4; Acts 26:9–11; 1 Corinthians 15:9). On several occasions, I have pondered the notion that I potentially become a vicarious participant in the sins of others by way of what I watch on television, at the movie theater, or on the Internet—not to mention what I choose to read. By consenting to watch or read a particular thing, it would seem that I approve of the content.

I will not be presenting you with a list of rules to govern what you can or cannot set before your eyes—you will have to sort that out with the Lord. Such matters of faith and conscience are between the believer and the Lord, as Paul made clear to the church at Rome:

> The faith that you have, keep between yourself and God. Blessed is the one who has no reason to pass judgment on himself for what he approves. (Romans 14:22)

Psalm 101 is a record of David's resolute prayer to be a man of integrity who does not delight in evil—especially in his home:

I will ponder the way that is blameless. Oh when will you come to me? I will walk with integrity of heart within my house; *I will not set before my eyes anything that is worthless.* I hate the work of those who fall away; it shall not cling to me. A perverse heart shall be far from me; I will know nothing of evil. (Psalm 101:2–4, emphasis added)

Let's take a closer look at two of the words in the above italicized text. David declared he would not *set* anything *worthless* before his eyes. Of the definitions given for the word *set* on the website blueletterbible.org, one seems to convey most accurately how this word is used in Psalm 101:3a: "to set, station, appoint, fix, set mind to."[3] Not only is there the sense of literally gazing upon something with our eyes, but also the notion of setting our mind on it—entertaining it in our thoughts, giving place and consideration to it. Of course, anything we see with our eyes has the potential to be replayed in the theater of our mind. This same Hebrew word is used in Proverbs 24:32 where Solomon describes passing by the field of a sluggard and the resulting impact it had upon him: "Then I saw and *considered* it; I looked and received instruction" (emphasis added).

According to blueletterbible.org, the word *worthless* in Psalm 101:3 comes from the Hebrew word for belial[4] and is translated as *wicked* in the KJV. In his exposition of Psalm 101 from *The Treasury of David*, Charles Spurgeon provides this commentary on the King James rendering of Psalm 101 verse 3a:

I will set no wicked thing before mine eyes. I will [not] delight in it, aim at it, or endure it. If I have wickedness brought before me by others I will turn away from it, I will not gaze upon it with pleasure. The psalmist is very sweeping in his resolve, he declines the least, the most reputable, the most customary form of evil—no wicked thing; not only shall it not dwell in his heart, but not even before his eyes, for what fascinates the eye is very apt to gain admission into the heart, even as [the fruit] first pleased [Eve's] sight and then prevailed over her mind and hand.[5]

When people are enticed to indulge in something they know goes against their better judgment, they often respond in jest by saying, "I could be persuaded to partake." As Spurgeon aptly points out, Eve was first drawn to the forbidden fruit because it was pleasing to the eye. It was the ultimate fatal attraction.

As marvelous as technology is, it makes us privy to things we would otherwise know nothing about. Before the days of mass media, news traveled slowly. Rarely did anyone know much of what went on in other parts of the world beyond their own town or burg. Today, information travels at the speed of light (or at least satellite).

We might as well be standing beneath the same tree in the same garden being offered the same fruit by the same devil.

On many mornings before going to work, I log about thirty minutes on an elliptical machine situated in front of twelve TV screens in my local fitness center. I am fascinated by how much information is presented to me in those thirty minutes, ranging from local news to national news to infomercials, sports analysis, history, weather, and so on. Those who market this news/ information know exactly how to manipulate their audience with teasers designed to pique our curiosity so we will continue tuning in, gobbling up whatever they are serving. We might as well be standing beneath the same tree in the same garden being offered the same fruit by the same devil. Wouldn't you have to agree that we are still feasting—gorging ourselves, in fact—on the fruit from the tree of the knowledge of good and evil?

It's been said that knowledge is power. Indeed, some knowledge is good and useful. But we would simply be better off not knowing some things, which perhaps makes Solomon's words more relevant today than ever before: "For in much wisdom is much vexation, and he who increases knowledge increases sorrow" (Ecclesiastes 1:18).

Soon after I became a Christian I questioned the fairness of God in allowing Adam's sin to be passed to all mankind. I was certain that if *I* had been the first Adam I would never have eaten from *that* tree. *Please*... I suggest that God imputed Adam's sin to the rest of us for the sake of efficiency. He knew we would all make the same choice, so He just cut to the chase—knowing also that He had already provisioned a Lamb to atone for our sin problem, long before He ever created mankind.

A Lesson in German

The final aspect we will consider with regard to 1 Corinthians 13:6a is its refusal to rejoice in the failures or misfortunes of others. Love does not delight in any form of "evil" be it sin or wickedness; neither does it derive pleasure when something bad happens to another person—even if that person is our enemy. Proverbs 24:17–18 says, "Do not rejoice when your enemy falls, and let not your heart be glad when he stumbles, lest the LORD see it and be displeased...."

Schadenfreude is a word of German origin that aptly encapsulates the above passage from the book of Proverbs. According to Dictionary.com, *schadenfreude* means to "delight in another's misfortune."[6] We see this often in the world of sports, as evidenced by the following example.

> *Love does not rejoice when something bad happens to another person, even if that person is our enemy.*

The University of Louisville's football program has gained national respect over the last decade or so, although it is still not among the elite programs. For most college football coaches, the head coaching job at Louisville remains a stepping-stone opportunity rather than a destination. Charlie Strong became the head coach in

2010, and transformed Louisville into a top-fifteen program over a four-year span. Before leaving for the top job at the University of Texas, Strong led the Cardinals to a 37–15 record and reached a bowl game each season, including a 33–23 victory over the Florida Gators in the 2012 Sugar Bowl and a 36–9 pounding of the Miami Hurricanes in the 2013 Russell Athletic Bowl.

Cardinal fans were understandably disappointed and upset when Strong left Louisville for a position that some consider to be one of the premier head coaching jobs in all of college football. But some fans allowed their displeasure to manifest as *schadenfreude* when Brigham Young thumped Texas 41–7 on September 6, 2014, handing Charlie Strong his first loss as coach of the Longhorns. Adam Himmelsbach of the Louisville *Courier-Journal* newspaper confirmed this in his article on September 8, 2014 when he wrote, "For some people around Louisville, it seemed, it was a source of delight. . . . Still, the celebratory tenor raises questions about the act of rooting for a person to fail."[7] It certainly does.

It is much more in keeping with the nature of love to rejoice in the successes of others instead of their failures. Love doesn't celebrate when someone stumbles and falls. Love doesn't say things like, "It serves them right. I'm so glad they got beat," or "I'm so glad that player got hurt." Such an attitude would reflect a selfishly perverse delight bordering on malice, while also bringing the probability of self-injury into play. As noted by Solomon in Proverbs 17:6, "he who is glad at calamity will not go unpunished."

Paul wrote to the church in Rome that we are to "Rejoice with those who rejoice [and] weep with those who weep" (Romans 12:15). Love not only shares in the joy of triumph and accomplishment, but also in the sadness and grief that accompany failure and loss.

That said, you will naturally be happy when your team wins, which by definition means you will also rejoice in the opposing team's loss. The two thoughts/emotions are inseparable. Still, love does not wish harm or misfortune on anyone, or take pleasure in it when it happens.

Now that we've explained that caveat, we also need to understand that a time is coming when the righteous *will rejoice* at the outpouring of God's judgments and avenging of the blood of his servants:

> After this I heard what seemed to be the loud voice of a great multitude in heaven, crying out, "Hallelujah! Salvation and glory and power belong to our God, for his judgments are true and just; for he has judged the great prostitute who corrupted the earth with her immorality, and has avenged on her the blood of his servants." Once more they cried out, "Hallelujah! The smoke from her goes up forever and ever." (Revelation 19:1–3)

Sharing in Christ's Delight

Once again, we look to our Lord as the superlative Example after whom we should pattern our lives. In what did Jesus delight? The book of Hebrews gives us insight into the heart of Jesus, and raises the possibility of a promise of greater joy to those who delight in the same:

> You have loved righteousness and hated wickedness; therefore God, your God, has anointed you with the oil of gladness beyond your companions. (Hebrews 1:9)

The GW translation uses much simpler language:

> You have loved what is right and hated what is wrong. That is why God, your God, anointed you, rather than your companions, with the oil of joy. (Hebrews 1:9 GW)

The presence of the word *therefore* in the ESV and the phrase *That is why* in the GW suggests a corollary between loving righteousness, hating wickedness, and being filled with joy—or so it was for Jesus. Is it reasonable to think that joy is a possible outcome of loving what is right and hating what is wrong?

We find in John 17 an account of the prayer Jesus prayed just before entering the Garden of Gethsemane for the last time with His disciples. He not only prayed for the ones God had given Him then, He also prayed for those He said "will believe in me through their word" (John 17:20). One of the things Jesus prayed was that we would all share His joy, and that the Father would sanctify us in the truth:

> But now I am coming to you, and these things I speak in the world, that they may have my joy fulfilled in themselves. I have given them your word, and the world has hated them because they are not of the world, just as I am not of the world. . . . Sanctify them in the truth; your word is truth. (John 17:13–14, 17)

We know from Hebrews 1:9 that Jesus loves righteousness and hates wickedness (iniquity); *therefore*, God anointed Him with the oil of gladness (joy). In John 17, we see that Jesus also places a premium on truth, which He defines as the Father's Word. He describes Himself and His disciples as being "not of the world," so we can safely infer that to love righteousness, hate iniquity, and rejoice in truth is not readily found in just anyone. Such individuals are not of this world, and have "set [their] affection on things above, not on things on the earth" (Colossians 3:2 KJV).

So, love does not delight in evil. It finds no pleasure in sin—not its own sin or being a partaker in the sins of others. We also know that love does not rejoice in the misfortunes of others.

It is a healthy practice to examine periodically the things in which we delight and that bring us pleasure, especially those things that enter the eye and ear gates and necessarily influence our thoughts. Long before Ralph Waldo Emerson penned "The ancestor of every action is a thought,"[8] Jesus taught that both good and evil originate in the heart (Matthew 12:34–35). Therefore, Paul's exhortation to the Philippians is a fitting yardstick for measuring our thought life given that all words and actions—good or bad, upright or underhanded—proceed from within:

> Finally, brothers, whatever is true, whatever is honorable, whatever is just, whatever is pure, whatever is lovely, whatever is commendable, if there is any excellence, if there is anything worthy of praise, *think about these things.* (Philippians 4:8, emphasis added)

We began this chapter by asserting that not delighting in evil and rejoicing with the truth can reasonably be characterized as *integrity.* Long ago, King Solomon personified wisdom as a voice crying out in the streets, on the heights, and at the crossroads and portals of life (see Proverbs 1:20-21, 8:1-3). I think it appropriate to end this chapter with a few words of wisdom from some notable figures who cry out to us from the pages of history:

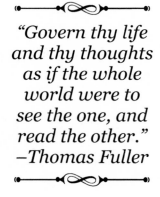

*"Govern thy life
and thy thoughts
as if the whole
world were to
see the one, and
read the other."
—Thomas Fuller*

Thomas Fuller, seventeenth-century English churchman and historian, said, "Govern thy life and thy thoughts as if the whole world were to see the one, and read the other."[9]

Early twentieth-century humorist Will Rogers put it this way: "Lead your life so you wouldn't be ashamed to sell the family parrot to the town gossip."[10]

Finally, physicist Albert Einstein said, "Whoever is careless with the truth in small matters cannot be trusted with important matters."[11]

These voices from the past speak to us today concerning the seriousness of truth and integrity. As should now be evident, integrity is so important in the life of a Christian that to violate it is to forfeit a good name and effectively perpetuate the list of excuses that many give for not following Christ.

For Further Study

"I will walk with integrity of heart within my house."
Psalm 101:2b

1. What single word does the author use to summarize the meaning of 1 Corinthians 13:6? What other word(s) could be used to summarize this verse?
2. When should I be honest, and when is it okay to be less than truthful?
3. How many areas of my life is God concerned with?
4. What lesson(s) do we learn from the life of Joseph as it relates to love not delighting in evil but rejoicing with the truth?
5. What quote is Andrew Lang generally credited with saying, and how does that apply to Christians?
6. How is it possible to be a partaker in the sins of others?
7. Explain how, to this day, people are still eating from the tree of the knowledge of good and evil.
8. Hebrews 1:9 tells us that Christ loved righteousness and hated iniquity. What does this same verse say was the corresponding result?

Part 5

The Practice

practice[1] [**prak**-tis]

—noun

5. *the action or process of performing or doing something....*
12. *to follow or observe habitually or customarily.*

15

The Winner and Still Champion

"Love... bears all things, believes all things,
hopes all things, endures all things. Love never fails."
1 Corinthians 13:7–8a (NKJV)

LOVE NEVER FAILS. What an encouraging thought! Yet I wonder how many of us have ever taken the time to seriously consider how potentially far reaching that is, and how those three words may not only impact our lives, but the lives of those around us. I don't intend to skip verse 7—we'll come back to that in a moment— but let me set the stage for what this chapter is about by saying, "Love triumphs over all. It *never* fails."

During the writing of this chapter, the Supreme Court of the United States (SCOTUS) ruled on a case that may forever impact the moral fabric of America. On June 26, 2015, a divided Supreme Court ruled to legalize gay marriage. Facebook and Twitter immediately went viral with posts of "Love Wins!" and the misguided hashtag of #lovewins. This was neither a victory nor a defeat for love, because this ruling has nothing whatsoever to do with the biblical definition of love (which will be addressed in chapter 16).

Prior to the SCOTUS ruling, the last sentence of this chapter's opening paragraph concluded with, "Let me set the stage for what this chapter is about by saying, 'Love wins—*always.*'" It is lamentable that such a meaningful expression has been subverted and hijacked, because love really does win. However, to say that love wins only makes sense when its underpinning is biblical truth.

Superlatively Solid Ground

One of my editors says that good writers rarely, if ever, use super-latives such as *never, always, best, least, greatest,* etc.; yet in this case, I'm on solid ground to say that love never fails. I'm simply telling you what the Bible says, and doing so in such a way as to leave no doubt. If you will learn to walk in love, you cannot fail. Oh, you may fail at a specific task, but you will not fail as a person—especially as you seek to honor Christ by walking in love. As stated in 1 Corinthians 13:7, those who walk in love are more apt to bear, believe, hope, and endure all things, and the same scribe (Paul) who wrote these words of encouragement to the church in Corinth was used by the Holy Spirit to pen a similar message for the church in Rome:

> Who shall separate us from the love of Christ? Shall tribulation, or distress, or persecution, or famine, or nakedness, or danger, or sword? As it is written, "For your sake we are being killed all the day long; we are regarded as sheep to be slaughtered." No, in all these things we are more than conquerors through him who loved us. For I am sure that neither death nor life, nor angels nor rulers, nor things present nor things to come, nor powers, nor height nor depth, nor anything else in all creation, will be able to sep-arate us from the love of God in Christ Jesus our Lord. (Romans 8:35–39)

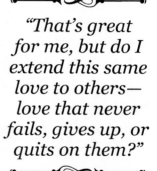

My church sings a song by the Jesus Culture band called *One Thing Remains.* The chorus is simple, and everyone seems to love singing about God's love that never fails, gives up, or runs out on them. Although the lyrics are assuredly com-forting and encouraging, not one time have I been able to sing this chorus

"That's great for me, but do I extend this same love to others— love that never fails, gives up, or quits on them?"

without thinking to myself, "That's great for me, but do I extend this same love *to others*—love that never fails, gives up, or quits *on them*?" I sometimes wonder how many people sing this song while picturing God's loving arms wrapped snugly around them, basking in the thought that He will never give up on them, nor will the endless supply of His love ever be exhausted. It is certainly not my intent to discredit the message of this lyric, but I wonder how often we fail to show even a scrap of that indefatigable love toward others.

It's time to challenge ourselves and take a hard look at that person in the mirror. We are going to discover in this chapter how love is an invincible force that enables us to face the torrid trials and challenging circumstances life sometimes throws at us. We are also going to see how this irresistible love of Christ shed abroad in our hearts has the power to transform how we deal with others, how they respond to us, and may even influence how they respond to Christ. The same love Jesus demonstrated from the cradle to the cross constrains us to bear, believe, hope, and endure all things for the sake of others, not just for our own wellbeing.

> *The same love Jesus demonstrated from the cradle to the cross constrains us to bear, believe, hope, and endure all things for the sake of others, not just for our own wellbeing.*

Do It for Love

My oldest son Ben works the assembly line at one of the Ford plants in Louisville, Kentucky. One evening less than a year after he started working there, Mindy and I had dinner with him at a local restaurant. Ben had been married for about two-and-a-half years, and he and his wife had a baby girl not quite one year old. As we ate our dinner, Ben began to describe how difficult his job was. For some reason—ignorance, I suppose—I had always thought that the most challenging aspect of blue-collar assembly-line work would be dealing with the monotony of doing the same thing over and over *and over* for the duration of the shift. I could not have been more wrong. As we listened to our son, we discovered not just the mental toll it was taking on him, but also the physical. The effects of repetitive motion and having to stoop or contort his 6'2" frame into uncomfortable positions made his hands, feet, and back hurt so much that he could hardly sleep some nights.

There came a point in the conversation when I knew that God wanted me to share some of my life experience with him to encourage him and give him the mental strength to do more than simply continue showing up for work every day. By applying what I was going to share with him, he could approach each shift in such a way as to turn dread into determination. Of course that would not eliminate the physical aches and pains, but it would help him find another motivational gear that would enable him to win at work in spite of the physical and mental toll it was taking on him. It's what I call the *Do it for love* principle.

It's no secret that love is either *the* most, or one of the most, powerful motivational forces in the world. You've probably heard of at least one instance of people lifting cars off of loved ones in order to free them—a feat not otherwise humanly possible for such individuals. The adrenaline rush generated by love is what enabled them to perform such an impossible exploit.

> *Many times I long to possess greater confidence in my own abilities to do whatever I need to do, and then the Holy Spirit reminds me of men like Gideon and Jehoshaphat, whom God used to accomplish great victories in spite of their lack of confidence in themselves.*

Gallup, Inc. is an organization not only known for its polling and data analysis, but also for providing services to help corporations leverage this information to improve associate/employee engagement and develop their people. One of the ways Gallup accomplishes this is by helping individuals discover and understand their unique strengths. Through my employer, I have benefited from taking the Gallup StrengthsFinder assessment. The focus is on learning to maximize your strengths—once you know them—rather than trying to strengthen (i.e., fix) your weaknesses. All who take the assessment are presented with a comprehensive list of thirty-four strengths, ranked in order from their top strength (1) to their bottom strength (34).

Strength number 34 for Steve Smith is *self-assurance*. I personally think there is a bit of semantics at work in this assessment, so I will frankly say that my score reflects a lack of confidence in my ability to do certain things. Not everything, mind you; but some things. That said, this particular "strength" forces me to rely on God's ability more than my own, which is not such a terrible thing when you think

> *With tears in my eyes, I simply said, "Ben, do it for love. Do what you have to do out of love for your wife and daughter."*

about it. Many times I long to possess greater confidence in my own abilities to do whatever I need to do, and then the Holy Spirit reminds me of men like Gideon and Jehoshaphat, whom God used to accomplish great victories in spite of their lack of confidence in themselves. Such accomplishments leave less room for fleshly boasting and more room for God to receive all the glory.

As previously mentioned in the introduction and in chapter 12, I spent two years working on an E-Commerce project based in New York City. I knew precious little about the inner workings of a major retail corporation's website and all the systems that have to be integrated in order to process a single transaction. Nevertheless,

I was assigned the role of being the technical lead for the integration of many of these systems. Mr. Self-Assurance felt a bit intimidated and overwhelmed at first. However, God put a thought in my mind early on in the project that revolutionized how I approached my work. The thought was to open my arms as wide as I could and embrace every challenge that was going to come my way instead of wasting energy fretting over how I might potentially fail.

In addition to the challenge of the work itself, during the first year of the project I spent nearly a third of my working days in Manhattan, which meant I was doing a fair amount of traveling between Louisville and New York. As the combination of the work and travel began to wear on me, the Lord gave me another thought that became a tremendous source of mental strength. On those days when I struggled to board another plane or find the resolve to work on a particularly challenging task, I thought about Mindy. I thought about my family. So I began to say to myself, "Do it for love, Steve. Do it for love." As I turned that thought into action, I discovered I was able to endure unpleasant circumstances more easily and accomplish things with greater resolve.

The best attitude in the world may have zero effect on my circumstances, but it does affect me and can also have a profound impact on the outcome of a situation or the people around me.

After listening to my son share the challenges he was facing with his job, that's when I knew I needed to share this principle with him. It was an emotional moment for me because I could truly empathize with his struggles—especially the mental aspect. So with tears in my eyes, I simply said, "Ben, do it for love. Do what you have to do out of love for your wife and daughter." I then told him how that same motivation had helped me find the inner strength necessary to persevere and to do more than simply *get through it*—although the reality is there were some days that bordered more on just getting through it than being Mr. Victorious. Then again, "love... *endures* all things," so sometimes we simply endure. The best attitude in the world may have zero effect on my circumstances, but it does affect *me* and can also have a profound impact on the outcome of a situation or the people around me.

A Formidable Foursome

Although we initially skipped over verse 7 of 1 Corinthians 13, we will now take a step back to cover four important aspects of love that coalesce to make it such an indomitable force.

1. Love *Bears* All Things

As defined by the website blueletterbible.org, the word *bears* in 1 Corinthians 13:7 means:

1) to protect or keep by covering, to preserve
2) to cover over with silence; to keep secret; to hide, conceal[1]

Consider the purpose of an umbrella. We hold it over our head—and sometimes the head of someone else—as a covering to protect ourselves from rain. Some even use an umbrella to shield themselves from the penetrating rays of the sun. In a similar way, love covers an offense instead of announcing it to others. Peter confirmed this by saying, "Above all, keep loving one another earnestly, since love covers a multitude of sins" (1 Peter 4:8). Proverbs 10:12 in the NIV says it this way: "love covers over all wrongs."

> *"Love stands in the presence of a fault with a finger on her lip."*
> – Charles Spurgeon

Here we see an attribute of love that is supremely sublime but doggedly difficult to practice consistently. Charles Spurgeon, teaching on *Love's Labours,* said, "Love stands in the presence of a fault with a finger on her lip. . . [and] covers all injuries by being silent about them, and acting as if they had never been."[2] How difficult it is at times to refrain from talking about the faults of others! There is not a single place in any of the gospels where Jesus is found talking about the sins of others. Yes, He confronted the scribes and Pharisees about their religiosity and He exhorted His disciples to beware of their hypocrisy, but He never discussed the faults of others the way a gossip would. Like David, we need a vigilant sentry keeping watch over our mouths: "Set a guard, O LORD, over my mouth; keep watch over the door of my lips!" (Psalm 141:3).

2. Love *Believes* All Things

The word *believes* in 1 Corinthians 13:7 means:

1) *to think to be true, to be persuaded of, to credit, place confidence in*
2) *to entrust a thing to one, i.e., his fidelity*[3]

In an ethical sense, this word essentially implies having confidence in the goodness of men.[4] It comes down to believing the best about an individual and giving them the benefit of the doubt—especially in the absence of all the facts.

Did you notice the words "to credit" in the definition? If I were to deposit funds into your bank account, your account would receive a credit for that specific amount of money—whether or not you had done anything to earn or deserve that money. Similarly, love credits goodness to others even when they don't deserve it. In fact, our demonstration of Christ is never greater than when we love unconditionally, and one of the ways we accomplish

Our demonstration of Christ is never greater than when we love unconditionally, and one of the ways we accomplish this is by believing the best about a person instead of judging them solely based on surface information.

this is by believing the best about a person instead of judging them solely based on surface information. There are often better qualities within a person than what meets the eye, but it is all too easy to focus on one's apparent faults instead of extending grace and looking for the good in that person.

We must not overlook another aspect of the word *believe*. The blueletterbible.org website also gives us this definition: "to trust in Jesus or God as able to aid either in obtaining or in doing something—saving faith."[5] Love is what constrains us to place our trust in Jesus, especially in the face of adversity or something we find particularly challenging. Love believes all things.

After our daughter Kristen graduated high school, she spent some time in Texas with the Teen Mania ministry. While she was there, I sent her a card to encourage her. In it I wrote these words:

> *My expectation for you is that you will far exceed anything I've done in the Kingdom. But my expectation is not based on your ability, but on God's ability within you. This takes all the pressure off of you. Whatever great things you are able to do in the Kingdom will be of God and to His glory, having been accomplished by Him through you.*

I believe this to be an apt expression of how love believes and trusts in God's ability to accomplish His purposes in and through us.

3. Love *Hopes* All Things

The word *hopes* in 1 Corinthians 13:7 means: "to wait for salvation with joy and full confidence."[6]

Although faith is the *substance* of things hoped for (Hebrews 11:1), love appears to be the *foundation* upon which hope is built. We are told that *love* ... hopes all things. And not only does love hope, but it joyfully waits with full confidence for the salvation of God. This is a hope that rests on the bedrock of faithful promises such as this: "When the righteous cry for help, the LORD hears and delivers them out of all their troubles" (Psalm 34:17).

Love is the basis of hope, especially when concerned for the welfare of others. The indwelling love of Christ enables us to have hope in situations that seem hopeless. It gives us that extra gear that refuses to give up or quit believing in the goodness and mercy of God to save, to deliver, or to restore someone who is overcome in a fault.

4. Love *Endures* All Things

The Greek word translated *endures* is used in several places in the New Testament. One of its definitions is particularly applicable to 1 Corinthians 13:7. It means "to remain, i.e., abide, not recede or flee,"[7] and suggests facing challenges and circumstances bravely and calmly, possessing an equanimity that is evident in one's countenance and conduct. Herein we find a characteristic of love that affords genuine peace in the face of adversity.

One of the things I have observed and admired about Pastor Bob for nearly forty years is his unflappable, reassuring aplomb in the face of difficult circumstances. He has a remarkable ability to comfort and encourage people in the midst of a crisis. I've watched him preside over funerals of close family members and friends, doing so with a grace at which I continually marvel. And yet, I should not be so amazed, because I know it to be an expression of the love of Christ that enables him to face these things calmly and courageously.

I'll Take Latin for $1000, Alex

Invictus is a Latin adjective meaning *unconquered*, and is perfectly apropos of love. Love is invincible, and cannot under any circumstances be conquered. There simply is no greater force this side of heaven. It subdues fear, supplants hatred, and is capable of vanquishing all its foes. It never quits, and never gives up.

During a particularly difficult time in my life, I once heard Pastor Bob say, "The only way you can ever lose is to quit." And I have discovered there is no quit in love, which is why love never fails. So remember this: no matter what you are going through, no matter what you are facing, no matter how far your loved one has strayed from God, the love of Christ prevails. No matter how much you want to retaliate, no matter how hard it is to forgive, and no matter how difficult it is to hold your tongue, mercy triumphs over judgment (James 2:13), which is why love will always be the Winner and still Champion.

For Further Study

"Nothing in all creation will ever be able to separate us from the love of God that is revealed in Christ Jesus our Lord."
Romans 8:39 (NLT)

1. In your own words, explain why love never fails.
2. When you think about the love of God, do you tend to reflect more on how much God loves you or on how much you should love others? What words would you use to describe these two different mentalities?
3. Explain how love is a powerful motivation that can sustain us through difficult times. What *principle* did the author share with his son?
4. What is another way to say that love *bears* all things? How did Charles Spurgeon explain this?
5. What two primary points does the author make concerning love's ability to believe all things?
6. Hebrews 11:1 teaches us that faith is the substance of things hoped for. The author suggests that love is the foundation upon which hope is built. State why you either agree or disagree with this premise.
7. Share some ways in which love enables us to endure circumstances, and whether or not you think it would ever be possible for love to fail.

16

Supremely Sufficient

"What we will be has not yet appeared."
1 John 3:2a

ARLY ONE MORNING while taking a walk, I passed by the house of a neighbor who, dressed in his house coat and slippers, was shuffling down his driveway to fetch his newspaper. It was obvious he had not been awake long, so I quipped, "Still trying to shake off the cobwebs?"

"Getting old is not for sissies," he riposted, running his hand over the top of his tousled hair from front to back and back to front.

"You got that right," I said in agreement, conscious of the sciatic nerve pain I was experiencing in my backside.

As I later reflected on that moment, I thought about the challenge of becoming Christlike, and realized that this too is not for the timid or faint of heart. Yet for those of us who sincerely want to be like Christ, God's Word is replete with promises and exhortations to encourage our faith and stir our hearts to action, fully trusting that God is all-sufficient to accomplish this singular work within us.

In a biblegateway.com devotional, theologian and author John Piper says, "I long for God to be glorified in our pursuit of holiness and love. But God is not glorified unless our pursuit is empowered by faith in his promises."[1] He continues by saying that "[God] is glorified when the power to be holy comes from humble faith in future grace."[2] I love the notion of having humble faith in a future grace, and Piper's words give us hope that this will lead to God being glorified as we pursue Christlikeness (what he synonymously describes as the pursuit of holiness and love).

Though Piper's premise is sound, I do not believe it to be disagreement to say that I also need humble faith for a *present* grace, because I need to be able to love with Christ's love *now*—as well as in the future. It would be a mistake to relegate becoming Christlike to some future point in time when I have at my disposal the tools to be like Him now.

> *"The Christlike Christian is one whose whole life is the outcome of divine love, welling up within him as the source and secret of all his motives and all his activities."*
> *— Unknown Christian*

In chapter 2 we spoke of how grace, faith, and works combine as a threefold cord to aid us in our pursuit of Christlikeness. We also have the Bible, the written expression of Jesus, the living Word of God, to serve as the plumb line for godly living. We've mentioned numerous times the indwelling love of Christ shed abroad in our hearts by the Holy Spirit, which constrains and compels us to love as Jesus loved. The perfect qualities of love are at our disposal to be expressed *now*, and the Unknown Christian reminds us that "the Christlike Christian is one whose whole life is the outcome of divine love, welling up within him as the source and secret of all his motives and all his activities."[3]

Grace and the Revelation of Christ

So we must put off procrastinating. Don't say, "I'll get to that someday. I'll get serious about becoming Christlike when I get older and have fewer demands upon my life." When does *that* day come?

In John's first letter to the Church, he writes:

> Beloved, we are God's children now, and what we
> will be has not yet appeared; but we know that when

he appears we shall be like him, because we shall see him as he is. And everyone who thus hopes in him purifies himself as he is pure. (1 John 3:2–3)

John affirms that we are God's children *now*, which means our lives should reflect that relationship now. That said, John continues with this thought, "What we will be has not yet appeared; but we know that when he appears we shall be like him, because we shall see him as he is."

Bible scholars generally agree that John was referring to the second coming of Christ when he said, "*When he appears* we shall be like him." The New King James Version renders this as, "*When He is revealed* we shall be like Him." I find additional meaning in these words. If you have been a Christian long, you have likely experienced a moment when the Holy Spirit revealed something new to you about the Lord Jesus. And I submit to you that the Holy Spirit uses such revelations of Christ to stir our hearts to desire more of His likeness.

Pastor Stormont recounts a conversation with Smith Wigglesworth that corroborates this point:

> One sunny day in our peaceful garden, we were discussing a criticism both of us had seen about Christians who went forward frequently at the end of services. Some thought it indicated insecurity, which perhaps it did. Yet Wigglesworth saw something important in it, saying, "Every fresh revelation calls for a new dedication."
>
> He perceived that while we have made, or should have made, once and for all a consecration of our lives to God, there will be all along the way further unveilings of the Lord, of His power, and of His purposes. As each fuller revelation comes into view, we commit ourselves afresh to God for its fulfillment in our lives (Rom. 12:1–2).[4]

Further confirmation of this is found in Peter's first letter to the church:

> Therefore, preparing your minds for action, and being sober-minded, set your hope fully on *the grace that will be brought to you at the revelation of Jesus Christ.* (1 Peter 1:13, emphasis added)

To borrow from Piper, I see this as future grace that lies before us—future grace that becomes present grace. Each time the Spirit of God reveals some facet of Jesus Christ to us, He brings with it the grace to walk in that revelation.

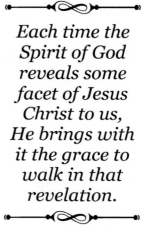

Each time the Spirit of God reveals some facet of Jesus Christ to us, He brings with it the grace to walk in that revelation.

John tells us that the reason we shall be like Him is "because we shall *see him as he is.*" When I *see* Christ *as He is*, my understanding of Him is enlarged and clarified, my faith is stirred, and with that comes the grace to be transformed into His image—from one degree of glory to another (2 Corinthians 3:18).

Time to Take Possession

In the introduction, I shared a bit of my experience with weight loss, and then compared that to our need to exercise ourselves toward godliness in order to remove the surrounding fatty tissue of those things in our lives that obscure the handsome physique of our Beloved, Jesus Christ. What I didn't share with you is my mental approach to losing weight.

When I finally get focused and determine to shed excess weight, I set short-term goals in increments of five pounds. So let's say my starting weight is 200 pounds and I want to lose 15 pounds. That would make 195 my first goal. When my weight finally drops—and stays—below 195 for at least a week, I consider myself to now *own* or possess that weight (or milestone). If you've ever made the effort to lose weight, you have probably experienced the frustration and discouragement that comes with getting on the scale and seeing little or no progress. But unless it is broken, the scale never lies. We tend to see the scale as our enemy when in truth it is our friend to help reveal whether or not we are progressing toward the ultimate goal. Becoming Christlike can be somewhat like losing weight in that we often struggle to make progress. Oswald Chambers reminds us that living as disciples of Jesus—which we expect would lead to becoming Christlike—requires effort, and is often difficult:

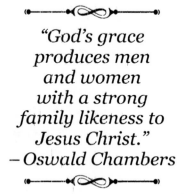

"God's grace produces men and women with a strong family likeness to Jesus Christ."
— Oswald Chambers

> If we are going to live as disciples of Jesus, we have to remember that all efforts of worth and excellence are difficult.... If we will only start on the basis of His redemption to do what He commands, then we will find that we can do it. If we fail, it is because we have not yet put into practice what God has placed within us. But a crisis will reveal whether or not we have been putting it into practice. If we will obey the Spirit of God and practice in our physical life what God has placed within us by His Spirit, then when a crisis does come we will find that our own nature, as well as the grace of God, will stand by us.... God's grace produces men and women with a strong family likeness to Jesus Christ.[5]

Chambers encourages us that our obedience flows out of redemption, and this gives us assurance that *we can do it*. Obedience out of redemption means that it's no longer I who live but Christ who lives in me (Galatians 2:20). In actuality, it is *Christ* who can do it.

Chambers next points out how God will use some crisis in our life—a disagreement with our spouse, an irritating co-worker, or the loss of our job while a close friend receives a nice promotion, etc.—to reveal whether or not we are making progress. For those attempting to lose weight, the crisis comes when they step on the scale. That is the moment of truth. For those pursuing Christlikeness, the moment of truth is revealed by the crisis God presents.

For me, it's not enough to always be pursuing but never possessing more of Christ, especially when it comes to loving others as described in 1 Corinthians 13. Paul spoke of owning it when he said, "Not that I have already obtained this or am already perfect, but I press on to make it my own, because Christ Jesus has made me his own" (Philippians 3:12).

God will use some crisis in our life to reveal whether or not we are making progress.

I want to own being longsuffering; I want to own being kind. I never want to be thought of as envious, boastful, or selfish. I want my spiritual house to be free of all pet peeves so that I am never provoked. I want my heart to be completely free of unforgiveness, and I want nothing to do with keeping a record of wrongs. I want to walk in integrity, always embracing a love for the truth. I want to own these godly qualities of love and I want them to own me since Christ has made me His own. I believe this to be the fulfillment of what we spoke of in the introduction: turning our *profession* of Christ into a *possession* of Christlikeness.

There's Nothing Here

The words of Jesus in John 14:30 provide a different perspective on this. He said, "The ruler of this world is coming. He has no claim on me." The ruler of this world is a reference to Satan, the prince of darkness. He had no claim on Christ because nothing of his nature (i.e., his character) existed in the Son of God. The New American Standard Version says, "He has nothing in Me." Stated differently, Satan had no case against Christ; nothing of which he could accuse Him.

This is certainly not anything we can ascribe to ourselves; for we were all born with a sinful nature and have all sinned. Yet all who receive Him become new creations in Christ (2 Corinthians 5:17), exchanging their old nature for His nature through the exercise of grace through faith as a gift from God (Ephesians 2:8). Therefore, it is not a stretch of the truth to say that Christians can—and should—possess these pre-eminent qualities of love to such an extent that nothing to the contrary exists within them. In other words, if Satan comes looking for anything within us that smacks of his nature, something that would give him some claim on us—impatience, meanness, envy, boastful pride, selfishness, petulance, unforgiveness, dishonesty, compromising of truth, etc.—he should find nothing!

Going to Extremes

In comparison to our natural inclinations, the love of Christ is extreme; extreme in long-suffering, extreme in showing kindness, extreme in its refusal to envy, to be selfish or boastful. We have discovered its resolve to shun provocation and keep no record of wrongs. Love is not confined within the boundaries of what is safe, comfortable, or beneficial to itself. It does not seek to protect or preserve its own interests. Love's defining characteristic is to give, and this is why it prefers the interests of others above its own.

> *Love is not confined within the boundaries of what is safe, comfortable, or beneficial to itself.*

Consider how extreme God's love is toward us, and His expectation for how we love others. Once again, Oswald Chambers articulates it well:

God loved me not because I was lovable, but because it was His nature to do so. Now He commands me to show the same love to others by saying, ". . . love one another as I have loved you" (John 15:12). He is saying, "I will bring a number of people around you whom you cannot respect, but you must exhibit My love to them, just as I have exhibited it to you." This kind of love is not a patronizing love for the unlovable—it is His love, and it will not be evidenced in us overnight. Some of us may have tried to force it, but we were soon tired and frustrated.[6]

Addressing the temptation to withhold grace from others, Chambers continues:

"I should look within and remember how wonderfully God has dealt with me. The knowledge that God has loved me beyond all limits will compel me to go into the world to love others in the same way. I may get irritated because I have to live [or work] with an unusually difficult person. But just think how disagreeable I have been with God! *Am I prepared to be identified so closely with the Lord Jesus that His life and His sweetness will be continually poured out through me?*"[7]

I truly believe the greatest gift this side of heaven is the ability to give and receive love. Not lust, not giving of ourselves as a means to an end, but pure, unadulterated, selfless love. There is no greater blessing than to exchange this currency with family, friends, neighbors, and co-workers; with our brothers and sisters in Christ; with complete strangers—even with our enemies and those who persecute us.

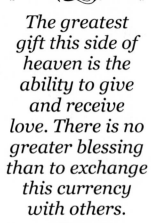

The greatest gift this side of heaven is the ability to give and receive love. There is no greater blessing than to exchange this currency with others.

Sermons from Songwriters

James Taylor, one of the greatest singer/songwriters of his generation, once wrote, "There ain't no doubt in no one's mind that love's the finest thing around."[8] I couldn't agree more! I think he nailed it, but what did JT mean by this?

The Beatles preached in song that all we need is love.[9] But what did John Lennon and Paul McCartney have in mind?

To some, love is a feeling. To some, it is family. To others, love is the freedom to live and express themselves however they want, which means love is tolerance and acceptance of differing beliefs and lifestyles. Many voices today espouse a seemingly untold number of opinions of what love is. Chambers says, "Love is an indefinite thing to most of us; we don't know what we mean when we talk about love."[10] But we need not look any further than God's Word to know exactly what love is:

> *We know what real love is because Jesus gave up his life for us.* So we also ought to give up our lives for our brothers and sisters. (1 John 3:16 NLT, emphasis added)

If what you call love is nothing more than an excuse to gratify your own lusts, pursue your own desires, or promote an agenda other than God's, then it is not love.

So there you have it. *We know what real love is....* Real love is *unselfish*. This is the litmus test for love. If what you call love is nothing more than an excuse to gratify your own lusts, pursue your own desires, or promote an agenda other than God's, then it is not love. Real love is giving up our lives, giving up our self-defined or even constitutional rights for others. Look again, and you will not find so much as a *skosh* of self-gratification, self-seeking, or self-fulfillment in anything Paul describes as love in 1 Corinthians 13:4–8.

To further underscore what real love is, John reminds us of why we are even able to love in the first place: "We love because *he first loved us*" (1 John 4:19, emphasis added).

God took the initiative and loved us while we were yet sinners (Romans 5:8), and He calls us to do the same. Jesus said we are to love others as He has loved us (John 13:34). This is not easy to do, and it is not my intention to suggest that it is. I find it quite difficult to love certain individuals, which is evidence that God is still working in me.

Although God has not yet finished His work in us, He has pledged to complete it (Philippians 1:6). What makes this so difficult to believe sometimes is that life gives us plenty of opportunities to witness the beginning of some particular vision or project that gets abandoned before completion. I will even venture to guess that you have started at least one thing in your lifetime that you've never finished. The same, however, cannot be said of God. As Moses recorded in the book of Numbers,

When God says He will bring to completion the good work He began in us, we need not be afraid that He will renege on His promise.

God is not man, that he should lie, or a son of man, that he should change his mind. Has he said, and will he not do it? Or has he spoken, and will he not fulfill it? (Numbers 23:19)

When God says He will bring to completion the good work He began in us, we need not be afraid that He will renege on His promise. Paul told Titus that God cannot lie (Titus 1:2), and the book of Hebrews uses even stronger language saying, "It is *impossible* for God to lie" (Hebrews 6:18 emphasis added).

Who Is Sufficient for These Things?

So we now come to the end of our quest. Or is it just the beginning? I suspect for most of us it's probably a continuation.

Surely we aren't so foolish as to think we can attain Christlikeness in our own strength or virtue. Paul said, "For I know that nothing good dwells in me, that is, in my flesh. For I have the desire to do what is right, but not the ability to carry it out" (Romans 7:18). Oh no! No matter how much I desire to be like Christ I cannot accomplish it! *Not on my own.* But there's no need to despair. On the contrary, we are to be confident. Read Paul's words to the church in Corinth:

> Such is the confidence that we have through Christ toward God. Not that we are sufficient in ourselves to claim anything as coming from us, but *our sufficiency is from God.* (2 Corinthians 3:4–5, emphasis added)

What powerful words! What words of hope and encouragement! We have God's promise to perfect that which concerns us and to fulfill His purpose for us (Psalm 138:8). We are assured that He who began a good work in us will bring it to completion at the day of Jesus Christ (Philippians 1:6). And let us not forget that we are *His* workmanship (Ephesians 2:10). So along with Paul, I ask, "Who is sufficient for these things?" (2 Corinthians 2:16). The answer, of course, is Christ in you, Christ in me, Christ in us, the hope of glory (Colossians 1:27)!

For Further Study

"Not that I have already obtained this or am already perfect,
but I press on to make it my own."
Philippians 3:12a

1. What gives us ample reason to trust in God's sufficiency to conform us to the image of Christ?

2. John wrote that we are God's children *now*. How should that influence our attitude toward becoming Christlike?

3. What would you say to someone who downplays either the importance or the possibility of being conformed to the image of Christ? What are some things you could say to encourage them to think otherwise?

4. What does God use to reveal whether or not we are progressing in our pursuit of Christlikeness? What examples of this can you share from your own life?

5. How do we turn our profession of Christ into a possession of Christlikeness?

6. God's love toward us is extreme. What does this say about the love we should have toward others?

7. There is no shortage of opinions in this world of what love is. What does the Bible say real love is, and what single word expresses this?

8. In light of our inability to attain Christlikeness in our own power, what should make us confident that we shall be transformed into His image?

A Final Word

"What then shall we say to these things?"
Romans 8:31a

S CRIPTURE ASSURES US that when we are born from above, the love of God is shed abroad in our hearts by the Holy Spirit (Romans 5:5). We also become new creations in Christ; the old life has passed away and all things have become new (2 Corinthians 5:17). We have been crucified with Christ; nevertheless, we live. He lives in us and we live by faith in Him (Galatians 2:20). By virtue of these things, we now possess what it takes to be a Christlike man or woman. The key lies in yielding to the work of the Holy Spirit such that the love of God is able to emerge in us as a true expression of Christ's nature and likeness.

The passage preceding this chapter's signature verse is a well-known favorite among Christians and altogether appropriate for examination, as we seek to put a bow on all that has been shared concerning the Christlike life:

> And we know that for those who love God all things work together for good, for those who are called according to his purpose. For those whom he foreknew he also predestined to be conformed to the image of his Son, in order that he might be the first-born among many brothers. And those whom he predestined he also called, and those whom he called he also justified, and those whom he justified he also glorified. (Romans 8:28-30)

What comfort, what encouragement, what resolve these verses have given to God's people for generations—particularly verse 28. "God makes all things work together for my good!" is how this verse is often paraphrased. What, then, is this *good* for which God is working all things together? Is it to guarantee my success in business or ministry? Is it to shield me from pain and heartache; or to bless me so abundantly that I lose all reliance upon God? Is it to encapsulate my life in a bubble so as to preserve me from trial and tribulation, or to ensure my continual happiness?

The answer could not be clearer. I can think of no greater good than what is described in verse 29—*to be conformed to the image of Christ.* If a greater good exists, then I confess I am blind to it. What higher ambition, what greater blessing could there be than to bear the likeness of Jesus Christ so that He is revealed to others through me?

Reviewing the Roadmap

In the opening pages of this book, we called attention to the crisis that exists in every Christian's life—to recognize the need for decisive change. To recognize that too often my life looks like *this*, and Christ looks like *that*. We spoke of how an un-Christlike life hinders the furtherance of the gospel. We progressed from there to explaining the importance of *aiming* to be Christlike, and how this is aided by utilizing the threefold cord of grace, faith, and works.

Continuing onward, we recognized the value in a daily reckoning of ourselves to be dead to sin and alive to God, and proceeded to lay a foundation for our pursuit of Christlikeness by defining what it means to be a Christian, and dispelling certain myths that keep people from experiencing a genuine faith in Christ.

We painted a picture of how daunting it can be to think how we could ever be like Christ, but offered hope that the love of God shed abroad in our hearts is the key to bridging the gap between a life that demonstrates Christ to the world and a life that does not. Finally, we explored each attribute of love described by Paul in 1 Corinthians 13:4-8.

Such is the consummation of all that has been presented in these pages—how to live Christlike through the demonstration of longsuffering and kindness; to neither envy others nor boast in ourselves; to shun selfishness and resist being provoked; to keep no record of wrongs and to walk in integrity, eschewing evil and delighting in the truth; to be motivated by love in everything we do, being supremely confident that love never fails.

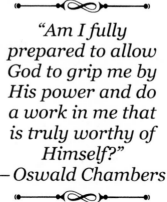

"Am I fully prepared to allow God to grip me by His power and do a work in me that is truly worthy of Himself?"
—Oswald Chambers

With these things freshly in mind, I believe it is fitting one last time to bring back our brother Oswald Chambers with a final word for us:

> The moment you are willing for God to change your nature, His recreating forces will begin to work. And the moment you realize that God's purpose is to get you into the right relationship with Himself and then with others, He will reach to the very limits of the universe to help you take the right road. Decide to do it right now.[1] ... *Am I fully prepared to allow God to grip me by His power and do a work in me that is truly worthy of Himself?*[2]

My expectation is that you *are* ready for God to do such a work in your life—a work that reflects the nature and likeness of Christ. Therefore, I pray as Paul did for the Thessalonians that God would "enable you to live a life worthy of his call. May he give you the power to accomplish all the good things your faith prompts you to do. Then the name of our Lord Jesus will be honored because of the way you live, and you will be honored along with him. *This is all made possible because of the grace of our God and Lord, Jesus Christ*" (2 Thessalonians 1:11-12 NLT, emphasis added).

For Further Study

*"We are confident of all this because of
our great trust in God through Christ."*
2 Corinthians 3:4 (NLT)

1. After reading this book, would you say you are more, or less, confident in God's sufficiency to make you like Jesus Christ?
2. Share with the group how this book affected you. Were you challenged? Were you inspired? Were you convicted?
3. How will you take and apply what you've read in order to live Christlike?

Special Acknowledgements

To Greg Burton, my first editor, whose kindred spirit I treasure. Greg, I enjoyed every moment of our time reviewing the manuscript—not to mention the Cinnamon Supreme pancakes at Bob Evans. I not only learned a great deal from you, but I am grateful that you weren't content to simply correct grammar and punctuation. You challenged the theology of this book, which made it a better read for all. Finally, I was glad to discover that the synapse between us is still working! Thanks for all the laughs, old friend.

To Cheryl Molin, my second editor: thank you for your help in putting the finishing touches on the manuscript, and for your patience with me throughout the editing process. Thank you also for challenging the content and theology of this work, and for taking the time to explain your perspective. I especially thank you for all the formatting work you did.

To Steve Mobley, one of my closest friends: Mobes, our friendship began with chasing a little white ball around a golf course, but has since grown from that of two buddies playing golf to two men who share a love for Christ. I'm thankful that God caused our paths to intersect when they did. You are a great friend and brother in Christ.

To Rich Elliott, also one of my closest friends: thank you for allowing me to use you as a sounding board. Rich, I thank God for your input into my life. I truly believe you are fulfilling your life purpose of helping others fulfill their life purpose—and I'm happy to be one of your assignments! God has given you the grace to challenge others in order to help them reach their potential. Thanks for the pushes and nudges, and thanks for putting up with all of my solicitations for feedback concerning the manuscript.

To Ted Baker, a true friend since we first met at Ball State University in 1977: thank you for your encouragement and advice, not only for this project but for so many other things over the years. I'm thankful our friendship has endured despite the miles that separate us.

To the following people (in no particular order) who read and reviewed all, or a portion, of the manuscript and/or its cover design and offered constructive feedback: Thank you Mindy, Julia, Kristen and son-in-law Bobby Gilles, Rich Elliott, Kristina Eddins, Pastor Bob Hauselman, Pastor Kaleb Lay, Ted Baker, Pastor G. B. Turner, Bob Allison, Geoff Dennis, Bob Kauflin, Trent Stivers, Steve Mobley, Jeff Hayes, Dave Hoeks, Dave Fischer, Miriam Flowe, Mandi Smith, Ron Ewing, Steve Elliott, and Trent Peyton.

To Dr. Robert Cornwall, the best gospel preacher and story teller I've ever had the privilege of hearing speak: thank you for reading through the first half of the manuscript in its early *rough* draft form, and for sharing helpful feedback. I am truly honored that you took the time to do so. May the fullness of God's grace, mercy, and peace be with you and your bride. I will never forget the first time you introduced our congregation to Trebor Llawnroc and Shirley Mae.

To Pastors Tony and Beverly Rezendes, thank you for being the first to read the entire manuscript and provide such positive feedback. Your unsolicited endorsement was perfect... and so encouraging to me! Thank you for allowing me to use it on the back cover.

To Joe Williamson, a friend and former pastor whose pastoral heart may prevent him from ever fully retiring: Joe, I cannot thank you enough for your gracious words of encouragement and suggestions for the book. It meant so much to me that you took the time to call and share your thoughts with me.

To Bill Womack, a co-worker, friend, and brother in Christ: thanks for reading the entire manuscript and offering some of the most helpful feedback of all—not to mention your kind and supportive words of encouragement. Truly means a lot.

To Jim Lee, a friend and brother in Christ whose passion for the Lord is evident to all who know you: thanks for reading as much of the manuscript as you could, and for calling to share some extremely encouraging feedback with me.

To Geoff Dennis, Bob Kauflin, Ted Baker, and Jeff Hayes: thank you for your advice and counsel concerning publishing and marketing.

To my project team at Xulon Press—Jason Gayle, Jennifer Kasper, Bethany Emerson, and Jason Fletcher: you guys were terrific to work with. Thank you for your support and guidance throughout the publishing process.

To my SICMA brethren, I thank God for all of you, and for your willingness to embrace the vision to develop meaningful, Christ-centered relationships with other men; and for endeavoring to live in a way that honors God and inspires others to want to know Him too.

To the men of the Heritage Classic, I thank God for our friendship in Christ, and it has been a privilege to meet with you annually now for so many years. You were the first ones to hear this message, and the opportunity to share it with you was one of the catalysts for writing this book. May your legacy continue impacting the lives of men for generations.

To my band of brothers, Steve Mobley, Dave Hoeks, and Jeff Hayes: I am thankful to have you in my life as accountability partners. I value your friendship, counsel, and wisdom, and I love our times of fellowship—on and off the golf course.

To Bob Hauselman, my pastor and brother-in-law: I thank God for your pastoral heart. It shines forth in all that you do. Thank you for taking time to critique the first draft of chapter 13. Thank you for never micro-managing the praise and worship ministry at RCC during my time as the director of worship. I am grateful for your implicit trust in me and God's hand on my life, and for the freedom to lead our congregation in worship under the direction of the Holy Spirit. Thanks for giving me print space in our church newsletter for so many years. This certainly contributed to my development as a writer, and has also provided a voice for my teaching gift. There are simply too many other things to list of which to express my sincere thanks to you. You are a godly example, and as concerns men... one of the finest I know.

To Mindy, my beautiful bride since 1979: you are my *best* friend, cheerleader, and encourager extraordinaire. You are the love of my life. Thank you for being all in with me on this. I also appreciate you being a good sport and allowing me to share some of our life's experiences with a larger audience. I know there were times when you grew weary of hearing me yammer on about "the manuscript," and it was not lost on me that you wondered if this project would *ever* come to an end. (Truthfully though, I'm expecting this to be a doorway into something God has purposed for us that is much greater than anything we ever imagined.) Thank you for extending grace to me, and for always loving me—*in spite of my caviling.*

To my heavenly Father and Jesus Christ His Son, who called me into His work and is fueling it by His grace. I treasure my early morning walks with You! Thanks for speaking to me during these times and for allowing me the privilege of being Your scribe/amanuenses to write this book. My heart's desire was simply to pass on the message you gave me (John 17:8a). May this book bring honor to Your name by inspiring all who read it to dare to be Christlike.

Recommended Resources

DARE *To Be* CHRISTLIKE—Articles and testimonials designed to challenge, encourage, and inspire Christians in their pursuit of Christlikeness. Contact Steve, purchase books, subscribe to email blogs, share feedback, view Steve's calendar of events, and more.
http://daretobechristlike.com

Southern Indiana Christian Men's Association (SICMA)—Information concerning the vision and mission of SICMA. Learn how you can establish an effective men's ministry in your local church, or how your men's group can become an affiliate of SICMA (regardless of your geographical location). View the SICMA calendar of events, and register for the annual *Man Up!* conference.
http://sicma-group.com

My Song in the Night—Articles on worship, songwriting, and effective church communication by Bobby and Kristen Gilles, staff deacons at Sojourn Community Church in New Albany, Indiana. You will also find articles of encouragement for anyone who has experienced the loss of a child.
http://mysonginthenight.com

Take Shape for Life (TSFL)—See how Mindy lost 64 pounds in less than five months eating healthy, tasty, nutritional foods. See how she can help you achieve your desired weight-loss goal AND obtain optimal health through this proven program.
http://mindysmith.tsfl.com
http://mindysmith.ichooseoptimalhealth.com

Notes

Preface

1. *The Princess Bride*. Dir. Rob Reiner. Writ. William Goldman. Perf. Carey Elwes, Robin Wright, Mandy Patinkin, Peter Faulk. Metro Goldwyn Mayer Studios;, 1987. VHS.
2. Pierre Bayle. https://www.goodreads.com/author/quotes/444184.Pierre_Bayle (accessed December 15, 2015).

Introduction: An Epic Enigma

1. Charles Kettering. BrainyQuote.com, Xplore Inc, 2015. http://www.brainyquote.com/quotes/quotes/c/charlesket181210.html (accessed December 30, 2015).
2. enigma. Dictionary.com. *Dictionary.com Unabridged*. Random House, Inc. http://dictionary.reference.com/browse/enigma (accessed April 3, 2013).
3. Unknown Christian, *The Christlike Christian* (Grand Rapids: Zondervan, 1988), 11.
4. caveat emptor. Dictionary.com. Dictionary.com Unabridged. Random House, Inc. http://www.dictionary.com/browse/caveat-emptor (accessed: October 24, 2014).
5. crisis. Dictionary.com. *Dictionary.com Unabridged*. Random House, Inc. http://dictionary.reference.com/browse/crisis (accessed October 24, 2014).
6. http://www.quotationspage.com/quote/33092.html (accessed December 27, 2015)
7. Taken from *My Utmost for His Highest*® by Oswald Chambers, edited by James Reimann, © 1992 by Oswald Chambers Publications Assn., Ltd., and used by permission of Discovery House, Grand Rapids, MI 49501. All rights reserved., December 27.

The Realization

1. realize. Dictionary.com. *Dictionary.com Unabridged*. Random House, Inc. http://dictionary.reference.com/browse/realize (accessed January 27, 2016).

1 – Once Upon a Word...

1. Taken from *Morning by Morning* by Charles H. Spurgeon Copyright © 2000 by Charles H. Spurgeon. Used by permission of Thomas Nelson. www.thomasnelson.com, 300.
2. caviling. Dictionary.com. *Dictionary.com Unabridged*. Random House, Inc. http://dictionary.reference.com/browse/caviling (accessed November 19, 2010).

2 – Aiming, Not Claiming

1. Taken from *My Utmost for His Highest*® by Oswald Chambers, edited by James Reimann, © 1992 by Oswald Chambers Publications Assn., Ltd., and used by permission of Discovery House, Grand Rapids, MI 49501. All rights reserved., May 15.
2. Ibid., July 21.
3. Ibid., April 24
4. Ibid., May 10.
5. Ibid.

3 – Day of Reckoning

1. reckon. *Merriam-Webster.com*. Merriam-Webster, 2011. http://www.merriam-webster.com/dictionary/reckon (accessed January 27, 2015).
2. "Greek Lexicon :: G3049 (KJV)." Blue Letter Bible (accessed January 28, 2015). http://www.blueletterbible.org/lang/Lexicon/Lexicon.cfm?Strongs=G3049&t=KJV
3. Ibid.
4. Taken from *My Utmost for His Highest*® by Oswald Chambers, edited by James Reimann, © 1992 by Oswald Chambers Publications Assn., Ltd., and used by permission of Discovery House, Grand Rapids, MI 49501. All rights reserved., March 21.

The Foundation

1. foundation. Dictionary.com. *Dictionary.com Unabridged*. Random House, Inc. http://dictionary.reference.com/browse/foundation (accessed January 27, 2016).

4 – A Defining Moment

1. http://www.gallup.com/poll/159548/identify-christian.aspx (accessed December 24, 2012)
2. http://www.britannica.com/event/United-States-presidential-election-of-1920 (accessed April 9, 2016)
3. Taken from *My Utmost for His Highest*® by Oswald Chambers, edited by James Reimann, © 1992 by Oswald Chambers Publications Assn., Ltd., and used by permission of Discovery House, Grand Rapids, MI 49501. All rights reserved., October 5.
4. http://www.blessitt.com/
5. Chambers, *Utmost,* August 6.
6. "Greek Lexicon :: G1247 (KJV)." Blue Letter Bible (accessed December 28, 2015). http://www.blueletterbible.orghttps://www.blueletterbible.org/lang/Lexicon/Lexicon.cfm

5 – Time for Some Fowl Language

1. Søren Kierkegaard. http://www.goodreads.com/author/quotes/6172.S_

ren_Kierkegaard (accessed January 19, 2015).

2. imitate. Dictionary.com. *Dictionary.com Unabridged*. Random House, Inc. http://dictionary.reference.com/browse/imitate (accessed June 18, 2013).

3. pretend. Dictionary.com. *Dictionary.com Unabridged*. Random House, Inc. http://dictionary.reference.com/browse/pretend (accessed June 18, 2013).

4. Taken from *My Utmost for His Highest*® by Oswald Chambers, edited by James Reimann, © 1992 by Oswald Chambers Publications Assn., Ltd., and used by permission of Discovery House, Grand Rapids, MI 49501. All rights reserved., November 29.

5. Ibid., September 16.

6. Burger King's ad slogan, "Have It Your Way" was created *circa* 1974, and was hugely successful because it revolutionized the fast food industry by meeting a customer demand to have a sandwich made to order hassle-free.

7. **tn** The word ἄνωθεν (anwqen) has a double meaning, either "again" (in which case it is synonymous with πάλιν [palin]) or "from above" (BDAG 92 s.v. ἄνωθεν). This is a favorite technique of the author of the Fourth Gospel, and it is lost in almost all translations at this point. John uses the word 5 times, in 3:3, 7; 3:31; 19:11 and 23. In the latter 3 cases the context makes clear that it means "from above." Here (3:3, 7) it could mean either, but the primary meaning intended by Jesus is "from above." Nicodemus apparently understood it the other way, which explains his reply, "How can a man be born when he is old? He can't enter his mother's womb a second time and be born, can he?" The author uses the technique of the "misunderstood question" often to bring out a particularly important point: Jesus says something which is misunderstood by the disciples or (as here) someone else, which then gives Jesus the opportunity to explain more fully and in more detail what he really meant. — https://bible.org/netbible/ Used by permission.

8. Taken from *Morning and Evening* by Charles H. Spurgeon, edited and revised by Alistair Begg, © 2003 p. 211. Used by permission of Crossway, a publishing ministry of Good News Publishers, Wheaton, IL 60187, www.crossway.org.

9. Taken from *The Liberation of Planet Earth* by Hal Lindsey Copyright © 1974 by Hal Lindsey. Used by permission of Zondervan. www.zondervan.com, 109.

10. If you prayed to receive Christ, I encourage you to begin reading the Bible. John's gospel would be a great place to start. I also encourage you to find a church in your area that will welcome you into the family of God and help disciple you in your growth as a Christian. Finally, I would love to hear from you! If this book helped you enter into a relationship with Jesus Christ, please visit my website http://daretobechristlike.com and let me—and others—hear your story.

11. Wikipedia contributors, "Jefferson Bible," *Wikipedia, The Free Encyclopedia*, http://en.wikipedia.org/w/index.

php?title=Jefferson_Bible&oldid=571715302 (accessed September 8, 2013).

12. Ibid.
13. Chambers, *Utmost,* January 24.

The Transition

1. transition. Dictionary.com. *Dictionary.com Unabridged.* Random House, Inc. http://dictionary.reference.com/browse/transition (accessed January 27, 2016).

6 – A More Excellent Way

1. Unknown Christian, *The Christlike Christian* (Grand Rapids: Zondervan, 1988), 18-19.
2. "Ephesians 3 (New American Standard Bible)." Blue Letter Bible (accessed November 8, 2014). http://www.blueletterbible.org/Bible.cfm?b=Eph&c= 3&p=0&rl=0&ss=0&t=NASB
3. Ibid.
4. Unknown Christian, *Christlike Christian,* 30.
5. Ibid., 29.
6. Ibid., 30.
7. Taken from *Morning and Evening* by Charles H. Spurgeon, edited and revised by Alistair Begg, © 2003 p. 55. Used by permission of Crossway, a publishing ministry of Good News Publishers, Wheaton, IL 60187, www. crossway.org.
8. George Stormont, *Smith Wigglesworth* (Tulsa: Harrison House LLC, 1989), 87.
9. Taken from *My Utmost for His Highest*® by Oswald Chambers, edited by James Reimann, © 1992 by Oswald Chambers Publications Assn., Ltd., and used by permission of Discovery House, Grand Rapids, MI 49501. All rights reserved., June 14.

The Precepts

1. precept. Dictionary.com. *Dictionary.com Unabridged.* Random House, Inc. http://dictionary.reference.com/browse/precept (accessed January 27, 2016).

7 – Take It Like a Man?

1. Taken from *My Utmost for His Highest*® by Oswald Chambers, edited by James Reimann, © 1992 by Oswald Chambers Publications Assn., Ltd., and used by permission of Discovery House, Grand Rapids, MI 49501. All rights reserved., February 3.
2. *RUDY.* Dir. David Anspaugh. Writ. Angelo Pizzo. Perf. Sean Astin, Ned Beatty, Charles S. Dutton, Lili Taylor, Robert Prosky. Tristar Pictures, Inc. All Rights Reserved; 1993. DVD.
3. For those who doubt whether God has a sense of humor, the following anecdote should serve to support the notion that He does:

Not long before this manuscript went to press, my writing was put to the test in a way I had not anticipated. A neighbor of mine, who lives just three doors away, began walking his dogs down our street in order for them to do their business *in someone else's yard*. Many times, that meant *my yard*.

Of course, that would not have been a problem had my neighbor cleaned up after his dogs, but he chose to leave the unwanted "gift" behind. I conferred with a couple of my neighbors and asked what they thought I should do. One suggested scooping it up and placing it on the man's front porch. Now as humorous as I found that to be, I had enough sense to know that was not an option—not for a man aspiring to be Christlike. However, I did scoop it up—under cover of darkness—and return it to the rightful owner's yard, feeling justified that that was where it belonged. After all, if he didn't think it was necessary to pick it up from my yard, then he should be fine with it in his yard, right?

It wasn't long before the Lord reminded me of what I had written in this chapter that being longsuffering means *putting up with the crap of others*. How ironic to have this opportunity to show longsuffering and kindness to a neighbor who has yet to pass Subdivision 101!

So here I was, having to apply my teaching quite literally. What was I going to do? It just didn't seem right that I should have to clean up after this man's dogs. After spending far more time praying about this than should have been necessary, I concluded I had two options: (1) leave it in the yard to decompose (not acceptable for a man who keeps his yard looking close to immaculate), or (2) scoop it up and flush it down my own toilet. As I have written in chapter 8, love is kind to the unkind, so I concluded that I should go with option 2, not only to show longsuffering to this man, but also to render kindness in return for his unkindness. Who knows what God may do with this? I'm hoping it will open a door to share Christ with this man.

4. crap. Dictionary.com. *Dictionary.com Unabridged*. Random House, Inc. http://dictionary.reference.com/browse/crap (accessed November 9, 2014).
5. https://bible.org/netbible/ Used by permission.

8 – Love's Secret Ingredient
1. kindness. Dictionary.com. *Dictionary.com Unabridged*. Random House, Inc. http://dictionary.reference.com/browse/kindness (accessed November 16, 2014).
2. Henry James, http://www.goodreads.com/author/quotes/159.Henry_James (accessed November 16, 2014).
3. Pierre de Marivaux, http://www.goodreads.com/author/quotes/7815558.Pierre_de_Marivaux (accessed November 15, 2014).
4. Leo Buscaglia, http://www.goodreads.com/author/quotes/27573.Leo_Buscaglia (accessed November 15, 2014).

5. I sometimes marvel at the goodness of God. While writing this chapter, I had the delightful blessing of running into Bob and his wife, Anne, at an outlet mall in Simpsonville, Kentucky, on October 16, 2014. Twenty-five years had passed since I left Doe-Anderson, and I had not seen Bob since. Quite frankly, I never expected to see him again. But God used this moment to confirm to me that this story belonged in this book. Thanks be to God for His indescribable goodness and perfect timing!

6. noblesse oblige. Dictionary.com. *Dictionary.com Unabridged.* Random House, Inc. http://dictionary.reference.com/browse/ noblesse oblige (accessed November 16, 2014).

7. Samuel Johnson, http://www.goodreads.com/quotes/265377-kindness-is-in-our-power-even-when-fondness-is-not (access November 15, 2014).

8. Unknown Christian, *The Christlike Christian* (Grand Rapids: Zondervan, 1988),84-85.

9. Ibid., 81.

10. John Tillotson, http://www.bartleby.com/348/authors/558.html (accessed November 15, 2014).

11. Unknown Christian, *Christlike Christian*, 75.

12. Ibid.

13. Mignon McLaughlin, http://www.goodreads.com/quotes/108653-don-t-be-yourself-be-someone-a-little-nicer (accessed November 15, 2014).

9 – Who Are You Sleeping With?

1. Harold G. Coffin, http://www.goodreads.com/author/quotes/753036. Harold_G_Coffin (accessed November 26, 2014).

2. Unknown Christian, *The Christlike Christian* (Grand Rapids: Zondervan, 1988), 96.

3. Ibid., 93.

4. Paul Bamikole. http://topfamousquotes.com/paul-bamikole-quotes/ (accessed November 26, 2014).

5. Aeschylus. BrainyQuote.com, Xplore Inc, 2015. http://www.brainyquote.com/quotes/quotes/a/aeschylus148572.html (accessed November 26, 2014).

10 – Flag on the Play

1. *When I Survey the Wondrous Cross*, Words and Music by Isaac Watts and Lowell Mason, Public Domain

2. "Nebuchadnezzar." Encyclopedia of World Biography. 2004. *Encyclopedia.com,* http://www.encyclopedia.com/doc/1G2-3404704711.html (accessed November 25, 2014).

3. Unknown Christian, *The Christlike Christian* (Grand Rapids: Zondervan, 1988), 98.

11 – The Secret to Becoming More Attractive

1. Unknown Christian, *The Christlike Christian* (Grand Rapids: Zondervan, 1988), 107-108.

2. Ibid., 108-109.

3. normal psychology. Dictionary.com. *Dictionary.com Unabridged.* Random House, Inc. http://dictionary.reference.com/browse/ normal psychology (accessed November 28, 2014).

4. Taken from *My Utmost for His Highest*® by Oswald Chambers, edited by James Reimann, © 1992 by Oswald Chambers Publications Assn., Ltd., and used by permission of Discovery House, Grand Rapids, MI 49501. All rights reserved., July 20.

12 – No Pets Allowed

1. girn. Dictionary.com. *Dictionary.com Unabridged.* Random House, Inc. http://www.dictionary.com/browse/girn (accessed: May 01, 2016).

2. *The Princess Bride.* Dir. Rob Reiner. Writ. William Goldman. Perf. Carey Elwes, Robin Wright, Mandy Patinkin, Peter Faulk. Metro Goldwyn Mayer Studios;, 1987. VHS.

3. Unknown Christian, *The Christlike Christian* (Grand Rapids: Zondervan, 1988), 111.

4. petulant. Dictionary.com. *Online Etymology Dictionary.* Douglas Harper, Historian. http://dictionary.reference.com/browse/petulant (accessed February 02, 2015).

5. Unknown Christian, *Christlike Christian*, 115.

6. Ibid., 111.

7. Ibid., 117.

8. Ibid., 120.

9. Ibid.

10. *RUDY.* Dir. David Anspaugh. Writ. Angelo Pizzo. Perf. Sean Astin, Ned Beatty, Charles S. Dutton, Lili Taylor, Robert Prosky. Tristar Pictures, Inc. All Rights Reserved; 1993. DVD.

11. Unknown Christian, *Christlike Christian*, 111.

13 – Scoreboards, Journals, and Do-overs

1. Confucius. http://www.goodreads.com/quotes/675653-those-who-cannot-forgive-others-break-the-bridge-over-which (accessed December 11, 2015).

2. Ansel Adams. http://www.goodreads.com/author/quotes/12115.Ansel_Adams (accessed February 24, 2015).

3. Taken from *The Christian Atheist* by Craig Groeschel Copyright © 2010 by Craig Groeschel. Used by permission of Zondervan. www.zondervan.com, 114.

4. Ibid., 115.

5. Ibid., 117-118.

6. Ibid., 119.

7. Ibid.

8. Ibid., 120-121.

9. Ibid., 121.

10. forgive. Dictionary.com. *Dictionary.com Unabridged.* Random House, Inc. http://dictionary.reference.com/browse/forgive (accessed February 16, 2015).

11. reconcile. Dictionary.com. *Dictionary.com Unabridged.* Random House, Inc. http://dictionary.reference.com/browse/reconcile (accessed February 16, 2015).

12. Unknown Christian, *The Christlike Christian* (Grand Rapids: Zondervan, 1988), 122.

13. Ibid., 123.

14. Ibid., 124.

14 – Joseph and Mrs. P.

1. http://www.goodreads.com/quotes/93716-he-uses-statistics-as-a-drunken-man-uses-lamp-posts-for (accessed April 16, 2016).

2. Robert Quillen, http://fiercemarriage.com/quote-author/robert-quillen (accessed July 29, 2015).

3. "Hebrew Lexicon :: H7896 (KJV)." Blue Letter Bible (accessed December 26 Dec, 2015). http://www.blueletterbible.orghttps://www.blueletterbible.org/lang/Lexicon/Lexicon.cfm

4. "Hebrew Lexicon :: H1100 (KJV)." Blue Letter Bible (accessed December 26 Dec, 2015). http://www.blueletterbible.orghttps://www.blueletterbible.org/lang/Lexicon/Lexicon.cfm

5. Charles H. Spurgeon, http://www.spurgeon.org/treasury/ps101.htm (accessed April 26, 2015).

6. schadenfreude. Dictionary.com. Collins English Dictionary—Complete & Unabridged 10th Edition. HarperCollins Publishers. http://dictionary.reference.com/browse/schadenfreude (accessed April 26, 2015).

7. Adam Himmelsbach, "Enjoying Strong's failure?," *Courier-Journal*, September 8, 2014.

8. http://www.goodreads.com/quotes/130817-the-ancestor-of-every-action-is-a-thought (accessed January 18, 2016).

9. http://www.goodreads.com/author/quotes/433477.Thomas_Fuller (accessed January 18, 2016).

10. http://www.goodreads.com/author/quotes/132444.Will_Rogers (accessed January 18, 2016).

11. http://www.goodreads.com/author/quotes/9810.Albert_Einstein?page=2 (accessed January 18, 2016).

The Practice

1. practice. Dictionary.com. *Dictionary.com Unabridged.* Random House, Inc. http://dictionary.reference.com/browse/practice (accessed January 27, 2016).

15 – The Winner and Still Champion...

1. "Greek Lexicon: G4722 (KJV)." Blue Letter Bible (accessed May 29, 2015). http://www.blueletterbible.org/lang/Lexicon/Lexicon.

cfm?Strongs=G4722&t=KJV

2. Charles H. Spurgeon, http://www.spurgeon.org/sermons/1617.htm (accessed November 19, 2015).

3. "Greek Lexicon: G4100 (KJV)." Blue Letter Bible (accessed May 30, 2015). http://www.blueletterbible.org/lang/Lexicon/Lexicon. cfm?Strongs=G4100&t=KJV

4. Ibid.

5. Ibid.

6. "Greek Lexicon: G1679 (KJV)." Blue Letter Bible (accessed May 31, 2015). http://www.blueletterbible.org/lang/Lexicon/Lexicon. cfm?Strongs=G1679&t=KJV

7. "Greek Lexicon: G5278 (KJV)." Blue Letter Bible (accessed June 19, 2015). http://www.blueletterbible.org/lang/Lexicon/Lexicon. cfm?Strongs=G5278&t=KJV

16 – Supremely Sufficient

1. John Piper, http://links.biblegateway.mkt4731.com/servlet/ MailView?ms=NDg5NDc3NTAS1&r=NDY2MDMzMTY5OTQS1&j= NzAzMTQ4MDcxSo&mt=1&rt=0 (accessed June 24, 2015).

2. Ibid.

3. Unknown Christian, *The Christlike Christian* (Grand Rapids: Zondervan, 1988), 130.

4. George Stormont, *Smith Wigglesworth* (Tulsa: Harrison House LLC, 1989), 50-51.

5. Taken from *My Utmost for His Highest*® by Oswald Chambers, edited by James Reimann, © 1992 by Oswald Chambers Publications Assn., Ltd., and used by permission of Discovery House, Grand Rapids, MI 49501. All rights reserved., July 7.

6. Ibid., May 11.

7. Ibid.

8. *Carolina in My Mind*, by James Taylor, © 1968 Emi Blackwood Music Inc., Country Road Music.

9. *All You Need is Love*, Writer(s): Gary Glitter, Mike Leander, Paul McCartney, John Lennon, © Sony/ATV Tunes LLC, MCA Music Ltd.

10. Chambers, *Utmost*, May 11.

A Final Word

1. Taken from *My Utmost for His Highest*® by Oswald Chambers, edited by James Reimann, © 1992 by Oswald Chambers Publications Assn., Ltd., and used by permission of Discovery House, Grand Rapids, MI 49501. All rights reserved., May 15.

2. Ibid., August 14.

CPSIA information can be obtained at www.ICGtesting.com
Printed in the USA
LVOW08s0340210516

489321LV00003B/33/P